ENVIRON-
MENTAL
GRAPHICS
PROJECTS
&PROCESS

ENVIRON-
MENTAL
GRAPHICS

PROJECTS
&PROCESS

WAYNE HUNT

HDi

HARPER
DESIGN
international

ENVIRONMENTAL GRAPHICS: Projects and Process
© 2003 by Wayne Hunt and Harper Design International,
an imprint of HarperCollins*Publishers*

Published by:
Harper Design International
an imprint of HarperCollins*Publishers*
10 East 53rd Street
New York, NY 10022

ISBN 0-942604-90-3
Library of Congress Catalog Card Number 2002112932

Distributed throughout the world by:
Harper Collins International
10 East 53rd Street
New York, NY 10022
Fax: (212) 207-7654

Designed by Michele Perez
Art direction by Hunt Design Associates
Jacket design by Tzumin Wen
Principal photography by Jim Simmons
    (Del Zoppo Simmons) and Wayne Hunt
Copyediting by Sherri Schottlaender
Printed in Hong Kong

While the publisher makes every effort possible to pub-
lish full and correct credits for each work included in this
volume, sometimes errors of omission or commission
may occur. For this we are most regretful, but hereby
must disclaim any liability.

All of this book is printed in four-color process; a few of
the designs reproduced here may appear to be slightly
different than their original reproduction.

Dedicated to Carla, Holly, Morgan, and Kelly
AND MY EXTENDED FAMILY AT HUNT DESIGN ASSOCIATES

CONTENTS

INTRODUCTION
A design discipline whose time has come

There are a lot of good books on graphic design. My own library is full of them. However, few interesting or truly valuable books have been published on one of the most exciting and relevant categories of graphic design—environmental graphics. That this engaging and fast-growing field is overlooked by most design writers is curious given the sheer scale of public graphics and their ubiquitous presence in our daily lives. Good or bad, environmental graphics are all around us every day and everywhere, from the mall to the museum, from the streetscape to the office complex, from the hospital to the airport. Signs, marquees, posted messages, billboards, exhibits, plaques, flags, banners—graphic elements by the hundreds confront us wherever we go, whether walking, driving, or traveling on public transit. Even simple trips to the market, work, or school invite interaction with myriad signs.

A recent study conducted by my office, Hunt Design, for a theme park client revealed that their typical guest encountered and had to react to more than forty signs on the property before climbing aboard the first thrill ride! And because each sign, no matter how humble, is a work of typography and visual composition, someone—a graphic designer, perhaps—inadvertently or otherwise exercised the processes presented in this book each and every time a sign was created. Signs and sign programs are inevitably works of graphic art, and as such they merit study, discussion, and criticism. This book aims to further reinforce signage design, or environmental graphics, as it has become known, as a recognized subdiscipline of the venerable and historic field of graphic design.

Who is this book for?
I intend the information presented in this book for anyone with a general interest in three-dimensional design, the built environment, or urban design, especially those who want to learn how graphic design applies to buildings, places, and spaces. My ideal readers are traditional graphic designers, accomplished in the principles of two-dimensional design, who want to expand their design horizons. They know the basics of typography, composition, color, symbols, and communication, but they have not applied these skills to the three-dimensional environment.

I want to also reach out to architects, urban designers, and landscape designers. They already know many of the design principles discussed, but they may not have considered the relevance to two-dimensional design media—and because as they are the primary collaborators of environmental graphics designers, an improved knowledge of how we think and work can only help make for better-designed environments.

The content
This book includes illustrated pages on several elemental three-dimensional design principles, many of which may seem obvious to the reader. However, I believe that taking a fresh look at the basics, perhaps forgotten or routinely assumed, can be a good idea even for a seasoned environmental graphics professional. In order to show examples of the design process, including many examples of preliminary design concepts and sketches that precede final design decisions, I am illustrating the book mainly with projects from Hunt Design. I've also included five topical expert essays by six good friends and respected specialist practitioners as well as a colorful summary of the materials and techniques of environmental graphics.

I hope you enjoy the book and find it useful.

Wayne Hunt

THREE DIMENSIONS vs. Two

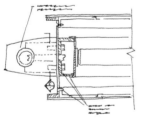

Environmental graphic design is different than "regular" graphic design

While environmental graphic design shares many principles with its two dimensional sibling, clear differences separate the two disciplines. Such fundamentals as proportion, contrast, figure/ground relationships, and basic composition underlie all graphic design. The use of color and application of typography comprise fundamental knowledge of all graphics practitioners.

However, when "flat" media becomes dimensional, new and additional principles and complexity emerge. The rules and conditions—and opportunities—are suddenly expanded. Here are ten ways environmental graphic design (EGD) differs from graphic design (GD).

1 Physicality

EGD exists in real space. It is tangible and touchable, not virtual and merely implied. It has thickness and dimension—a side view. An EGD element can cast a shadow; one can stand next to it or view it from different angles. EGD designs are fabricated, not just printed or projected on a screen.

2 Scale

The elements considered and designed in EGD often exist at human scale and larger. From people-sized map kiosks to sign pylons of eighty feet or more, these EGD designs demand a different process of creative development—the understanding and use of scale, both human and architectural.

3 Context

The designs and results of EGD have to coexist with an existing setting or context. Signs are inevitably next to something else; a landscape background exists; the sun is shining in a set direction; the architect has specified certain materials for the building. While designers of GD may consider such quasi-contextual factors as demographics and brand positioning, they don't need to consider the color of the reader's desk when designing a catalog.

4 Complexity

The projects, processes, and elements of EGD can be very complex. Finished projects are often made up of hundreds of individually designed but integrated pieces. One assignment can require knowledge of multiple materials, difficult fabrication techniques, and even engineering—all in addition to the conventional skills of the graphic designer. Also, more than just production or camera-ready art is called for: detailed fabrication and installation drawings, bid sets, and technical specifications are needed to implement the work.

5 Viewed in motion

EGD is frequently viewed, understood, and used while in motion. The human factors of perception for drivers and active pedestrians place different demands on the EGD practitioner. Design solutions need to be effective from multiple angles and viewed and understood from great distance as well as close up.

6 Durability

Graphics printed on paper not only usually have time-limited content, but they are prepared on an ephemeral medium—paper. EGD, conversely, is usually designed and executed to last for years. Durable media, from metals to stone, withstand the test of time; Roman inscriptions from 200 B.C. are still with us today.

7 The environment

Light conditions change during the day; moisture, salt air, and sunlight have physical effects; colors look different in the shade than in bright sun. Environmental graphic design must, in fact, engage and react to the environment.

8 Teamwork

A conventional graphic design is often the product of a single individual; one designer can design a logo, brochure, or a package and all that goes with it. EGD, on the other hand, is not only usually created by a team made up of signage programmers, designers, and drafting technicians, but it is often co-designed with an architect, landscape architect, lighting designer, and other specialists in a multidisciplined process.

9 Production time

Graphic design projects take from a few weeks to a few months from start to completion. EGD assignments, conversely, can require years to design and implement. The creative process is often parallel to architecture in sequence and pace.

10 Part of something bigger

The biggest single difference between these two design fields is that the results of EGD are seldom ends in themselves. EGD is inevitably part of something larger—a building, an airport, an entire theme park, or even a city. As complex as the work is, EGD is but one element in a designed, coordinated place.

Even though man first decorated caves with colorful graphics thousands of years ago, historically speaking the design discipline of environmental graphics is a new field—so new that its traditions and standards of practice are only now emerging. Unlike poster design or packaging design, each with more than 150 years of refinements and professional development, environmental graphics as a definable discipline is still in its adolescence.

Now, early in the fourth decade of self-recognition, environmental graphic design is still evolving and being redefined continually by design practitioners as they respond to new technologies and changing opportunities in the marketplace.

Architectural signing: The beginning
As graphic design gradually separated itself from the umbrella of the advertising business and became a defined field in the middle of the twentieth century, the full-service design firm was born. With offerings such as visual identity, package design, poster design, corporate communications, and book design, a professional model emerged, practiced by thousands of large and small graphic design firms during the 1950s, 1960s and early 1970s.

Among the services provided by graphics firms was the infrequent sign design assignment—a logo sign here, a storefront there; occasionally, a client needed a set of signs for a real estate development or public event. These were the first sign programs—informal systems of diverse sign types unified by common colors, typography, materials, and design details. Early examples of such coordinated sign programs are the seminal designs for the Fashion Island shopping center in California by design pioneer John Follis, and on the East Coast, the exuberant signage designed for corporate buildings by New Yorker Rudy de Harak.

At the same time, without any fanfare, talented designers working at W.E.D. Enterprises (later known as Walt Disney Imagineering) were creating highly detailed, beautifully crafted sign "packages" for Disney rides and theme parks. And like the consulting design offices, they developed methods for organizing many sign types, managing sign wording, and documenting sign locations.

This early formalization came to be known as architectural signing. Soon designers around the U.S. were offering the service or even shaping entire practices around the programming and designing of signing systems. Major real estate developments, hospitals, airports, and theme parks made up most of the assignments.

As projects proliferated, design standards and professionalism improved, especially when architectural firms began to budget for signing design services just as they did for landscape design. However, the focus of the projects and the design solutions was on func-

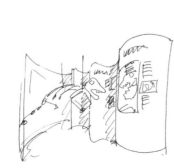
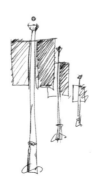

tion and blending into the architecture. Architects and corporations such as ARCO and IBM drove the designs. The best signing design work reflected the modernist understatement popular throughout the era's contemporary architecture and corporate culture.

Placemaking: The second generation

In the early eighties a parallel but separate trend evolved: graphics went beyond the display of directions and building identification. Graphic design came to life to enhance and even define public spaces in innovative projects. Colorful signs, festive banners, and thematic graphics were designed and deployed to create interest, differentiation, and even entertainment in otherwise predictable environments. First seen as decorative or artistic directional signage in breakthrough shopping malls, this image-driven approach quickly evolved into arresting floor-to-ceiling and wall-to-wall graphics. Influential designers Deborah Sussman, RTKL's Ann Dudrow, and Denver's Communication Arts, working with progressive retail developers such as the Rouse Company, led the exciting trend.

Then, in 1984 the diverse and widespread venues of the Los Angeles Olympics were unified and defined solely with colorful large-scale site graphics, generating additional momentum for environmental graphics. The potential power for public spaces of all kinds was revealed. Graphics could now transform existing places and define districts and zones within previously neutral environments. Graphics could be the

lead, the image-setter of a built environment. And it wasn't expensive: even complex graphic media cost much less than conventional image-oriented architectural finishes. The descriptive term "environmental graphics," coined years earlier, now made real sense and gained acceptance by designer and client alike.

This designing of the environment, whether large or small, retail or civic, was actually placemaking—a process heretofore limited to architects and urban designers. Now graphic designers were at the table, participating in the design and definition of public space.

Interpretive design: The third aspect

Exhibition design is not a new discipline. Museum exhibits and international expositions have been an important part of our culture since the nineteenth century, but exhibit design had traditionally been practiced primarily by formal exhibition design firms. Although graphic design was part of most exhibits, it played a secondary role.

As placemaking with graphics spread through retail, sports, entertainment, and civic environments, the museum world took notice. Museums had begun a struggle to keep visitors coming back, especially young visitors more attracted to active contemporary diversions such as malls and video games. Progressive institutions such as science centers, and new museums such as the Holocaust Museum offered total-immersion environments where media of all kinds combined

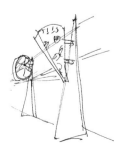

to provide compelling guest experiences. Not the least of these environmental media was graphics, fresh from success in energizing retail and sports venues. Graphic designers had moved up the exhibit design food chain, taking a lead role in designing interpretive environments.

Now known as interpretive design, this rediscovered exhibit design discipline began to appear on the services rosters of environmental graphics firms. More young designers found total environment design to be interesting; their passion for intelligent and creative typography could be expressed in large doses in learning places.

Another trend in the museum business also piqued the interest of designers: the need to offer temporary exhibits created with funding shared by multiple institutions. These movable displays are, by definition, lightweight and more dependent on engaging graphics than more permanent exhibits. Entertainment design firms—creative powerhouses that previously concentrated on theme park and attraction design—also joined forces with museums. They had a high respect for the impact graphic design can have in environment design and often brought with them their preferred graphics consultants.

Fission and fusion

The three faces of environmental graphic design—wayfinding, placemaking, and interpretive design—now make up the split personality of this eclectic field. Thirty-plus years of professional practice, innovation, and opportunity have resulted in a kind of professional fission, the splitting of a discipline into new forms. Now, to use another physics term, a sort of fusion is occurring. But this reuniting of design disciplines is not driven as much by the designers as by ever more complex and interesting projects and their demanding clients. Formerly distinct building types with definable purposes and users are beginning to overlap in programming and function: shopping centers look more like theme parks, hospitals have themes, and airports are acting like shopping centers.

What's next? No one knows; however, environmental graphics will certainly become even more interesting and relevant to the built environment.

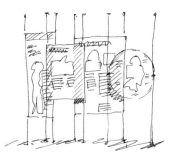

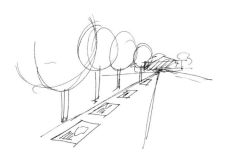

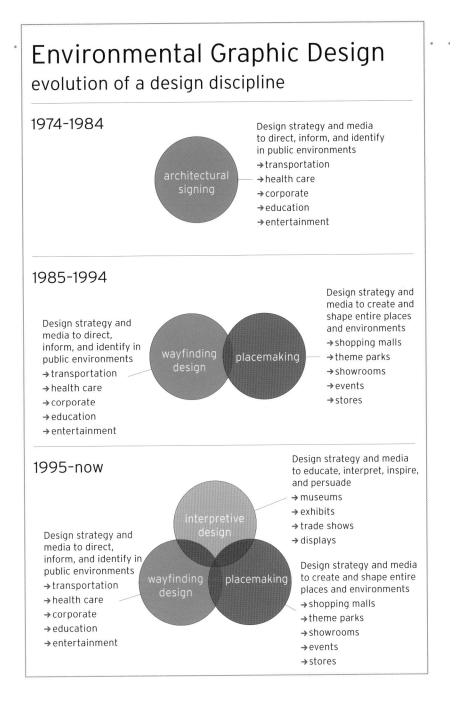

Environmental Graphic Design
evolution of a design discipline

1974-1984

architectural signing

Design strategy and media to direct, inform, and identify in public environments
→ transportation
→ health care
→ corporate
→ education
→ entertainment

1985-1994

Design strategy and media to direct, inform, and identify in public environments
→ transportation
→ health care
→ corporate
→ education
→ entertainment

wayfinding design

placemaking

Design strategy and media to create and shape entire places and environments
→ shopping malls
→ theme parks
→ showrooms
→ events
→ stores

1995-now

interpretive design

Design strategy and media to educate, interpret, inspire, and persuade
→ museums
→ exhibits
→ trade shows
→ displays

Design strategy and media to direct, inform, and identify in public environments
→ transportation
→ health care
→ corporate
→ education
→ entertainment

wayfinding design

placemaking

Design strategy and media to create and shape entire places and environments
→ shopping malls
→ theme parks
→ showrooms
→ events
→ stores

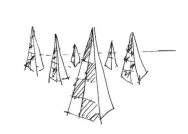

WAYFINDING PROJECTS
Environmental graphics that orient, direct, and identify

McCARRAN International Airport

Major identification signs can often be designed to play a second role as popular backdrops for visitor photos.

A new terminal gets the Las Vegas treatment

When McCarran International, now the seventh-largest airport in the U.S., planned a new freestanding terminal of fifty-two gates, airport management wanted to create a state-of-the-art, beautifully designed, and efficient building. They also desired to communicate to travelers that they had arrived in Las Vegas. The resulting structure is a work of world-class architecture with equally good design details, including fine art, lighting, and of course, graphics. Veteran Las Vegas architect Tate Snyder Kimsey designed the new terminal and in turn selected Hunt Design as their signage and graph-

ics consultant—one of more than fifteen specialty subconsultants on the design team!

Planning, designing, and building an all-new aviation facility is one of the most complex development projects imaginable. The required integration of systems and components, both on the land side and air side, has made airport design a specialty. Also, the execution of a signage and graphics program is doubly complicated in air-transport environments—coordination with many disciplines well beyond landscape

Gate signs "stand off" canted columns by means of the yellow bracket.

Plan

AVIATION complexity project

A floating ring of letters above the information counter.

Typical hanging directional sign.

9'-0"

3'-11"

DIRECTORY

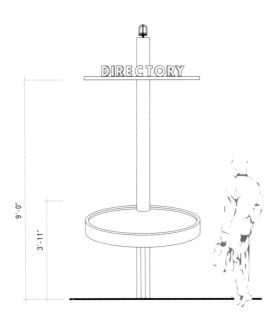

Elevation

DIRECTORY

Side

McCARRAN INTERNATIONAL AIRPORT

D GATES

Directory map for the first two legs of the D Gates terminal.

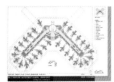

and lighting is required. Specialties such as security, public information, and display advertising play critical roles and need careful interaction with graphics. In addition, Federal Aviation Administration requirements and the often conflicting needs of airline tenants add even more complexity to the design process.

Wayfinding in airports is critical—passengers, already under some stress just getting to the airport, must be processed through ticketing, check-in, and security, and then must easily find their departure gates. A system of quick-reading signs with clear, understandable wording is paramount. And unlike those in many built environments, airport signs need to be read and reacted to as travelers are in motion.

Respecting and complementing the architecture is also important, especially in a major new air terminal. The architect was concerned that the many signs needed for successful wayfinding might diminish the grand and dramatic building design—many airports have become cluttered with mismatched signs.

McCarran International's designs reflect a close working relationship between the graphics designers and the architect, and they borrow colors and details from the building's high-tech design palette. Sign brackets, supports, and other hardware match materials in the building.

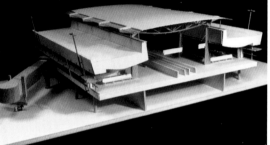

The graphics team used models prepared by the architect to establish sign sizes and typical locations.

Architect's site plan shows the spatial relationships of the new D Gates to the existing terminal.

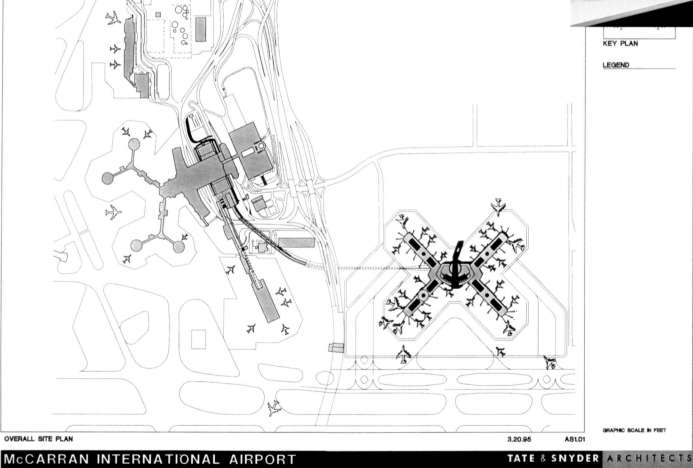

KEY PLAN

LEGEND

OVERALL SITE PLAN

GRAPHIC SCALE IN FEET

3.20.95   AS1.01

McCARRAN INTERNATIONAL AIRPORT
SATELLITE D PROJECT

TATE & SNYDER ARCHITECTS

12

PROJECTS

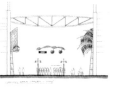

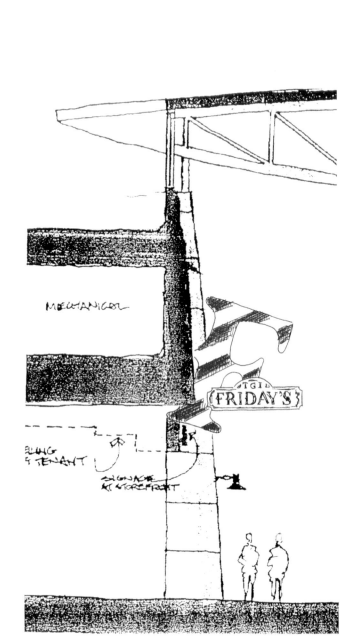

Early sketches of the retail/gaming area, McCarran Air Strip.

Computer rendering shows the presence of signage elements within the architectural space.

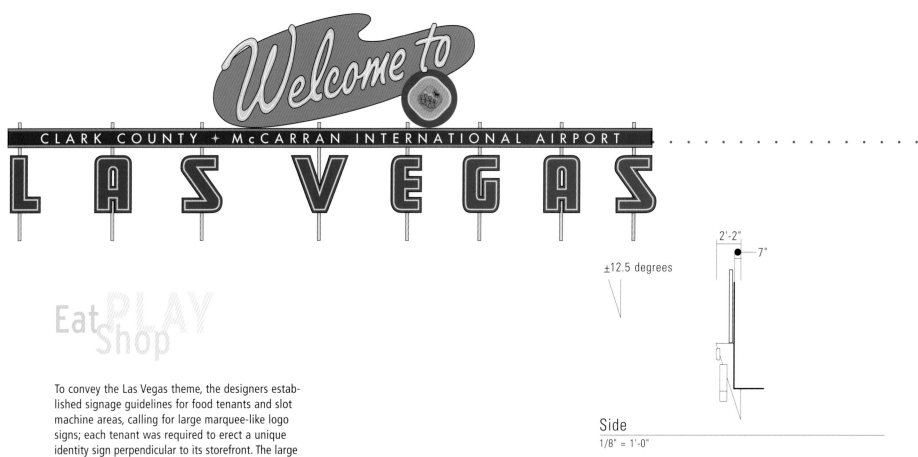

Welcome to

CLARK COUNTY ✦ McCARRAN INTERNATIONAL AIRPORT

LAS VEGAS

2'-2"
7"
±12.5 degrees

Side
1/8" = 1'-0"

Eat PLAY
Shop

To convey the Las Vegas theme, the designers established signage guidelines for food tenants and slot machine areas, calling for large marquee-like logo signs; each tenant was required to erect a unique identity sign perpendicular to its storefront. The large illuminated blade signs that resulted define the food areas as special spaces and create a colorful counterpoint to the more disciplined wayfinding signs.

And to let visitors know they've really arrived in Las Vegas, the design team added a bright neon gateway above the escalators which features the famous local salutation, "Welcome to Las Vegas."

illuminated letters

Flat cut out aluminum copy with exposed centerline neon on face.

Fabricated aluminum kidney shaped panel.

Fabricated aluminum prismatic stars

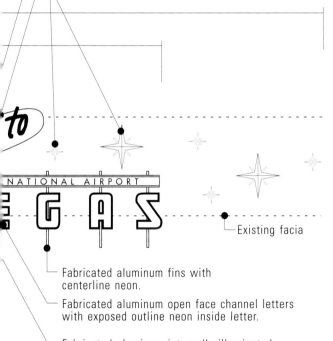

Existing facia

Fabricated aluminum fins with centerline neon.

Fabricated aluminum open face channel letters with exposed outline neon inside letter.

Fabricated aluminum internally illuminated cabinet with routed out letters and push thru acrylic.

Sign logo for children's area.

Logo and banner for the Air Strip.

Neon Air Strip logo signs were integrated into the flight information directories.

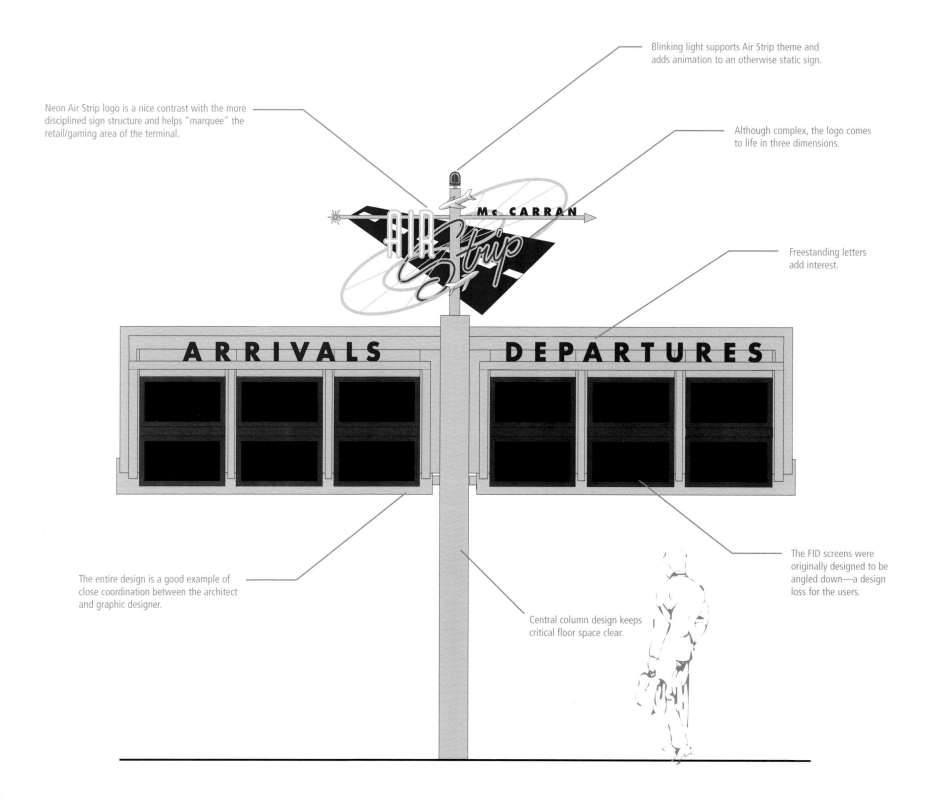

Blinking light supports Air Strip theme and adds animation to an otherwise static sign.

Neon Air Strip logo is a nice contrast with the more disciplined sign structure and helps "marquee" the retail/gaming area of the terminal.

Although complex, the logo comes to life in three dimensions.

Freestanding letters add interest.

The entire design is a good example of close coordination between the architect and graphic designer.

Central column design keeps critical floor space clear.

The FID screens were originally designed to be angled down—a design loss for the users.

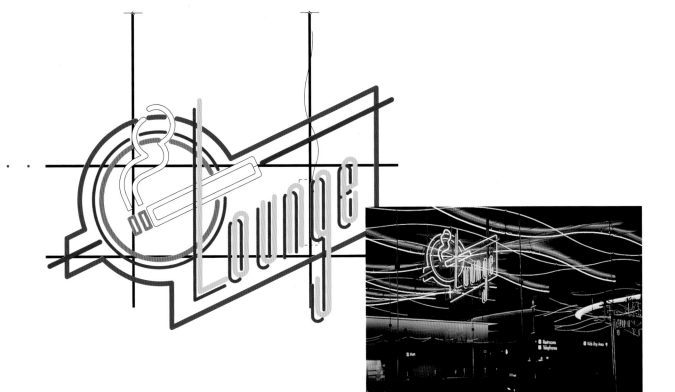

Formed in neon, a real
Las Vegas–style sign.

This view shows the integration
of all categories of signage:
wayfinding, FID, retail, food,
and gaming.

PROJECT OVERVIEW

Integrated signage and graphics program
for the new fifty-two gate terminal.

PROJECT FACTS

Client:
   McCarran International Airport
Architect:
   Tate Snyder Kimsey
Graphic Design Team:
   Hunt Design:
   Christina Allen, Wayne Hunt,
   Dinnis Lee, Sharrie Lee, John Temple
Sign Company:
   AHR Ampersand
Schedule:
   Three years
Photography:
   Jim Simmons (Del Zoppo Simmons)

MATERIALS & TECHNIQUES

Aluminum sign cabinets with pushthrough
letters, exposed neon, aluminum open-face
channel letters; inset electronic message
units; ceramic tiles with glazed graphics.

UNIQUE ASPECTS

The program features two personalities:
first, a function-driven wayfinding system
well matched to the modernist architecture, and second, colorful "Las Vegas"
graphics elements that establish a strong
sense of place.

WICHITA

A colorful graphics program helps revitalize a classic downtown

As a classic Midwestern city, Wichita was laid out in the nineteenth century in a neat grid of equal-sized blocks. However, two winding rivers, the Arkansas and the Little Arkansas, curve through the city, converge, and divide the downtown, creating substantial circulation challenges for drivers and walkers. Many streets are discontinuous, and destinations can be seen or sensed but not reached by intuitive routes. Bridges form primary links between areas, but many destinations are hard to find. This situation is difficult for local residents, but daunting for visitors. To help vehicular circulation, many mismatched and inconsistent signs had been added over the years, creating a condition of sign clutter while not substantially improving the understanding of the downtown.

In addition to circulation difficulties, the two rivers had another profound effect—the ad hoc creation of public districts and neighborhoods. Development on one side of the river differed from that on the other: a civic center evolved on the river's east side, bars and hotels on the west side. Later, arts-oriented destinations emerged along the river, and the original Wichita city center was preserved as an entertainment-based Old Town.

Compounding the situation, during the last forty years Wichita, like many cities in postwar America, grew away from its downtown; the sprawling suburbs attracted most of the new development and infrastructure. Downtown Wichita languished. New construction was rare, activity slowed, and people forgot about downtown in the state's largest city.

River Center

Government Center

Looking up at one of the five gateway structures shows the contrast between the solid base and the fanciful top.

But as in countless other cities with similar decaying downtowns, city government, downtown businesses, and the citizens of Wichita came to the rescue. A new riverfront was planned and built, new development occurred, and the city began to rediscover downtown. Major streets were improved, landscaping was upgraded, and with a surprising commitment to the arts, the downtown emerged as a center for public art. All that was missing was a way to help visitors (and locals) find their way around and discover the dozens of interesting downtown destinations.

The city formed a wayfinding committee of interested downtown businesspeople and arts leaders. Hunt Design was chosen to plan, and as a first step, design a comprehensive wayfinding program for the central city area. The design firm conducted a brainstorming

Each district greets visitors with a colorful twenty-foot-high gateway.

The sign system was designed for single- and double-panel signs. Each district has a unique color to further show the downtown diversity.

Old Town

Museums on the River

Playful, whimsical, COLORFUL...

This sign-location plan is presented in "drivers" format for easy message-checking by the client.

Historic County Courthouse 510

Major civic buildings are signed with vertical monument signs.

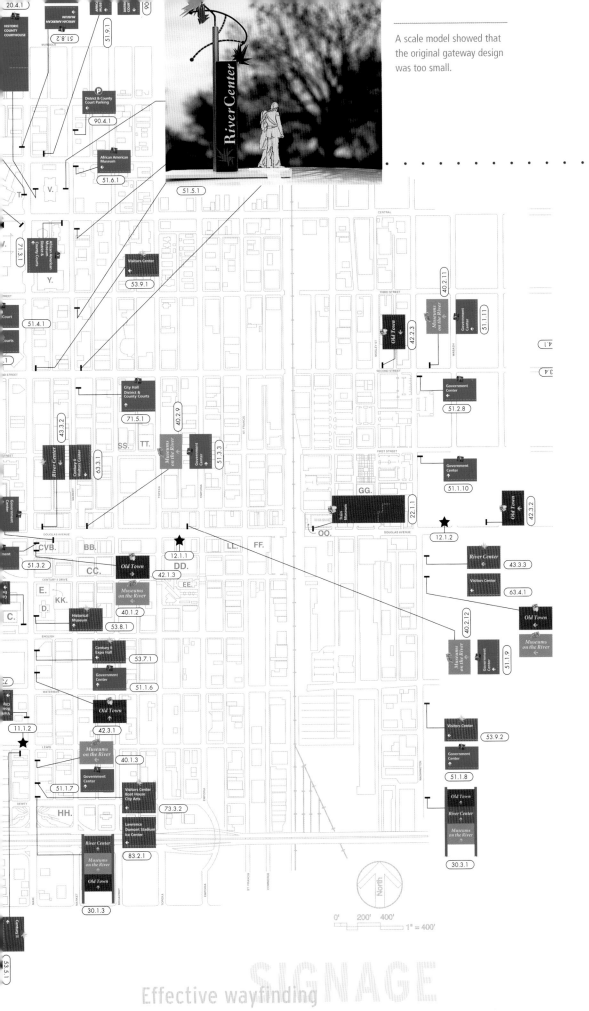

A scale model showed that the original gateway design was too small.

session with the committee to help further assess the issues and define the goals of the proposed program. This meeting not only helped to identify more than fifty deserving downtown destinations, but it also clearly showed the need to identify and present four distinct downtown districts. This multidistrict approach guided the entire process from beginning to end and led the design team to create a set of distinctive district icons and a color-coding system for the signs.

Preparing the final project "punch list" for vendor completion.

Effective wayfinding SIGNAGE

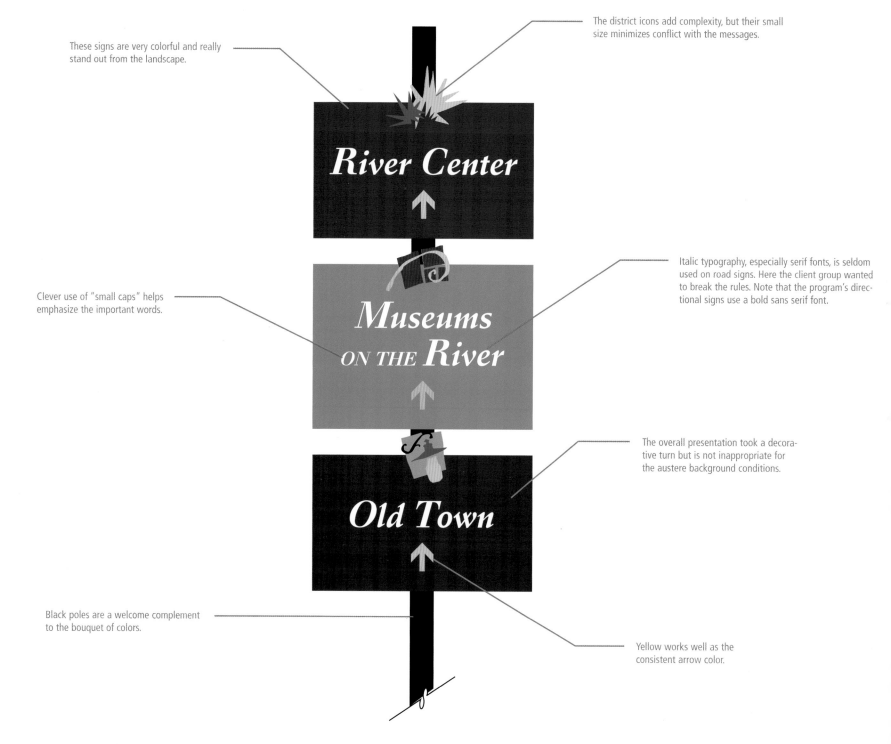

The district icons add complexity, but their small size minimizes conflict with the messages.

These signs are very colorful and really stand out from the landscape.

Italic typography, especially serif fonts, is seldom used on road signs. Here the client group wanted to break the rules. Note that the program's directional signs use a bold sans serif font.

Clever use of "small caps" helps emphasize the important words.

The overall presentation took a decorative turn but is not inappropriate for the austere background conditions.

Black poles are a welcome complement to the bouquet of colors.

Yellow works well as the consistent arrow color.

Urban wayfinding programs can take a variety of forms, from straightforward and function-driven to colorful and even flamboyant. After the designers presented a wide range of conceptual sketches, it was clear that Wichita's wayfinding committee wanted a colorful, image-oriented approach. The designers responded with a rich program of colors and forms, including fanciful sculptural gateways for each district.

Even in historic Old Town the gateway looks right.

The system included blade signs for building façade applications.

The success of the program depends on its application to all sign categories. Each district has color-coded parking signs with district icons.

PROJECT OVERVIEW

A four-district downtown identity and wayfinding program featuring more than sixty directional signs and five artful district gateways.

PROJECT FACTS

Client:
    City of Wichita
Graphic Design Team:
    Hunt Design:
    Christina Allen, Jennifer Bressler,
    Wayne Hunt, Dinnis Lee
Sign Company:
    Heath
Schedule:
    Twenty-four months
Implementation Budget:
    $400,000

MATERIALS & TECHNIQUES

Aluminum sign panels on steel poles; aluminum sign cabinets with steel "art" structures; monolithic aluminum sign cabinets with applied graphics.

UNIQUE ASPECTS

Dramatic color and strong signage presence were desired from the city from the very beginning of the project.

23

Jack Biesek on EDUCATIONAL ENVIRONMENTS

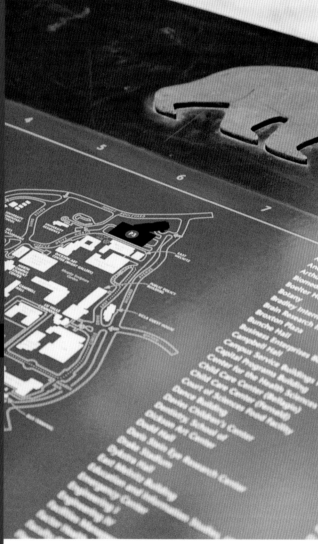

The campus map expressed
in porcelain enamel on steel.

In this modern world, colleges and universities might do well to rethink how they present themselves to their students, visitors, and the outside world. Too often campuses are layered with signs and graphics, yet it still can be difficult to find one's destination. Campuses that want to improve their stature and their curbside appeal should consider improved wayfinding and signage as a means to revitalize campus environments and create positive first impressions. Successful campuses understand that they need to be engaging, friendly, and accessible. The campus of the future will embrace signage as a communications and information delivery system, as well as an architectural building block that enhances the environment, provides guidance, and contributes to a sense of place.

Thomas A. Gaines, in **The Campus as a Work of Art,** said, "Education is an endeavor that is most sensitive to ambience; students respond all their lives to memories of the place that nourished their intellectual growth." A leading authority on campus settings, Mr. Gaines has studied many campus environments, and his assertion succinctly summarizes the feelings of students. Successful campuses that use signage as an information tool will efficiently connect their visitors with arterial roads that lead to the campus, identify convenient parking, and provide easy-to-understand information throughout the entire facility. These schools understand that seamless wayfinding provides an experience for the first-time visitor which is compellingly simple. In fact, when signage is done well it is nearly invisible—it recedes nicely into the background. It is only when signage is badly done that it sticks out like a sore thumb. This creates an irony for designers: when we do a good job nobody notices, but when signs are poorly placed or worded improperly, many people notice (and complain).

University campuses are by nature vast and complex environments with an assortment of roads, parking lots, footpaths, and buildings. These structures and open spaces typically develop over many decades. Finding a destination in this kind of environment can often be a daunting challenge, especially if you are a first-time visitor. A smart signage system on a university campus provides a gracious and seamless welcome experience as you transition from driving or public transportation to parking, to walking, and ultimately to arriving at your destination.

Working with campus stakeholders is also an integral part of the equation. In a unique environment such as a university, it is important to understand the approval process. You'll want to know who will be reviewing your ideas and how decisions will be made. Planning presentations that will connect with twenty people is quite different than meeting one-on-one with the campus architect. In an academic environment, consensus-building usually is essential and may require an ongoing, thoughtful approach, with the stakeholders participating or observing the process.

When possible, work directly with the people who have a vested interest in the campus and ask questions of people who will actually be using the system, including those responsible for campus upkeep. Working through other professionals—such as a consulting architect or engineering firm—may limit your ability to connect with actual decision makers and may complicate the communications process. Unless the project architect is willing to fully integrate a comprehensive sign program into the project, it is usually better to work directly with the campus as your client.

Signage offers an opportunity to provide two powerful communication tools: information that helps orient people to the environment, and graphic design that enhances the environment by providing attractive and trustworthy messaging. Wayfinding and signage can

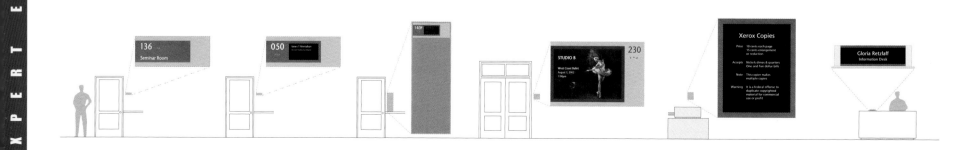

be major players in campus life by providing necessary guidance through maps, directional signs, disabled-access information, and identifying devices, making a campus logical and easy to navigate. Wayfinding graphics make a powerful first impression. Effective, functional, and practical, well-planned signage dramatically improves the campus environment.

Chris Stinehour hand-carves beautiful letters in UCLA Gothic typestyle.

Polished stainless steel letters set an elegant tone.

UCLA CAMPUS

At UCLA, with nearly five hundred acres of campus, we approach wayfinding as a work of art. Whether we are carving letters in limestone, gold-leafing inscriptions, or casting letters in bronze, all signage follows a singular theme and uses a unique typeface (UCLA Gothic) that we developed.

In 1993 we began developing campus wayfinding standards in collaboration with the campus architects, facility managers, and the Chancellor's Office on Accessibility. We started with a visual audit of the campus to evaluate the "look and feel" of the environment to help integrate new signage into the architectural style and design vernacular. Included were vehicular and pedestrian wayfinding, architectural signage, sign nomenclature, directory maps, an original typeface used exclusively for signage, and a distinctive color scheme of statuary bronze, soft white, and wrought-iron black. To ensure ongoing correct implementation of future signage, we prepared the UCLA Campus Sign Guidelines.

Triangular granite monolith features aluminum letters and etched stainless steel.

a singular
THEME

JACK BIESEK heads Biesek Design, a California design consultancy noted for their environmental graphic design expertise as well as the ability to manage large-scale projects. The group specializes in wayfinding and sign system master planning for colleges, universities, and public spaces. Jack has more than twenty-five years' experience working with a diverse range of clientele, including world-renowned architects as well as educational and institutional clients.

Mr. Biesek lectures about technology, design business practices, and a broad range of issues related to the field of wayfinding. He has served as president of the Society for Environmental Graphic Design (SEGD) and received the SEGD Angel Award for personal commitment and contribution to the direction and growth of the Society. The firm has received many awards for environmental graphic design excellence. Examples of their enthusiastic problem-solving approaches have appeared in several books and magazines.

Although this profile is centered on Jack's personal vision, the firm's success is a collaborative effort that includes the expertise of Jack's wife and business partner, Susan Mackenzie Biesek, and the talented designers who have helped shape the firm, including Gerry Stamm, Julie Frankel, and Karilyn Taylor—over the last twenty years they have established themselves as industry leaders. It is this collective group, along with Jack's vision, which gives Biesek Design a dynamic perspective and garners the respect of the design community.

The **Good Sign** Theory

Twenty years ago, conservative theorists James Wilson and George Kelling published an article in the **Atlantic Monthly** introducing a new crime-fighting premise known as the "broken window theory." The theory states, "If the first broken window in a building is not repaired, then people who like breaking windows will assume that no one cares about the building and more windows will be broken. Soon the building will have no windows." The theory demonstrates that vandalism is a result of lack of upkeep as well as lax police efforts, and that stricter law enforcement and good house-keeping promote safer communities.

Apply this concept to college campuses and you trigger a topic that few campus officials want to discuss—controlling and managing campus signage. Like a headache you just don't want to admit you have, signage has a blight factor that is similar to the broken windows muddle. Hastily prepared signboards and quick-printed paper signs with out-of-date messages, attached randomly to walls and windows, represent the "broken window theory of wayfinding"; they are evidence that the environmental communication system has broken down and needs repair. As a result of lax policing efforts, this ubiquitous degradation of the environment is a problem that many campuses face today. Not all are out of control, but the majority of school environments are certainly showing the strain. Fortunately, there is hope for campuses seeking to clean up their act: the remedy is diligence.

The "Good Sign Theory," as put forward by Biesek Design, is the opposite of the broken window theory. When signage is well thought-out and carefully planned, it not only communicates on many levels, but it also perpetuates interest in adding only well-designed signs. As landscape elements, as decorative components that enhance architecture, and as graphic design statements, signs are powerful tools that add value to the campus. Positive impressions of a campus come to life with good signs. A feeling develops that suggests that behind these good graphics are thoughtful people creating order and overseeing the well-being of a valued place.

Controlling the environment with signage is not rocket science. It requires some systematic thinking and an effort to make order out of chaos. The goal is fairly simple: to provide just enough accurate information to welcome a first-time visitor with dignity, grace, and style. Don't overdo it, use restraint when necessary, keep it simple and clean. Using the theory, simple diligence—removing obsolete and temporary signs—is a simple way of improving a campus which can be accomplished in a matter of days. Leaving old signs in place long after they are needed implies a lack of care by those who run the institution. Good signs with thoughtful messaging, strategically placed and scaled for legibility and easy comprehension, are not only the hallmarks of wayfinding and of a professionally developed architectural signage system, but also of an enlightened administration.

Signage design complements elegant architecture.

Parking bollard features internal lighting.

Dimensional bronze letters.

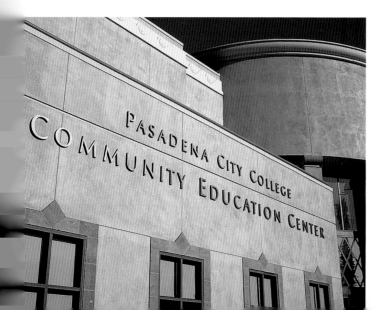

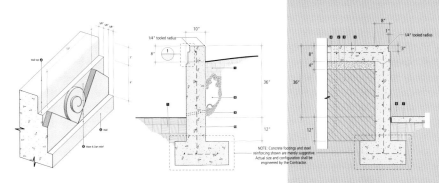

a sophisticated look for
CAMPUS
SIGNAGE

Library directory sign is
understated but effective.

Sketches for decorative
concrete details.

PASADENA CITY COLLEGE

With a student population of 25,000 students, PCC is
one of California's largest community colleges. Over
the years we have built a working relationship with
the college which has allowed us to create a signage
master plan by the simplest means possible: on a proj-
ect-by-project basis. This economical yet far-reaching
approach began with our very first assignment, a
sign system for the architectural crown jewel of the
campus—the new Shatford Library, designed by
Gruen Architects. Our wayfinding program was
highly successful and was deemed appropriate for
campus-wide applications.

Today, with more than twenty major projects completed, we've created a sophisticated look for campus
signage and in the process established master plan
guidelines for nearly every aspect of campus wayfinding, including vehicular, parking, pedestrian, shuttle
system, architectural signage, and donor recognition.

A major electronic sign
greets drivers.

Bronze logo and shield
set in terrazzo floor.

echoes of original materials

DOHENY MEMORIAL LIBRARY

Biesek Design created a comprehensive wayfinding and signage program for the Edward L. Doheny Jr. Memorial Library at the University of Southern California. The work included planning, design, construction documents, and contract administration. A sign guidelines binder with project signage and templates for changeable signs was included, as well as digital versions on CD-ROM. Reordering signs or changing sign inserts is as simple as opening a sign template, changing text, and printing it out on a laser printer.

Utilizing bonded bronze, antique brass, and low-glare acrylic, the wayfinding and signage program echoes the original materials utilized in this classic 1932 Mediterranean and Romanesque architectural gem. The 167,000-square-foot facility's signage program included a complex wayfinding program for five-story perimeter floors and seven stories of book stacks in the center of the building.

Interior signs feature bronze finishes with hand-rubbed patinas. Sign backing panels were made from high-tech gypsum (by Formglass), then bonded with a metallic bronze powder that wears and ages like bronze but costs far less than traditional cast metal. The Biesek team had cast-bronze samples made and presented them alongside the bonded bronze, and without prejudice the client picked the bonded bronze—when we explained that they just saved thousands of dollars, the material got a quick approval.

Signs had to be appropriate for the classic stone walls, floors, and moldings.

Cast bronze sign (circa 1930).

Bas relief frieze and original inscriptions influenced the designs.

Bronze letters with antique finish.

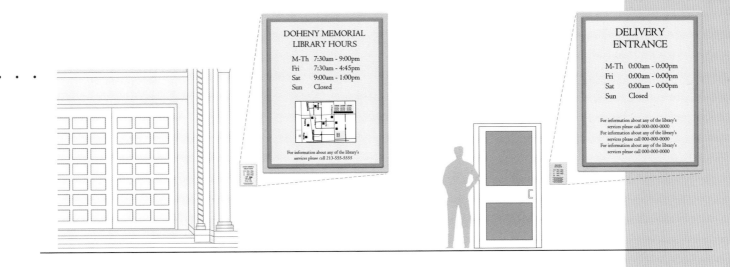

DOHENY MEMORIAL
LIBRARY HOURS

M-Th   7:30am - 9:00pm
Fri   7:30am - 4:45pm
Sat   9:00am - 1:00pm
Sun   Closed

For information about any of the library's
please call 213-555-5555

DELIVERY
ENTRANCE

M-Th   0:00am - 0:00pm
Fri   0:00am - 0:00pm
Sat   0:00am - 0:00pm
Sun   Closed

For information about any of the library's
services please call 000-000-0000
For information about any of the library's
services please call 000-000-0000
For information about any of the library's
services please call 000-000-0000

NO
ENTRY

Please use
west entrance

Bonded bronze signs:
new technology, old look.

Directory is bronze and acrylic
but features a paper insert.

ZION NATIONAL PARK

In collaboration with the National Park Service, Biesek Design creates signage master plans that include a broad range of planning, design, and coordination. Our projects have included the Franklin Delano Roosevelt Memorial in Washington, D.C.; Carlsbad Caverns; Lake Mead; and Zion National Park, our largest project to date. As Zion entered the twenty-first century, vehicular traffic was shifted to a tram and shuttle system to accommodate the 2,500,000 yearly visitors. Biesek Design provided services for a wide range of transportation signage, wayfinding graphics, park directories, trailhead maps, and site-specific interpretive panels. The work included roadway signing, shuttle and tram information graphics, vehicular parking control, a sign system for the Zion Visitor Center, as well as maps and graphics throughout the park. Starting in the town of Springdale, Utah, the sign system leads guests to the park entrance, to the shuttle station, and throughout Zion National Park.

In addition to wayfinding signage, the project included more than thirty interpretive displays that teach visitors about the unique features of the area: history, geology, flora, and fauna. High-fidelity porcelain signs with Corten steel posts were used extensively. Some initial concepts were reminiscent of "lodge architecture," prevalent in many of the national parks. The park staff contributed to the sign planning and design selection process, and they were pleased that the wayfinding elements helped establish a parkwide sense of unity and authority without being overly decorative. Signage elements utilize venerable and durable materials such as bronze, porcelain enamel on steel, weatherproof steel, and kiln-dried wood. In addition to the several hundred signs added to the park, we helped identify and remove more than one hundred obsolete signs.

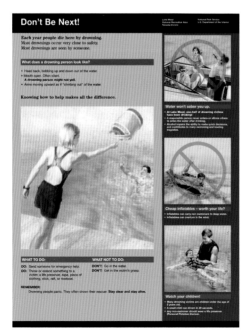

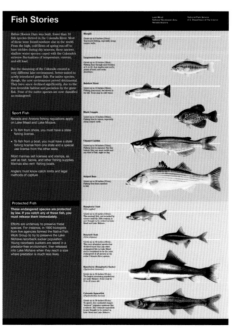

Interpretive panels present
lifesaving tips and fish stories.

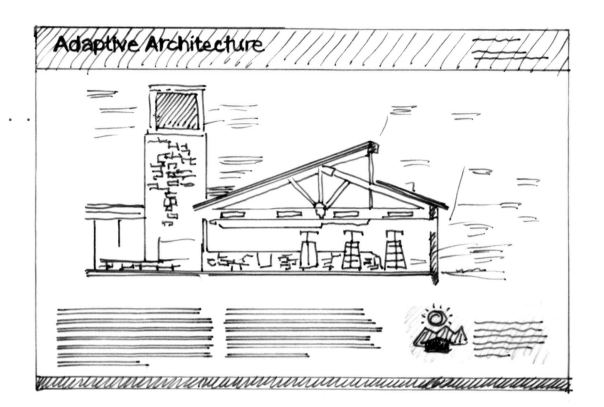

Adaptive Architecture

To Templ
of Sinawa

31

Adaptive Architecture

Entrance fee sign flips to
second message.

Study sketch and finished
porcelain panel.

SHUTTLE
ROUTE

FRANKLIN DELANO
ROOSEVELT MEMORIAL

Shuttle sign of porcelain enamel
and weatherproof steel.

MGM GRAND Las Vegas

Wayfinding for the world's largest casino

When the mammoth MGM Grand opened in the early 1990s, it also opened to mammoth wayfinding problems. Few customers at the elegant casino resort could find their way around the 300,000-square-foot public spaces or the 100-acre site. Featuring more than five thousand hotel rooms, the biggest gaming areas anywhere, fourteen restaurants, two shopping malls, assorted other stores, and ancillary rooms, the sprawling facility seemed to defy understanding. To help blunt the criticism of lost guests, soon all visitors entering the main lobby were automatically handed maps of the property by casino staff.

Fast-forward five years: a massive facility improvement and expansion program was underway, which included a new conference center, themed shopping areas, a five-pool swimming complex, a state-of-the-art salon and spa, and a doubling of the already expansive parking garage. With these fundamental changes came, finally, all new wayfinding. Hunt Design won the project in a competitive proposal process, and the biggest assignment in the firm's history began.

Interior wayfinding at the resort

Tackling the casino first, Hunt's team learned that there were more than forty named destinations to be organized and displayed on directional signs—more than triple that of a typical major hotel. And in a facility this large, there was a desire from each area manager to display as many destinations as possible on each sign; stimulating foot traffic to the far reaches of the property was important. On peak Saturdays, pedestrian traffic crossing the bridge between the neighboring New York New York casino and MGM was said to total 50,000 visitors! The MGM Grand needed an effective and comprehensive approach to message-organizing and sign design.

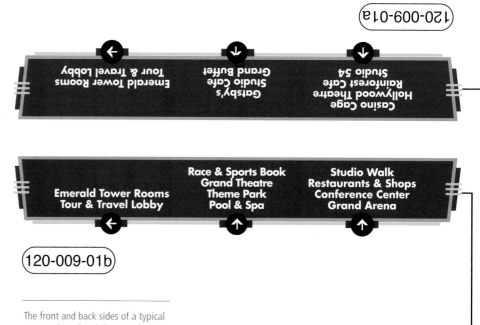

The front and back sides of a typical proposed overhead directional sign.

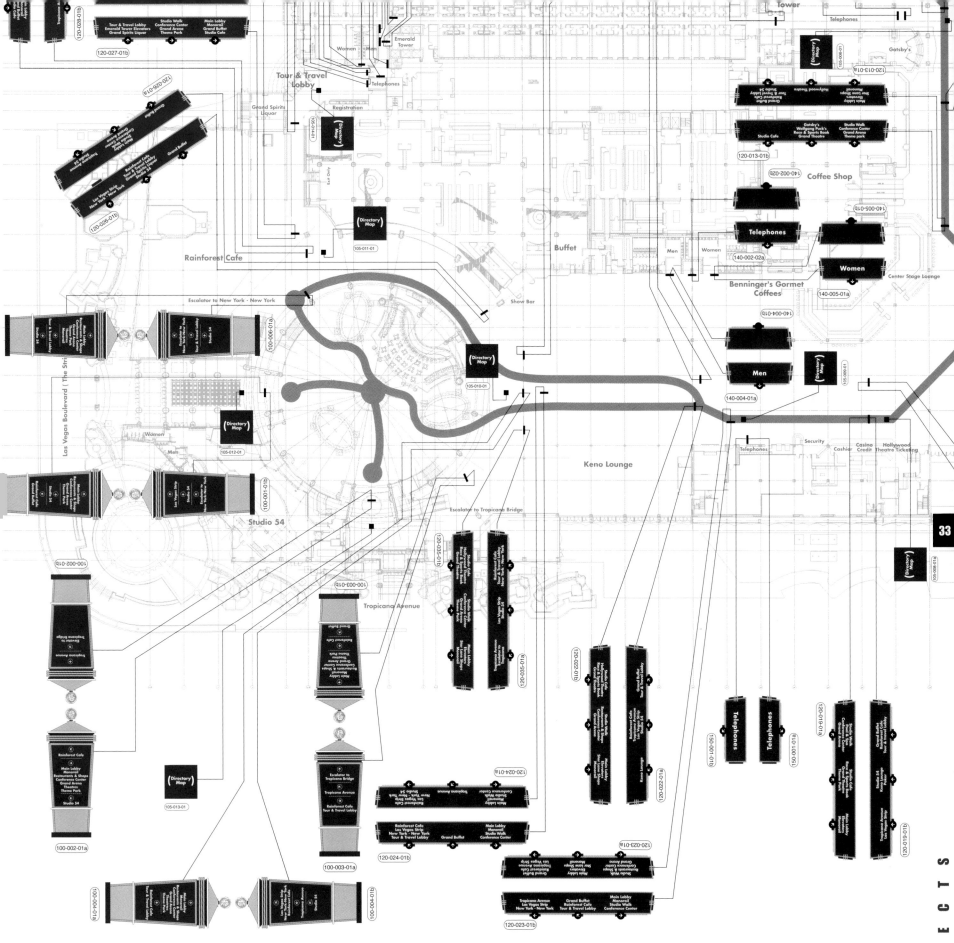

A portion of the interior wayfinding plan, delineated to allow review by turning the drawing to follow the pathways.

STRATEGIC Wayfinding

Restrooms

Buffet
Hollywood
Theatre
Studio 54
New York
New York

Hotel Elevators
Grand Arena
Shops &
Restaurants
Grand Theatre

Restrooms

Buffet
Hollywood
Theatre
Studio 54
New York
New York

Restrooms

Hotel Elevators
Grand Arena
Shops &
Restaurants
Grand Theatre

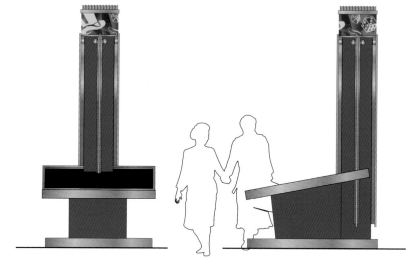

Multiple concepts were explored
to marry functional wayfinding
with the hotel's Art Deco theme.

Restrooms

A quick survey of other Las Vegas hotels showed that current industry wayfinding practice was not based on function, but instead on projecting an image—usually an image expressed in polished brass and decorative typography. Typical casino signage was designed and fabricated by local sign companies without the benefit of a strategic wayfinding plan. What the MGM Grand situation demanded was an entirely different way of implementing directional signage.

The solution posed by the designers acknowledged that, from a circulation and wayfinding perspective, the MGM Grand was as much like a hospital or an airport as it was a resort. An organized review of the many destinations and pathways, accompanied by intensive interviews with staff from all departments, showed that continuous, twenty-four-hour-a-day multiple destination circulation was the norm. Not surprisingly, some of the best information about confused guests and their needs came from security staff and cocktail waitresses.

The floor plan was organized into major pathways or streets, and large directional signs were placed along the way and at each intersection. The designers set a practical display limit of twelve destinations per sign; only in this way could the messages be large enough to be effective. With the client's request to "serve" all destinations, negotiation was required to select the twelve choices to be listed on each sign. Even more study and negotiation followed in order to shorten destination names to twelve letters to fit the text on the sign layouts. For example, "MGM Grand Garden Arena" was shortened to "Grand Arena" for display.

The designers developed large, simple layouts for maximum visibility and understanding but contained them in a system of decorative Art Deco frames in keeping with the hotel's architectural theme. The sign faces are straightforward three-column designs with bold arrows in round brass frames. Most signs are double-sided and mounted directly above the path of travel.

The program featured freestanding signs in casino areas with high ceilings.

theme and FUNCTION

The selected scheme framed straightforward sign face layouts with thematic edges and details.

Exterior wayfinding on the immense site

With thousands of vehicles entering the MGM Grand site each day, improving vehicular wayfinding was critical. Awkward access from two arterial streets culminating in a complicated six-lane porte cochere made for daunting decisions and difficult turns by arriving drivers. The existing signs were too small, and too decorative, to be effective.

The designers again turned to a function-driven solution, creating a system of large sign elements displaying simple, clear messages. Discipline was required to keep the wording clear and to a minimum. The sign bases and supports bring in the property's Art Deco theme, and in a gesture toward decoration, the sign faces of the internally lit signs are covered with a subtle diamond pattern expressed in digital vinyl.

Final designs deliver bold messages on sign cabinets decorated with a digital vinyl pattern.

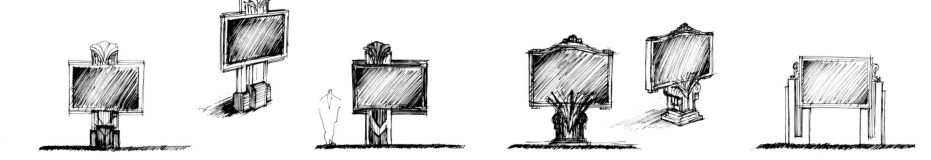

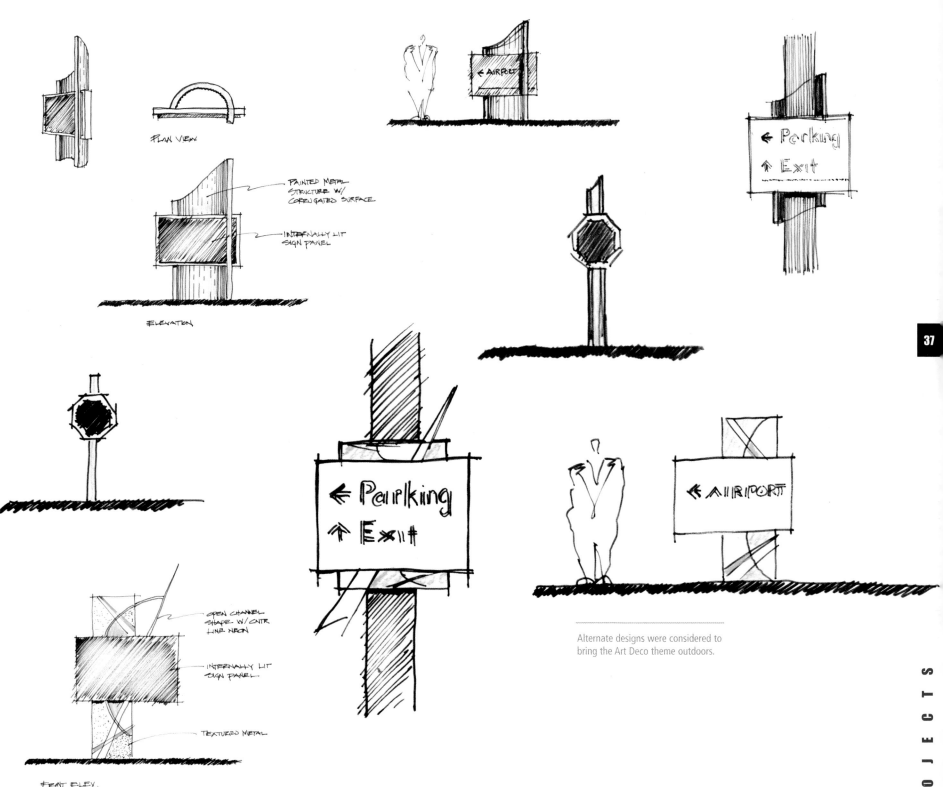

PLAN VIEW

PAINTED METAL
STRUCTURE W/
CORRUGATED SURFACE

INTERNALLY LIT
SIGN PANEL

ELEVATION

← AIRPORT

← Parking
↑ Exit

← Parking
↑ Exit

← AIRPORT

OPEN CHANNEL
SHAPE W/ CNTR
LINE NEON

INTERNALLY LIT
SIGN PANEL

TEXTURED METAL

FRONT ELEV.

Alternate designs were considered to
bring the Art Deco theme outdoors.

PARKING LEVEL I.D.
PARKING STRUCTURE SIGNAGE

The biggest parking structure in Nevada
If large parking garages are frequently difficult for drivers, the parking buildings in Las Vegas are especially confounding. The MGM Grand's five-story garage had an ambitious but ineffective signage system with zone identification based around characters from **The Wizard of Oz**, an early theme of the entire property. Already the area's largest, the structure was set to expand to 8,500 spaces. The time was right for an all-new sign program.

First came an all-new alpha-based zone nomenclature to organize the long floors into easy-to-remember areas. Next, strong color coding distinguished the parking levels. Then a bold graphics approach was

adopted to unify more than one hundred vehicular signs. To help relate the look of the signs to the hotel, a graphic interpretation of an Art Deco form was included in the design.

Separating vehicular and pedestrian information in parking structures not only brings clarity, but also safety. Here, the seemingly endless walking path on each parking level was signed with specially designed inner-illuminated signs to create a point of difference from the driver's signage. The designers also enhanced the lighting along the path for further differentiation.

1" = 1'-6"

sign panel

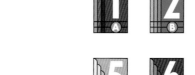

LOCATION ELEVATION
3/16" = 1'-0"

The huge parking structure has its own version of Art Deco; again, function was paramount.

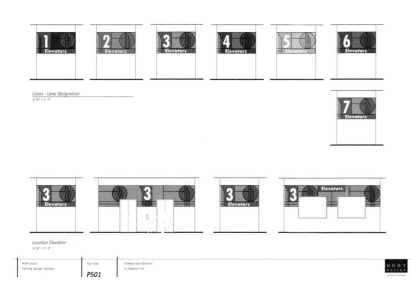

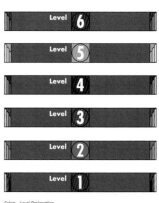

3/8" 11 3/4" 1/4"   5 1/4"
Center arrow   4"cap ht.   1/4" 3/8"

6 7/8"

6 1/4"

L
P

1/4" rule

Layout Detail   Typical Dimensions, (same at opposite hand)

1-1/2"

Parking & Exit

Upper Level
Parking & Exit

Elevator enclosures are decorated
on all sides for visibility.

Pedestrian signs are illuminated to
mark the pathway to the activities.

Layout A

Layout B

Eq.   Eq.
Eq. Align Eq.

Exit   Upper Level
Parking

Layout S

Layout T

Exit
Park

4"   4"   4"   4"

Layout C

Layout D

Layout E

Layout F

Layout G

Not a
Thru Aisle

4"   4"

Layout H   Parking   Exit

Exit
Koval
Return

1'-0" 11 1/2"

Layouts

1/4"

39

P R O J E C T S

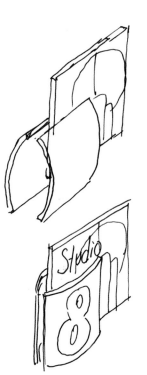

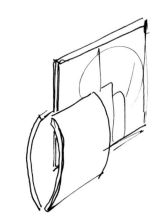

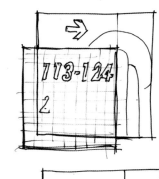

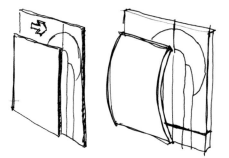

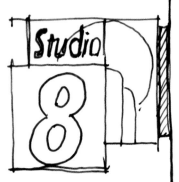

style by area

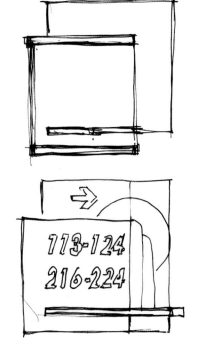

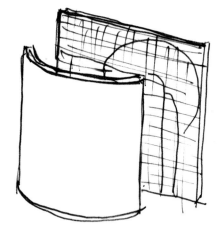

Photo-illustration shows early concept to project the logo onto the arena walls.

Sketches for meeting-room signs.

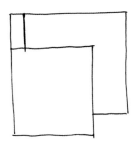

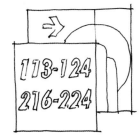

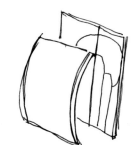

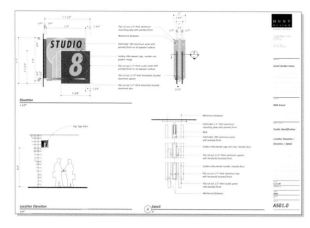

A unique design variation for the family of signs at the MGM Grand Arena.

Round building configuration leads to a complex numbering system.

RESTROOMS

BLADE MOUNT - FRONT ELEVATION
1 1/2" = 1'-0"

SIDE
1 1/2" = 1'-0"

WOMEN

WALL MOUNT - FRONT ELEVATION
HALF SIZE

LOCATION ELEVATION
1/4" = 1'-0"

LOCATION ELEVATION
1/4" = 1'-0"

Double column base provides style and a Las Vegas touch (as well as a small footprint).

Brass logo works well as a focal point and lends corporate identity.

Digital vinyl pattern adds richness.

← **MGM Grand Conference Center Parking**

The Futura type family, used throughout the property, helps present visual continuity.

All exterior signs are asymmetrical, adding a dynamic quality.

ACADEMY POOL & SPA
BACKLOT BAR &
RIVER POOL
OBSERVATION DECK
CABANAS 1 - 8
RAFT RENTALS
CABANA GRILLE
MARGARITA BAR

A special grouping of signs was
created for the five-pool garden area.

Etched-glass signs add an elegant
feel to the luxurious spa.

ACADEMY
POOL & BAR

PRODUCERS

ACADEMY
POOL & BAR

PRODUCERS
POOL

ACADEMY BAR

PRODUCERS POOL
ACADEMY BAR

PROJECT OVERVIEW
One of the largest single-property
wayfinding projects ever implemented.

PROJECT FACTS
Client:
  MGM Grand, Inc.
Graphic Design Team:
  Hunt Design:
  Karen Aseltine, Esteban Hernandez,
  Wayne Hunt, Dinnis Lee,
  Brian Memmott, Sharon Persovski,
  Perry Shimoji, John Temple,
  Kevin Stevens
Consultant, Parking Areas:
  Signologists:
  Ted Wu, Eileen Avery
Sign Companies:
  Casino, Site, Parking:
  AHR Ampersand;
  Pool: YESCO
Schedule:
  Two years
Photography:
  Jim Simmons (Del Zoppo Simmons)

MATERIALS & TECHNIQUES
Casino: Suspended and freestanding aluminum cabinets with decorative polished
brass trim; dimensional polished brass
"circles"; internal fluorescent and neon
illumination; translucent acrylic panels
with surface-applied opaque vinyl.

Site: Aluminum cabinets wrapped with
digitally printed pattern on vinyl; routed
graphics with pushthrough acrylic or
wrapped acrylic panels; internal fluorescent illumination; brushed stainless steel
accent bands.

UNIQUE ASPECTS
Highly complex environment with multiple, often conflicting wayfinding needs.

43

MGM GRAND
CAST MEMBERS
ONLY

MEN

PROJECT FACTS

MARKET STREET

The logo/emblem looks appropriate when integrated with existing street poles.

Graphics for a prototype streetscape

Covering only two blocks, this modest wayfinding/ identity program was created as a demonstration project for the city of Inglewood, a moderate-to-low-income Southern California city completely surrounded by Los Angeles sprawl. To help the aging downtown, no longer thought of as a shopping or pedestrian destination, the city initiated a sample streetscape improvement effort of landscape, lighting, and façade upgrades. To help communicate and reinforce the changes, an identity program for the downtown was added to the design scope.

Hunt Design, working as part of a multidisciplinary team, developed alternative design approaches for a set of basic signage elements, including off-site directional signs, gateway pylons, and thematic banners. Because integration with the other streetscape improvements was important, several design concepts were developed and presented.

The designs required extensive public review, a process that does not always go smoothly. Here, consideration of the design proposals continued to get tangled up in the often heated discussion of other, non-design issues. This is not an unusual problem: the public, brought together to discuss one issue, often uses the forum to address other topics.

Eventually the city settled on a traditional, "Victorian" graphics concept based on a symmetrical abstract leaf pattern. From among several more colorful options presented, a blue and light gray palette was selected—the city has a tradition of blue signage. The signs were then detailed by the designers and expressed in a bid package for implementation.

Research photographs show a previous urban graphics effort.

Once the sign types were selected, the designers developed three design directions for review.

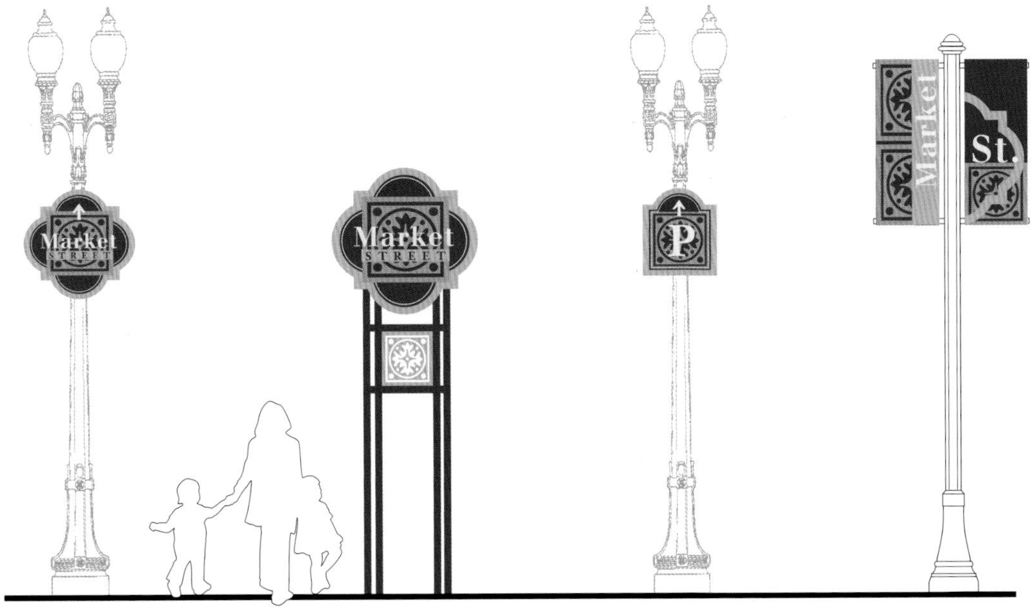

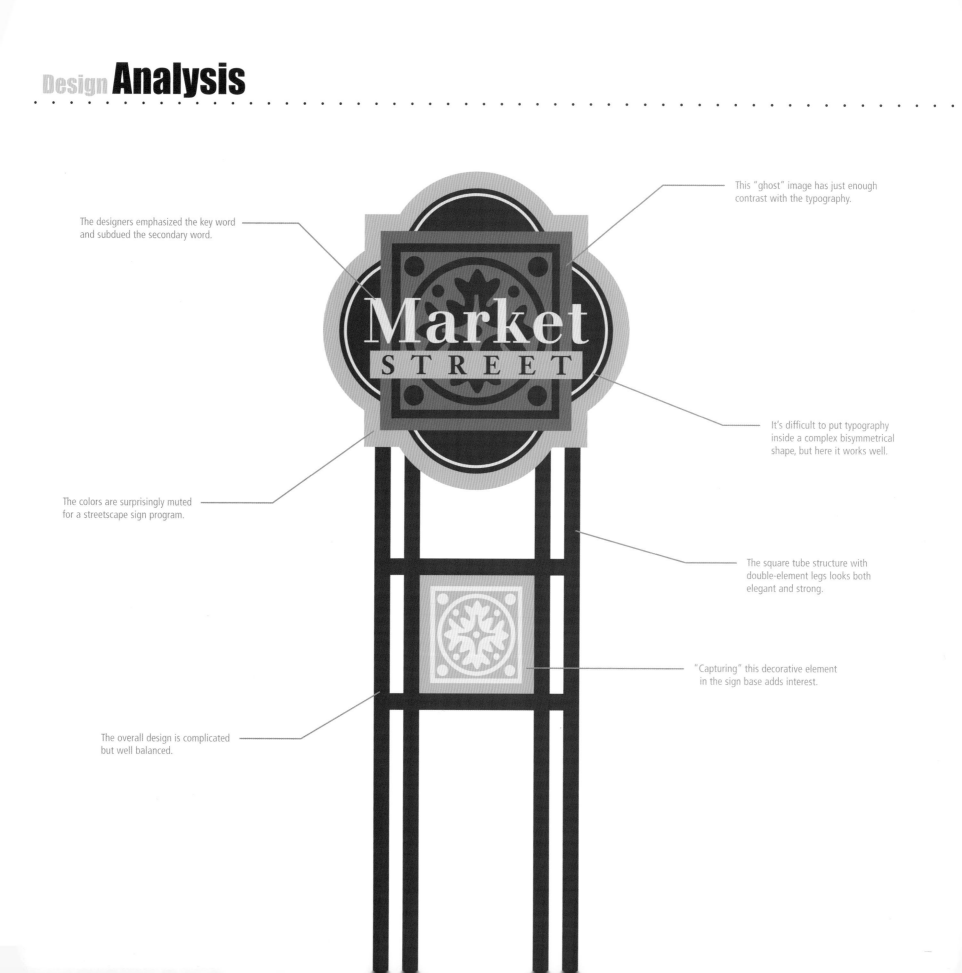

This "ghost" image has just enough contrast with the typography.

The designers emphasized the key word and subdued the secondary word.

It's difficult to put typography inside a complex bisymmetrical shape, but here it works well.

The colors are surprisingly muted for a streetscape sign program.

The square tube structure with double-element legs looks both elegant and strong.

"Capturing" this decorative element in the sign base adds interest.

The overall design is complicated but well balanced.

WIDTH VARIES · PARALLEL PARKING BEYOND   13'-0"   8'-0"   ...GONAL PARKING BEYOND

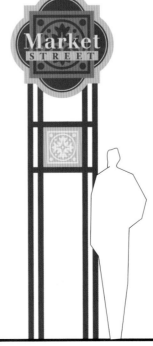

Understated street banners were designed to complement the more functional elements.

Custom parking signs can extend and reinforce city graphics programs.

PROJECT OVERVIEW
Two-block identity and graphics demonstration project.

PROJECT FACTS
Client:
   City of Inglewood
Graphic Design Team:
   Hunt Design:
   Jennifer Bressler, Dinnis Lee,
   Sharrie Lee
Sign Company:
   Bravo Sign & Design
Schedule:
   Six months

MATERIALS & TECHNIQUES
Aluminum panels with retro-reflective vinyl film and translucent ink graphics; inset aluminum squares with silk-screened graphics; inset aluminum square tube structure with powder-coated finish; four-color silk-screened fabric banners.

UNIQUE ASPECTS
Although the designs look non-controversial, the project itself required extensive public review.

Jeffry Corbin on MEDICAL ENVIRONMENTS

One of the guiding principles of wayfinding theory is that wayfinding programs should be designed for the first-time visitor. Among the many types of public facilities and environments, medical facilities probably have the highest number of first-time visitors. And not only are a high percentage of users making their first visit, they are often doing so while dealing with stressful medical situations. It is imperative to orient visitors properly and to make them as self-sufficient as possible in finding their way—to do so supports their personal dignity and gives them added feelings of comfort and security, to say nothing of reducing time lost as staff members help confused visitors.

Good wayfinding is intuitive, but not all medical environments are as intuitively designed as they might be. Given the choice, people will naturally turn right instead of left. Many hospitals, however, require a series of left turns as drivers drop patients off at building entrances in order to let the patient exit on the building side of the driveway. Signage, therefore, has to compensate for the anti-intuitive circulation pattern that results. Further examples of anti-intuitive situations are: multiple or hard-to-find public entrances; arbitrary floor-level designations; highly technical terminology; elevators that are unnecessarily hidden; and the illogical relationship of related services.

The most effective wayfinding leads—not points—the way. People are more comfortable walking toward something than following a series of signs with arrows pointing the way. Examples of worthy "targets" are: natural light; landmarks such as sculpture, artwork, or significant plantings; and architectural features such as atriums, crossroads, or areas of refuge.

By using similar colors for vehicular directional signs and hospital entrances, the designers provided wayfinding that leads the way. Canopy identifiers also provide quick identification for emergency entrances and other top destinations.

Good wayfinding is intuitive

The primary purpose of this site-identification sign is to identify the hospital from the nearby elevated freeway. The sign also reinforces the Clarian Health brand.

Wayfinding programs should be designed for the **first-time** visitor.

Wayfinding elements should be comfortably integrated with the environment, yet they must be designed consistently to increase their "anticipatory value." Just as people anticipate the message on large green-and-white signs along interstate highways, they should be able to anticipate the next sign along the way in a hospital. Institutions should resist the desire to customize the signage design for various centers or parts of the facility (such as the Women's Center or Oncology Suites): while variations on the overall theme are certainly permissible, sudden changes in color, scale, or logic defeat the purpose of a comprehensive wayfinding program.

Wayfinding programs benefit from functional redundancy. Different people use different parts of wayfinding programs more effectively. The same information should be presented in various formats: maps, words and arrows, and landmarks. Signage should show a person where they are, as well as where they want to go. Certain destinations benefit from redundant terminology (radiology/X-ray; patient cluster names together with room number ranges, etc.).

Typical wall-mounted direction sign.

Upon entering the hospital at any public point of entry, a main directory is available, defining the universe of information. The directory's map diagram illustrates the main public corridors, much as a road map illustrates the main highways. Public elevators and entrance locations are also highlighted.

On the main floor of the hospital, corridor maps function much like rapid-transit maps, illustrating the destinations along the corridor, or "street," in the order in which they occur.

Jeffry Corbin established Corbin Design in Traverse City, Michigan, in 1976. Under Jeff's leadership, the firm now known simply as Corbin has grown to become a national leader in the field of wayfinding and environmental graphic design, having designed wayfinding programs for more than fifty major medical centers nationwide.

Jeff's expertise in information architecture and wayfinding design has made him a popular public speaker before a wide range of audiences, including the American Hospital Association, Symposium on Healthcare Design, American Institute of Architects, International Downtown Association, and Society for College and University Planning.

Before forming Corbin, Jeff was a vice president and director of Interior and Graphic Design for Caudill Rowlett Scott (CRS), a large full-service architectural/engineering firm in Houston, Texas. He holds bachelor of arts and bachelor of architecture degrees from Rice University, Houston, where he won the William Ward Watkin Traveling Fellowship in 1967, using it to tour Europe to study architectural and design history.

Jeff is a founder and past president of the Society for Environmental Graphic Design. He has also served as president of the Association of Professional Design Firms, an organization dedicated to improving the performance of design firms.

Wayfinding information should be readily adaptable to various media. The information created for the wayfinding program can have great application to the facility's Web site, its patient-referral materials, and internal patient passports. It is important to the success of the entire program that terminology and graphic depictions of the facility be consistent across the range of these elements.

An effective wayfinding process will: orient the visitor to the environment; define the destinations in the space; route the individual properly; periodically reconfirm their route; and finally, celebrate their arrival!

Elevator directories are located in every elevator lobby. The smaller directory lists all the destinations that the elevator serves. The larger one lists all the destinations in the hospital in case the viewer selected the incorrect elevator.

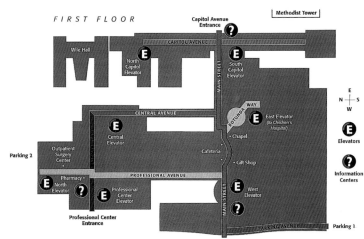

At Methodist Hospital, the designers gave public corridors unique "street" names. "Street signs" identify the various corridors, while wall-mounted directional signs point the way to nearby destinations.

Information should be **adaptable** to various media.

People are more comfortable
walking toward a
VISIBLE LANDMARK ·

Artwork, properly placed, can serve as a landmark, such as this sculpture that marks the main lobby and the transition to the elevators leading back to the parking garage.

Site maps help pedestrians locate the proper building on the fifteen-block urban medical campus.

Vehicular signage for this urban medical center had to have a heightened sense of presence to overcome commercial signage prevalent in the area.

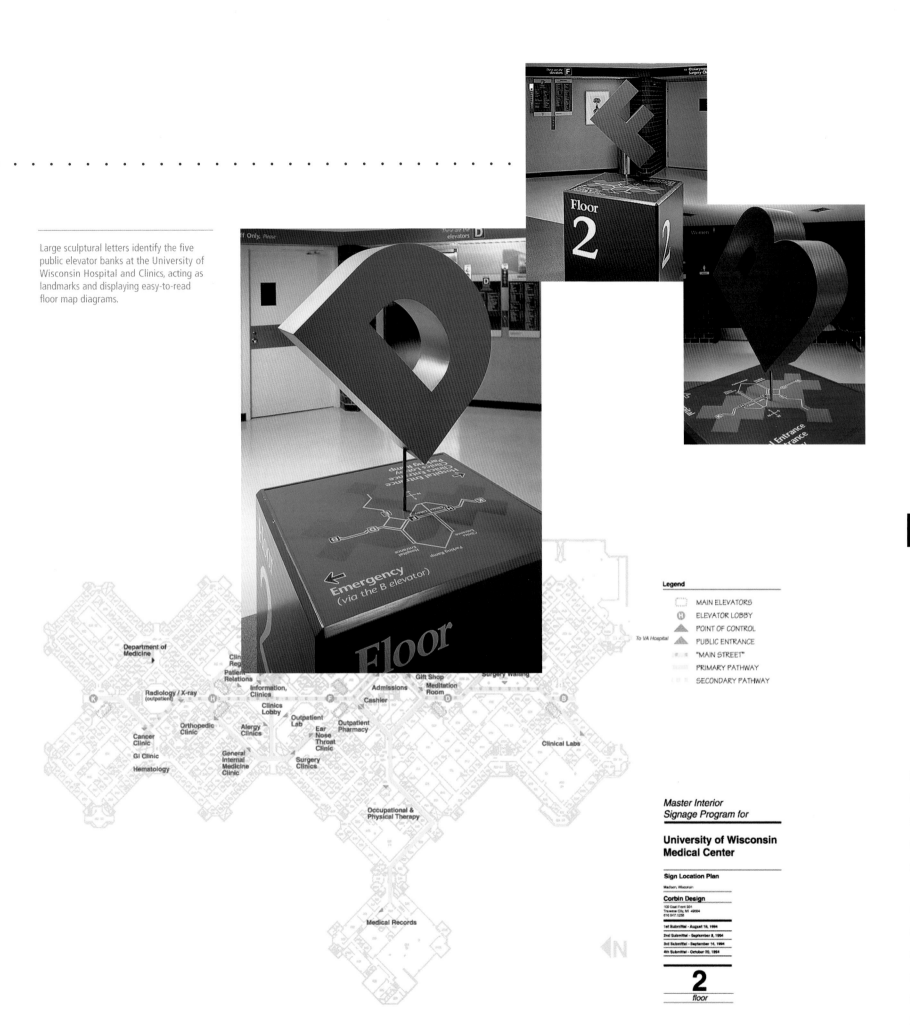

Large sculptural letters identify the five public elevator banks at the University of Wisconsin Hospital and Clinics, acting as landmarks and displaying easy-to-read floor map diagrams.

Floor 2

Emergency
(via the B elevator)

Floor

Legend

- ⬚ MAIN ELEVATORS
- Ⓗ ELEVATOR LOBBY
- ▲ POINT OF CONTROL
- ▲ PUBLIC ENTRANCE
- "MAIN STREET"
- PRIMARY PATHWAY
- SECONDARY PATHWAY

Department of Medicine

Radiology / X-ray (outpatient)

Cancer Clinic

GI Clinic

Hematology

Orthopedic Clinic

Clin Reg

Patient Relations

Information, Clinics

Clinics Lobby

General Internal Medicine Clinic

Allergy Clinics

Outpatient Lab

Ear Nose Throat Clinic

Surgery Clinics

Admissions

Cashier

Gift Shop

Meditation Room

Outpatient Pharmacy

Surgery Waiting

Clinical Labs

To VA Hospital

Occupational & Physical Therapy

Medical Records

*Master Interior
Signage Program for*

**University of Wisconsin
Medical Center**

Sign Location Plan

Madison, Wisconsin

Corbin Design

109 East Front 304
Traverse City, MI 49684
616 947-1236

1st Submittal - August 16, 1994
2nd Submittal - September 8, 1994
3rd Submittal - September 14, 1994
4th Submittal - October 22, 1994

2
floor

53

EXPERT ESSAY

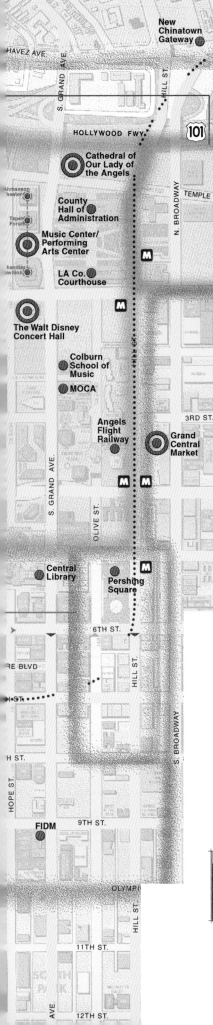

Two design firms tackle wayfinding in thirteen urban districts

When nine often competitive business districts in a dense three-hundred-block downtown area agree to cooperate on joint improvement projects, it is big news. That is what happened when the Confederation of Downtown Associations was formed in Los Angeles in 2000. And among the first shared efforts—which included joint security, sidewalk cleaning, and promotion—was what has turned out to be one of the largest urban wayfinding efforts in the U.S.

Downtown Los Angeles has had several false starts in rebuilding a city center that would be appealing to the area population of more than five million residents. As in many major American cities, the pull of suburbia had attracted department stores, entertainment venues, and hundreds of vital businesses away from downtown. While the western edge of downtown had regained some credibility with the construction of high-rise office buildings, little or no evening or weekend activity existed, and there was certainly little appeal as a destination. But by 2000, early signs of life and urban vitality were becoming visible. Older buildings were being restored as residential lofts; the Fashion District started attracting weekend crowds; and people began talking about "going downtown." What was also apparent was a lack of knowledge about the many diverse districts of downtown, what they were and where they were, and most important, what visitors could do there—the perfect scenario for an urban wayfinding program.

The Confederation requested proposals from across the country, received a dozen or so, interviewed five finalists, and selected the team of Corbin and Hunt Design to execute the newly named "Downtown Los Angeles Walks" signage program. Corbin's role was weighted toward the programming and documentation phases of the project; Hunt's staff focused on the design issues and implementation coordination. The Confederation also a hired a consultant, Urban Place Consulting Group, to coordinate the input of the nine districts and the myriad city agencies.

From the start the design team recognized that while Downtown consisted of nine official districts with legal names and distinct boundaries, the general public had its own perception of what and where districts were: for example, the well-known and geographically unique Bunker Hill area had been subsumed by the Downtown Center district, and the Civic Center wasn't included in any of the formal districts. The solution, after much negotiation, was to slightly regroup the districts into "publicly understandable" areas. Only in this way could a sign system based on named districts be effective. The resulting network of thirteen perceivable districts became the programmatic core of the wayfinding project.

Next came designs for icons for each area. As they emerged, these logo-like images began appearing as lead items on the early sign design concepts.

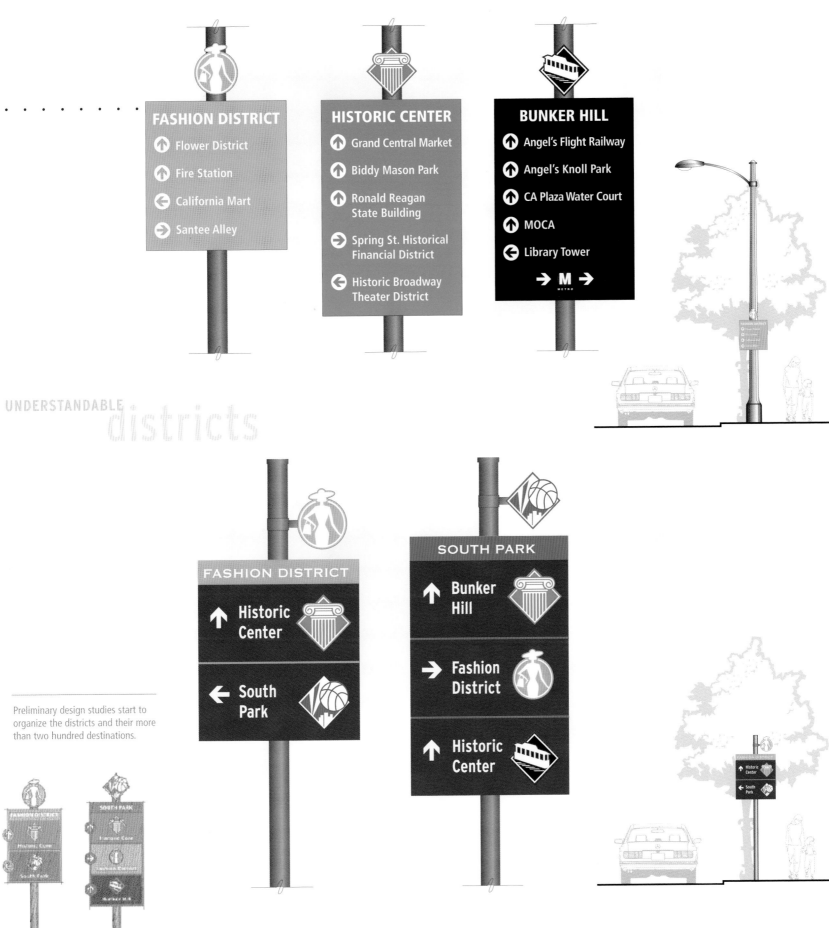

FASHION DISTRICT
- ⬆ Flower District
- ⬆ Fire Station
- ⬅ California Mart
- ➡ Santee Alley

HISTORIC CENTER
- ⬆ Grand Central Market
- ⬆ Biddy Mason Park
- ⬆ Ronald Reagan State Building
- ➡ Spring St. Historical Financial District
- ⬅ Historic Broadway Theater District

BUNKER HILL
- ⬆ Angel's Flight Railway
- ⬆ Angel's Knoll Park
- ⬆ CA Plaza Water Court
- ⬆ MOCA
- ⬅ Library Tower
- ➡ **M** ➡
  METRO

UNDERSTANDABLE districts

FASHION DISTRICT
- ⬆ Historic Center
- ⬅ South Park

SOUTH PARK
- ⬆ Bunker Hill
- ➡ Fashion District
- ⬆ Historic Center

Preliminary design studies start to organize the districts and their more than two hundred destinations.

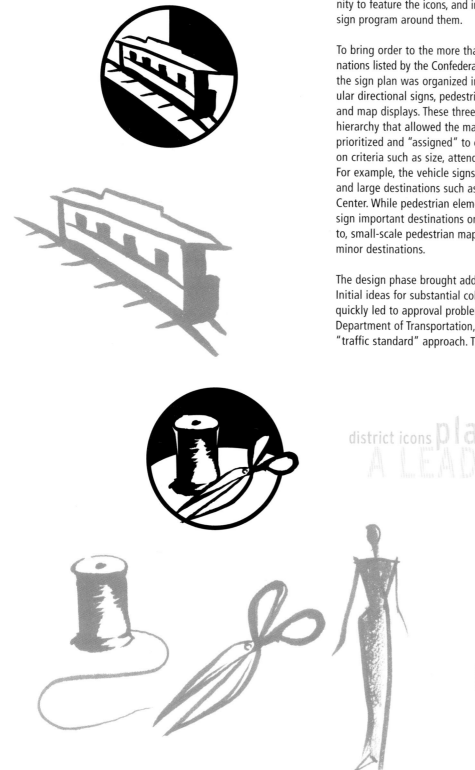

The designers and the Confederation saw the opportunity to feature the icons, and in fact, build the entire sign program around them.

To bring order to the more than two hundred destinations listed by the Confederation's district members, the sign plan was organized into three groups: vehicular directional signs, pedestrian directional signs, and map displays. These three elements formed a hierarchy that allowed the many destinations to be prioritized and "assigned" to certain sign types based on criteria such as size, attendance, and "findability." For example, the vehicle signs present district names and large destinations such as the popular Staples Center. While pedestrian elements display on any one sign important destinations one can reasonably walk to, small-scale pedestrian maps address the more minor destinations.

The design phase brought additional challenges. Initial ideas for substantial color and visual vitality quickly led to approval problems from the city's Department of Transportation, which wanted a more "traffic standard" approach. The design process evolved into a more straightforward visual vocabulary with the district icons playing the lead role. Each vehicular sign features an icon header element displaying the district name, as well as a sign with a neutral green background. Each pedestrian sign is the color of its respective district and presents the icon as a "ghost" image under the message typography. The result is a highly systematic, logical system with function and communication as priorities.

The Confederation's commitment to include pedestrian mapping in the system led to an innovative approach to map design. Unlike maps that show the entire downtown, these maps display nine-square-block areas. As a pedestrian moves through the area, the map "window" changes with each map encountered, keeping the walker roughly on center in the map segment. A small key map shows one's relative location to all of Downtown.

The original plan included a program of banners to support the district identities, but some districts later chose to create banners independent of the system.

district icons play
A LEAD ROLE

Central to the program are these district icons, each the result of district-by-district negotiation.

= 15

57

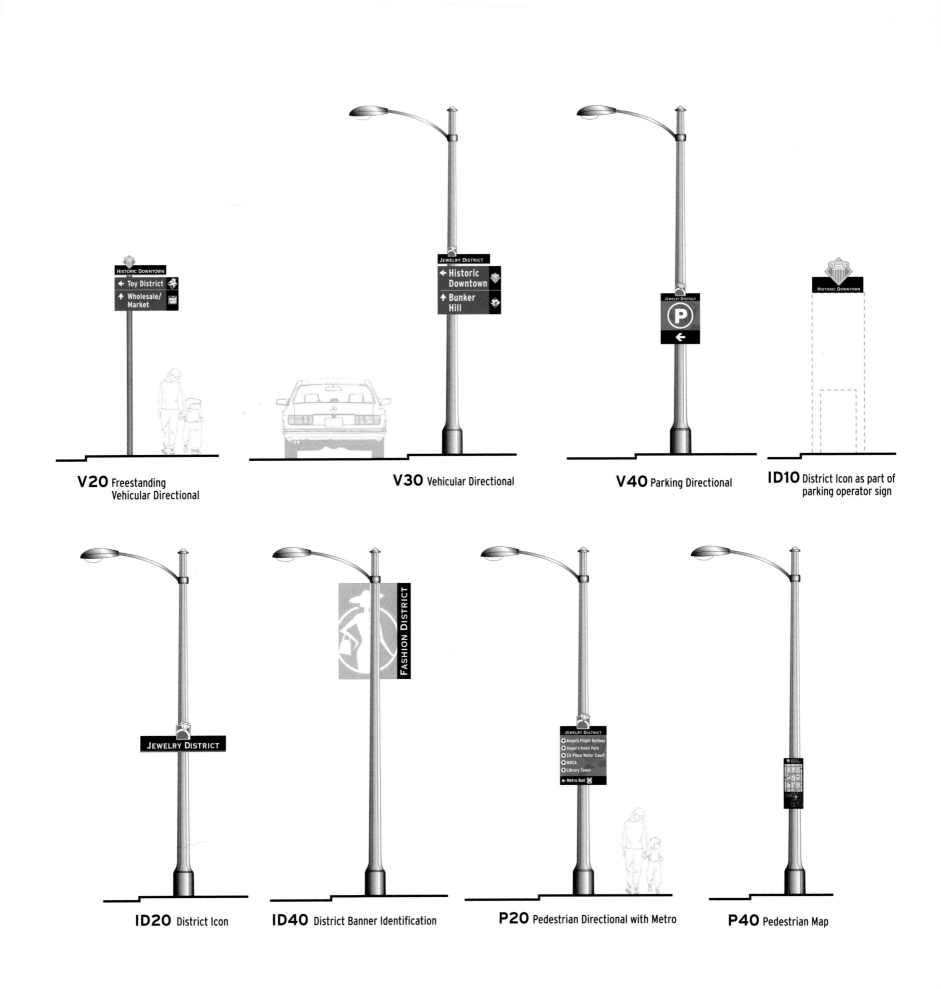

V20 Freestanding Vehicular Directional

V30 Vehicular Directional

V40 Parking Directional

ID10 District Icon as part of parking operator sign

ID20 District Icon

ID40 District Banner Identification

P20 Pedestrian Directional with Metro

P40 Pedestrian Map

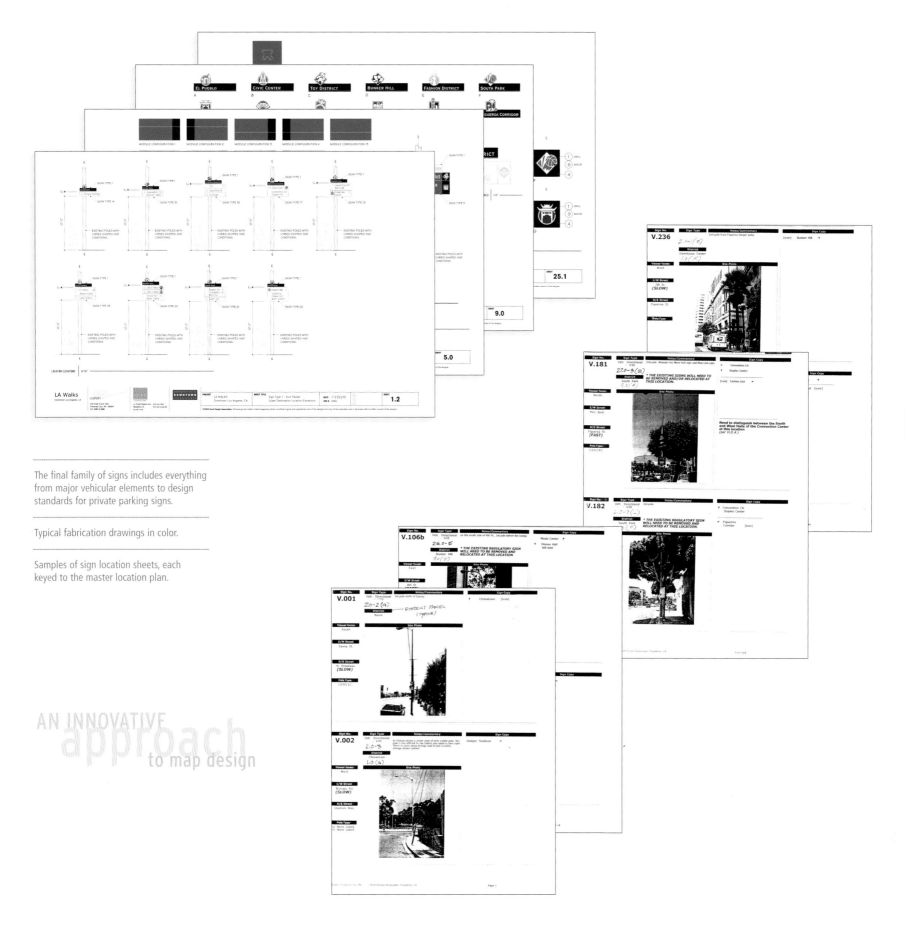

The final family of signs includes everything from major vehicular elements to design standards for private parking signs.

Typical fabrication drawings in color.

Samples of sign location sheets, each keyed to the master location plan.

AN INNOVATIVE
approach
to map design

Design **Analysis**

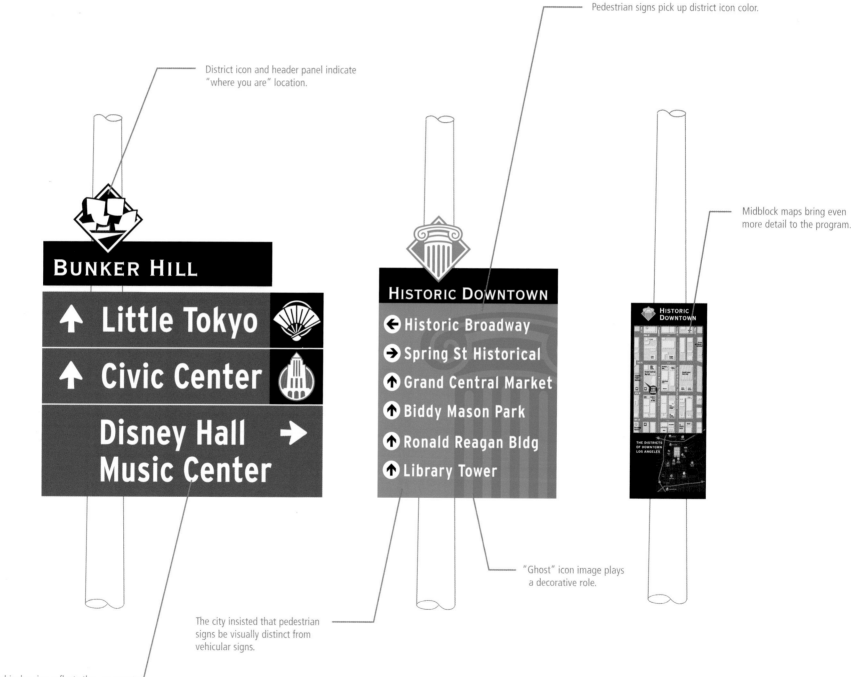

District icon and header panel indicate "where you are" location.

Pedestrian signs pick up district icon color.

Midblock maps bring even more detail to the program.

"Ghost" icon image plays a decorative role.

The city insisted that pedestrian signs be visually distinct from vehicular signs.

Final vehicular sign reflects the strong influence of the city's Department of Transportation.

BUNKER HILL

↑ Little Tokyo

↑ Civic Center

Disney Hall
Music Center →

HISTORIC DOWNTOWN

← Historic Broadway

→ Spring St Historical

↑ Grand Central Market

↑ Biddy Mason Park

↑ Ronald Reagan Bldg

↑ Library Tower

HISTORIC DOWNTOWN

THE DISTRICTS
OF DOWNTOWN
LOS ANGELES

Super/Major Destinations

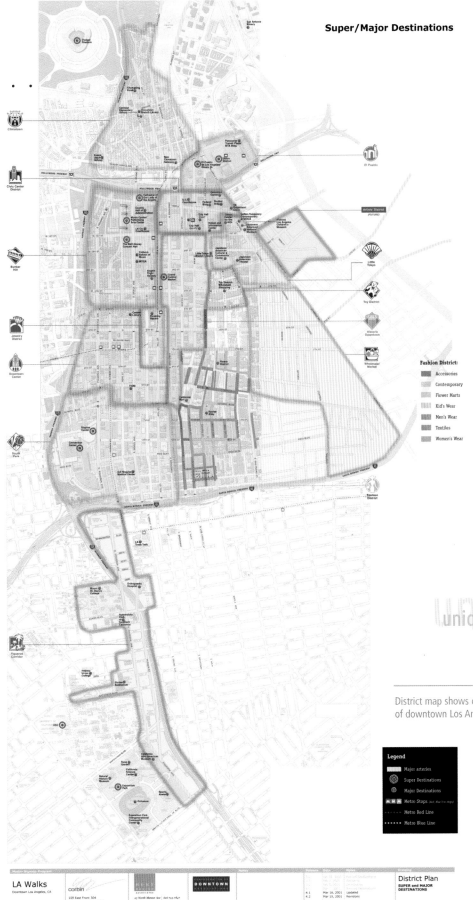

Fashion District:

- Accessories
- Contemporary
- Flower Marts
- Kid's Wear
- Men's Wear
- Textiles
- Women's Wear

District map shows complex layout
of downtown Los Angeles.

Legend

- Major arteries
- Super Destinations
- Major Destinations
- Metro Stops *(incl. Blue line stops)*
- Metro Red Line
- Metro Blue Line

unique areas OF DOWNTOWN

LA Walks
Downtown Los Angeles, CA

corbin
109 East Front 304
Traverse City, MI 49684
231 947.1236

DOWNTOWN
ASSOCIATES
17 North Marion Ave
Pasadena, CA
91104-1709

CONFEDERATION OF
DOWNTOWN
ASSOCIATES

4.1	Mar 16, 2001	Updated
4.2	Mar 19, 2001	Revisions

District Plan
SUPER and MAJOR
DESTINATIONS

PROJECT OVERVIEW
Vehicular and pedestrian wayfinding
program for downtown Los Angeles.

PROJECT FACTS
Client:
  Confederation of Downtown Associations
Graphic Design Team:
  Corbin:
  Jeff Corbin, Jim Harper,
  Matt McCormick
  Hunt Design:
  Christina Allen, Wayne Hunt,
  In Sung Kim, Dinnis Lee,
  Perry Shimoji, John Temple
Consultant:
  Urban Place Consulting Group
Map Source:
  Cartifact
Schedule:
  Two years (design only)

MATERIALS & TECHNIQUES
Aluminum sign panels and decorative
icon shapes with retro-reflective vinyl
film and translucent ink graphics.

UNIQUE ASPECTS
Multiple approval agencies, challenging
field conditions, diverse client group.

61

PROJECT FACTS

OXNARD Downtown Wayfinding

An old downtown gets a colorful face-lift

Oxnard, California, a thriving city with more than 182,000 residents, is often overshadowed by its well-known coastal neighbors, Ventura and Santa Barbara. While Oxnard has an active marina and some of the area's best beaches, it is best known to Southern California visitors as an agricultural center. Seen from the busy 101 Freeway, Oxnard is a patchwork of green fields, windrows of trees, and unsightly highway sprawl.

What the passerby cannot see is a charming, once vibrant downtown. As the former center of community and commerce, this twenty-four-block area of primarily one-story retail buildings survived the bulldozer and retained its pedestrian scale and urban qualities. Though rundown and with many empty storefronts, the district was primed for a comeback. As in many other California cities, Oxnard's city leaders came to appreciate the downtown area as a valuable civic asset with substantial civic and commercial potential. A streetscape enhancement program was initiated with new landscaping, historic lighting, and freshened storefronts.

To complement the renewed streets and buildings, and to let people know that downtown Oxnard was back, new signage was needed. The city formed a wayfinding committee of local businesspeople, arts groups, and preservation leaders, all managed by city staff. Hunt Design was selected to design and execute a downtown identity and wayfinding program. The committee met regularly as the creative team helped identify significant downtown destinations and began to organize a system of sign types to meet the needs of drivers and pedestrians.

Agreement on which destinations to feature in which sign locations and preferred wording came easy; how the signs should look proved more controversial. The design team presented a range of visual solutions, from sophisticated retail mall styling to rough-edged Western themes. After much discussion, a contemporary abstraction of converging rows of farmland was selected for further development. These agricultural lines could also be interpreted as sun rays or seen merely as a design motif.

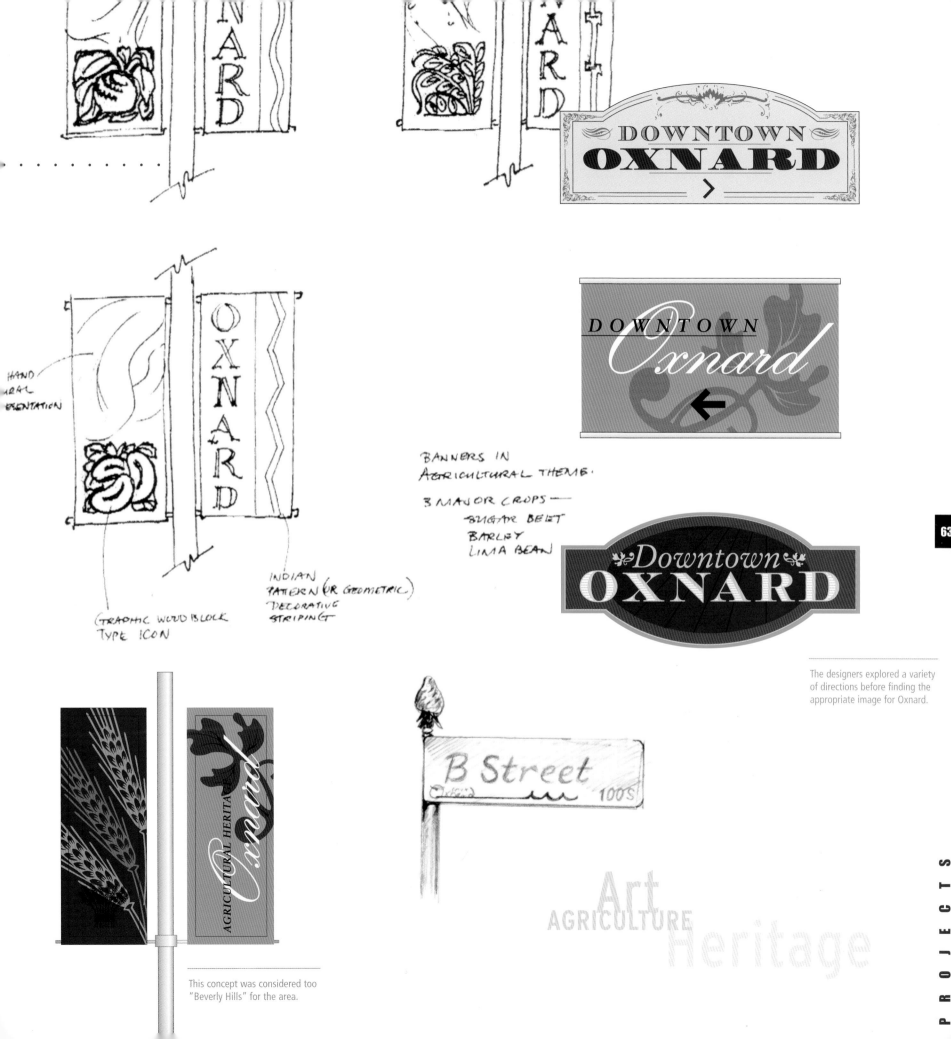

DOWNTOWN
OXNARD
>

DOWNTOWN
Oxnard
←

❧*Downtown*❧
OXNARD

BANNERS IN
AGRICULTURAL THEME.

3 MAJOR CROPS —
SUGAR BEET
BARLEY
LIMA BEAN

HAND
MURAL
PRESENTATION

GRAPHIC WOODBLOCK
TYPE ICON

INDIAN
PATTERN (OR GEOMETRIC)
DECORATIVE
STRIPING

The designers explored a variety
of directions before finding the
appropriate image for Oxnard.

AGRICULTURAL HERITAGE *Oxnard*

B Street
Oxnard   100 S

This concept was considered too
"Beverly Hills" for the area.

Art
AGRICULTURE
Heritage

Each sign location in the program was photodocumented and depicted in the construction drawings.

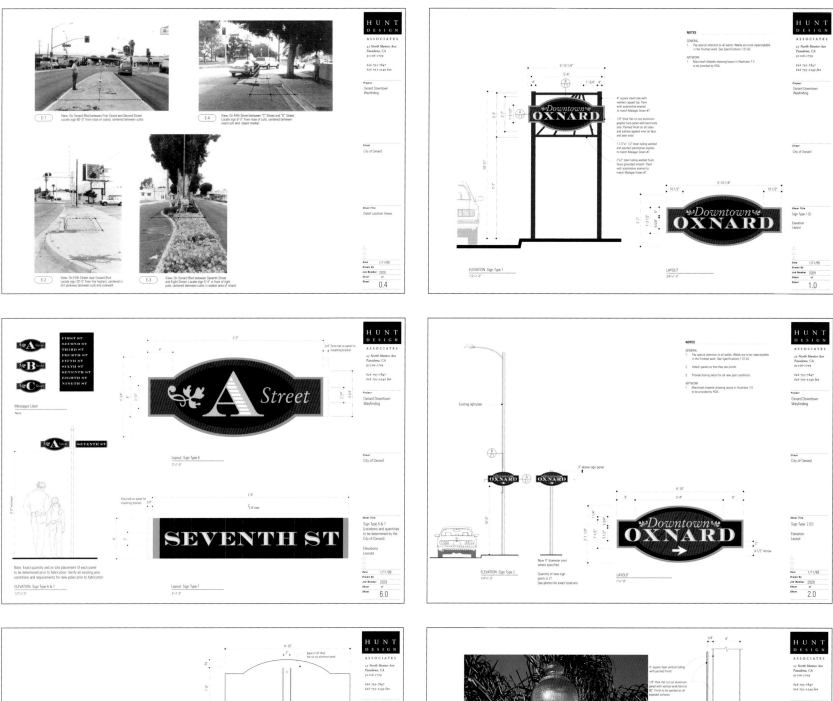

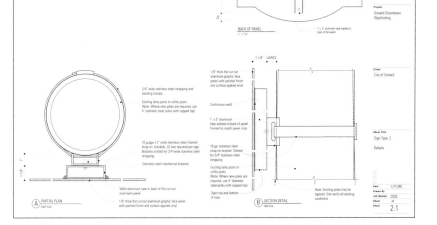

Construction drawings were 11 x 17 inches and presented the sign faces in color.

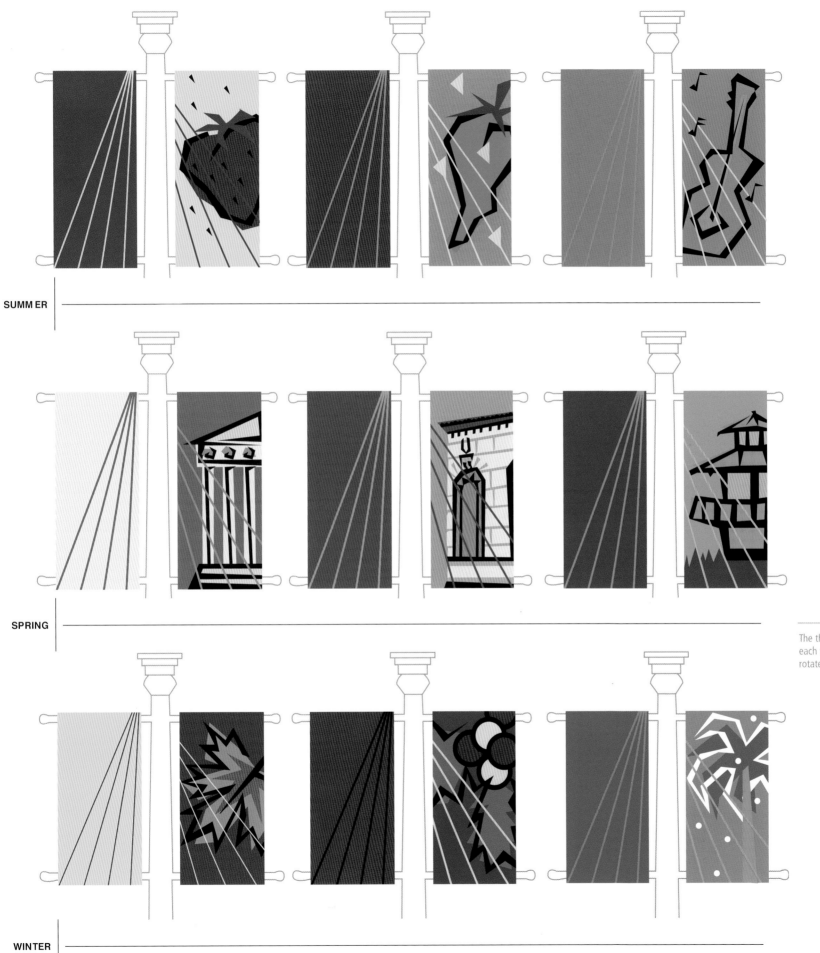

SUMMER

SPRING

WINTER

The three sets of street banners, each with a seasonal theme, are rotated every four months.

These converging lines represent Oxnard's agricultural past and underlie all of the sign types in the program.

Curved shape adds further distinction from typical signs.

The short messages allowed the use of decorative typography, usually not appropriate on street signs.

Devoting one panel to each message helps compensate for the decorative design theme.

The bright colors came from a scarf worn by a client team member; this is not your ordinary roadside sign program!

Secondary message provides location of destination above.

Colorful downtown "logos" on decorative square-tube structures greet downtown visitors.

When it was time to select the color scheme for the sign elements, controversy again reigned. Hunt Design's team demonstrated numerous color combinations without consensus. Some committee members wanted a simple conservative approach, others a bold, colorful look consistent with Oxnard's Hispanic culture. In a climactic meeting, one of the group's more outspoken members referred everyone's attention to a bright shawl worn by another member. There, displayed in one garment, was a beautiful palette of strong and appropriate colors.

The designs, organized into downtown signs and off-site sign groups, were then developed into detailed construction drawings and advertised for public bid to qualified sign companies. A unique design for the downtown street-name signs added another dimension to the scope. Hunt's team helped oversee the fabrication and installation of the program.

As a parallel project, three sets of banners were designed as a seasonal program to enliven the downtown streets. Each set of four designs remains in place for four months and is then replaced with the next set in a continuous rotation.

11 3/4"

2'-3"

1"=1'0"

Double Faced Sign

1/8" Flat Cut out Metal
Porcelain Enamel Graphics
Background

2'-6"

6"

Double Faced Sign

1/8" Flat Cut out Metal
Porcelain Enamel Graphics
Background

Vinyl applied Lettering

Attached with
U Bracket and Strap

Sign Type 5 & 6

1/2"=1'0"

PROJECT OVERVIEW
A downtown identity and wayfinding program of directional signs, street-name signs, and three sets of seasonal banners.

PROJECT FACTS
Client:
    City of Oxnard, California
Graphic Design Team:
    Hunt Design:
    Jennifer Bressler, Wayne Hunt,
    Dinnis Lee, Perry Shimoji
Sign Company:
    Zumar Industries
Schedule:
    Eighteen months

MATERIALS & TECHNIQUES
Aluminum panels with retro-reflective vinyl film and translucent ink graphics; screened-fabric banners.

These custom street-name signs add much to the district's sense of place.

LOS ANGELES ZOO Signage Master Plan

Visual guidelines for a famous zoo

The venerable eighty-acre Los Angeles Zoo was well underway with the implementation of an ambitious master plan—two of ten major new exhibits were open and three more were in final planning stages. At this critical point it became apparent that in addition to the dramatic new attractions, improvements to the zoo's infrastructure were needed as well. Landscaping, lighting, and of course, signage deserved consideration if the master plan was to be fully appreciated and enjoyed by the public.

Like many zoos, the Los Angeles Zoo had spent little on major improvements to signage. The Zoo's own graphics department focused primarily on replication and maintenance of existing designs and themes. Just keeping up with basic animal identification and event graphics consumed their resources. During recent years, signage of many kinds proliferated in all of the Zoo's public areas and became a substantial distraction for visitors. Especially problematic were two important categories of signs: wayfinding and donor recognition. Visitors seemed to be continually lost in spite of more than one hundred directional signs and map kiosks, and the large quantity of mismatched donor signs cluttered many exhibits.

Hunt Design was selected by the Greater Los Angeles Zoo Association, the Zoo's private fund-raising organization, to create and oversee a complete reworking of signage throughout the property. The firm had previously designed a successful outdoor children's exhibit for the Zoo and had extensive knowledge of the facility, as well as a real appreciation of the difficulty facing any attempt to upgrade the Zoo's signage.

The first step was a formal evaluation of existing conditions. The design team photographed hundreds of signs, interviewed Zoo staff, and spoke to dozens of visitors. They observed key parts of the zoo at various times of day and night and on busy and light attendance days. They noted the behavior of families, couples, and school groups. The result was a thirty-page critique with chapters on each category of zoo signage, including wayfinding, operations, food and retail, parking, and donor recognition. Recommendations for improvements to each area were presented.

The report noted that even though there were more than forty map directories on the property, visitors could not stay oriented. The Zoo's many curving walkways and paths combine with hilly terrain to make wayfinding difficult. The designers convinced the Zoo that a new approach to direction-giving was needed. And because visitor orientation is fundamental to wayfinding, the team began to explore ways to help visitors "know where they are" at all times. They needed a way to break the Zoo into smaller, more understandable pieces, as is done in theme parks.

orientation is fundamental to
WAYFINDING

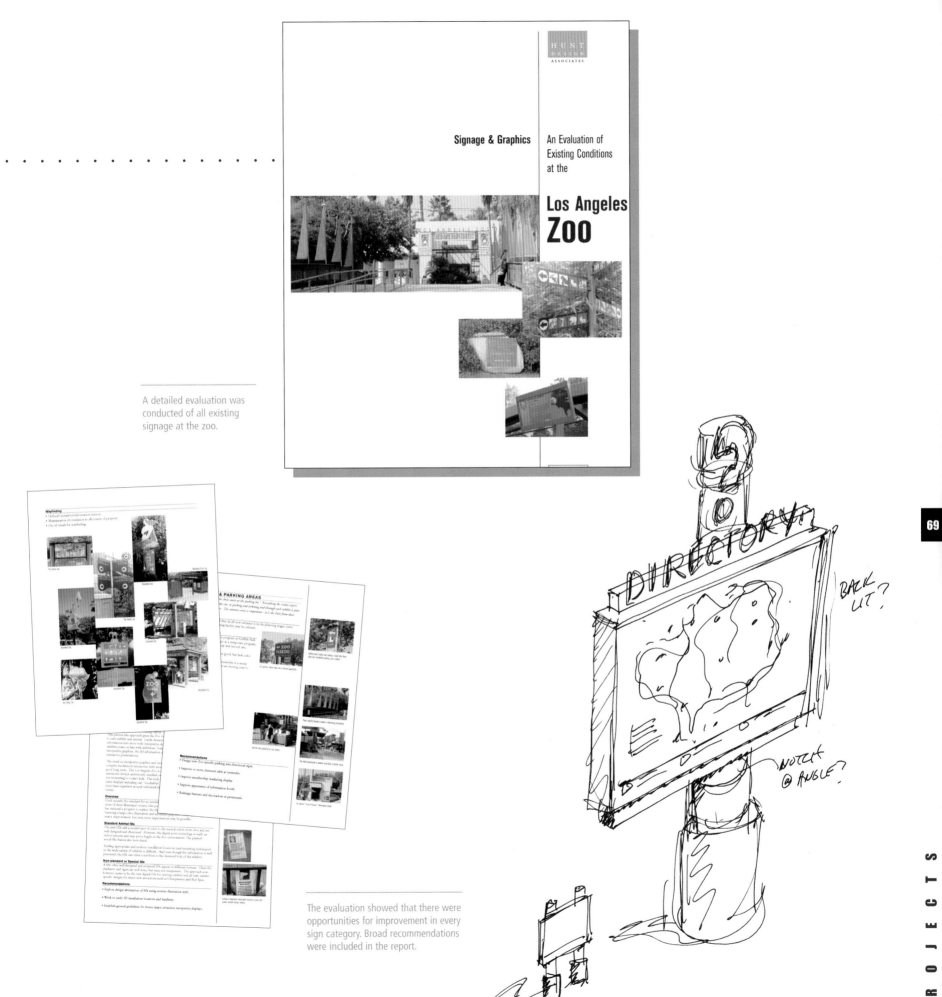

Signage & Graphics | An Evaluation of Existing Conditions at the

Los Angeles Zoo

A detailed evaluation was conducted of all existing signage at the zoo.

The evaluation showed that there were opportunities for improvement in every sign category. Broad recommendations were included in the report.

DIRECTORY

BACK LIT?

NOTCH @ ANGLE?

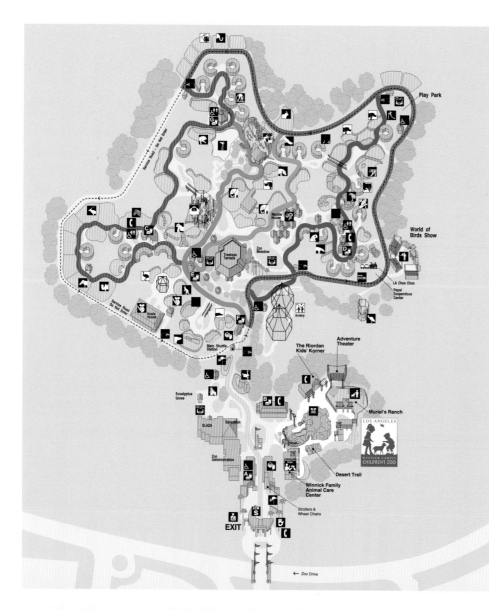

The complex facility did not neatly subdivide into quadrants or cardinal direction groupings (north, south, etc.), nor did it offer opportunities for geographic organizing (Africa, Asia, etc.). After considering several approaches, the designers hit upon the idea to create perceivable subareas by simply color-naming five of the primary trails and to build the entire wayfinding system around a visual and verbal design of colors: Blue Avenue, Red Road, etc. This back-to-basics approach made the handsome but heretofore confusing zoo map suddenly functional. Directional signs also fell into place with logical, color-based designs.

The final signage master plan features a new site gateway sign, new alpha-pictorial parking signs, a botanical background theme for the many operational signs, and guidelines for the design by others of retail and food operation graphics. Designs for off-site directional signs to the zoo were developed.

Donor signage was reorganized to recognize benefactors in two major categories, the capital campaign and the general fund. And except for major donors to master plan exhibits, all recognition displays will be incorporated into the new public entrance.

Early attempts to find a wayfinding organizing principle for the zoo included a concept based on compass directions.

Working over the existing map, the designers created a system of color-based trail names: Green Street, Blue Avenue, Red Road, etc.

The families of sign types defined by the master plan: site, parking, wayfinding, operations, animal identification, and donor recognition.

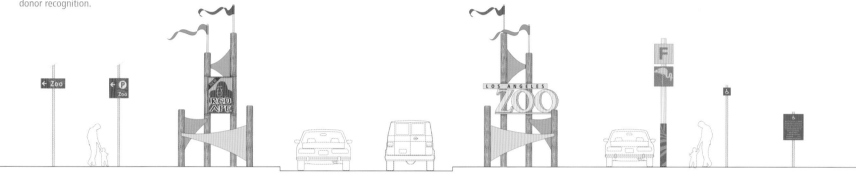

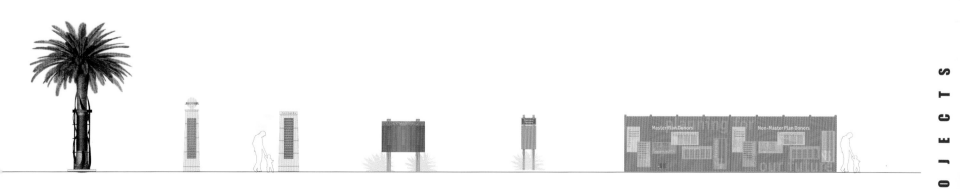

Information is broken into separate panels for visual interest and modular accessibility.

In a departure from tradition, photographs replace illustrations on the new ID displays.

Provocative titles invite reading.

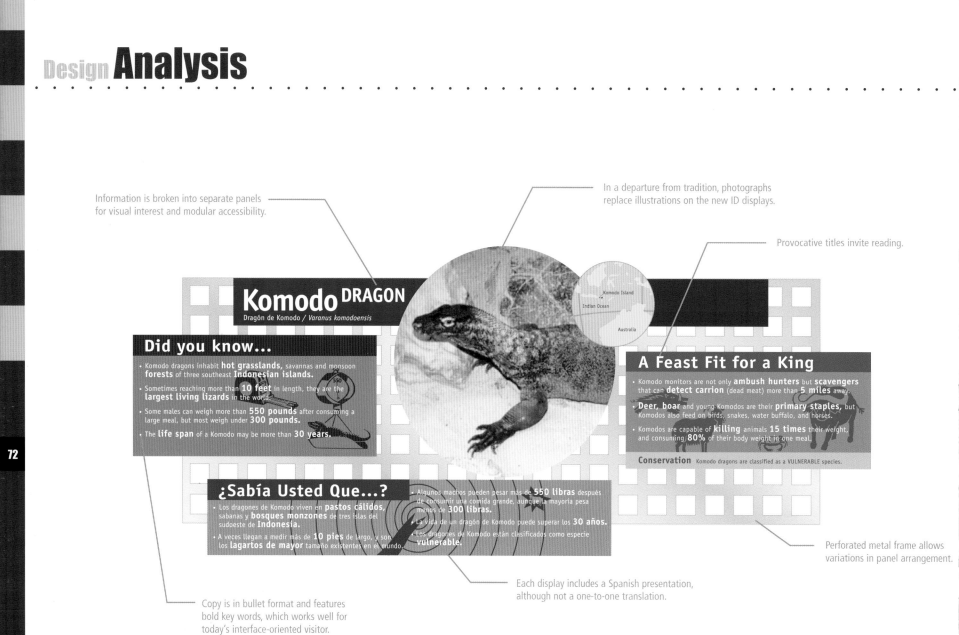

Komodo DRAGON
Dragón de Komodo / *Varanus komodoensis*

Did you know...
- Komodo dragons inhabit **hot grasslands**, savannas and monsoon **forests** of three southeast **Indonesian islands.**
- Sometimes reaching more than **10 feet** in length, they are the **largest living lizards** in the world.
- Some males can weigh more than **550 pounds** after consuming a large meal, but most weigh under **300 pounds.**
- The **life span** of a Komodo may be more than **30 years.**

Komodo Island
Indian Ocean
Australia

A Feast Fit for a King
- Komodo monitors are not only **ambush hunters** but **scavengers** that can **detect carrion** (dead meat) more than **5 miles** away.
- **Deer, boar** and young Komodos are their **primary staples**, but Komodos also feed on birds, snakes, water buffalo, and horses.
- Komodos are capable of **killing** animals **15 times** their weight, and consuming **80%** of their body weight in one meal.

Conservation Komodo dragons are classified as a VULNERABLE species.

¿Sabía Usted Que...?
- Los dragones de Komodo viven en **pastos cálidos**, sabanas y **bosques monzones** de tres islas del sudoeste de **Indonesia.**
- A veces llegan a medir más de **10 pies** de largo, y son los **lagartos de mayor** tamaño existentes en el mundo.
- Algunos machos pueden pesar más de **550 libras** después de consumir una comida grande, aunque la mayoría pesa menos de **300 libras.**
- La vida de un dragón de Komodo puede superar los **30 años.**
- Los dragones de Komodo están clasificados como especie **vulnerable.**

Perforated metal frame allows variations in panel arrangement.

Each display includes a Spanish presentation, although not a one-to-one translation.

Copy is in bullet format and features bold key words, which works well for today's interface-oriented visitor.

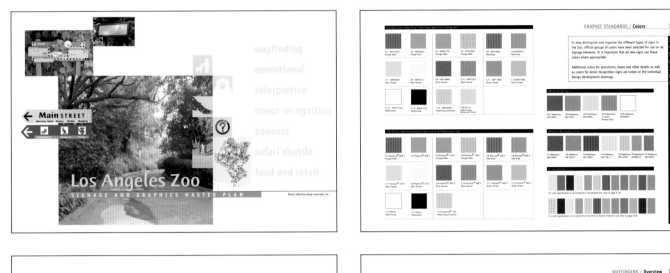

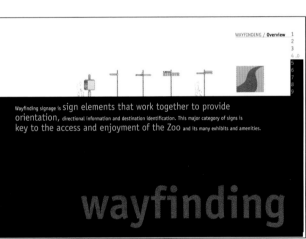

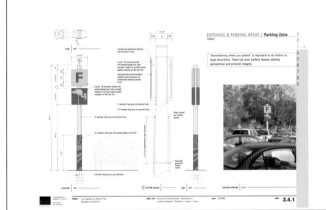

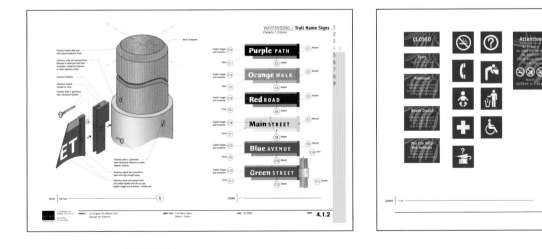

Typical pages from the master plan.

PROJECT OVERVIEW
A comprehensive long-term plan for signage and graphics of all types.

PROJECT FACTS
Client:
   Los Angeles Zoo
Graphic Design Team:
   Hunt Design:
   Christina Allen, Jennifer Bressler,
   Wayne Hunt, Dinnis Lee, Perry Shimoji
Schedule:
   Six months (design only)

MATERIALS & TECHNIQUES
Flat and curved aluminum panels with vinyl graphics on painted steel poles and pressure-treated cedar posts; phenolic resin panels with impregnated digital print on painted aluminum frames; dimensional aluminum letters; wood posts; phenolic resin graphics panels applied to powder-coated perforated steel background shapes, mounted on natural weathered posts or exhibit handrails; translucent digital prints set into existing exhibit light boxes.

Acrylic and aluminum plaques with screened graphics, existing palm tree surrounded by formed sculptural aluminum leaves, bands, and tubing on concrete pad; formed aluminum donor strips with etched and filled copy; banners with graphic images on existing wood armatures.

UNIQUE ASPECTS
Required input from all departments of the zoo and extensive review by the zoo's volunteer fund-raising organization.

Designing in HUMAN SCALE

Much of the man-made world is scaled for people—nearly everything not provided by nature relates in some way to the size of the human body. Signage and graphics are especially dependent on direct size relationships to people and how they perceive, access, and interact with their surroundings. An understanding and working knowledge of human scale is important for success in any three-dimensional design effort.

74

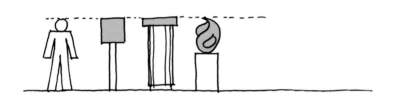

AS A GENERAL RULE, OBJECTS THAT ARE THE SAME SIZE AS PEOPLE ARE NOT VERY INTERESTING.

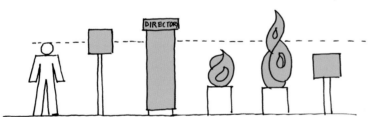

OBJECTS LARGER OR SMALLER THAN PEOPLE ARE INHERENTLY INTERESTING.

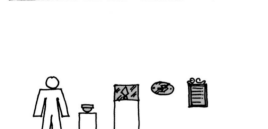

SMALL OBJECTS ARE "DOMINATED" BY HUMAN SCALE AND OFTEN HAVE A PERSONAL FEEL. EXTREMELY SMALL OBJECTS OFTEN SEEM PRECIOUS AND EVEN JEWELLIKE.

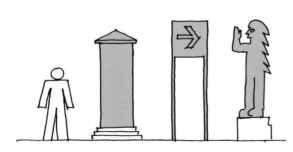

LARGER OBJECTS "DOMINATE" HUMAN SCALE AND CAN PROJECT A HEROIC SENSE.

Human size influences the design of the environment.

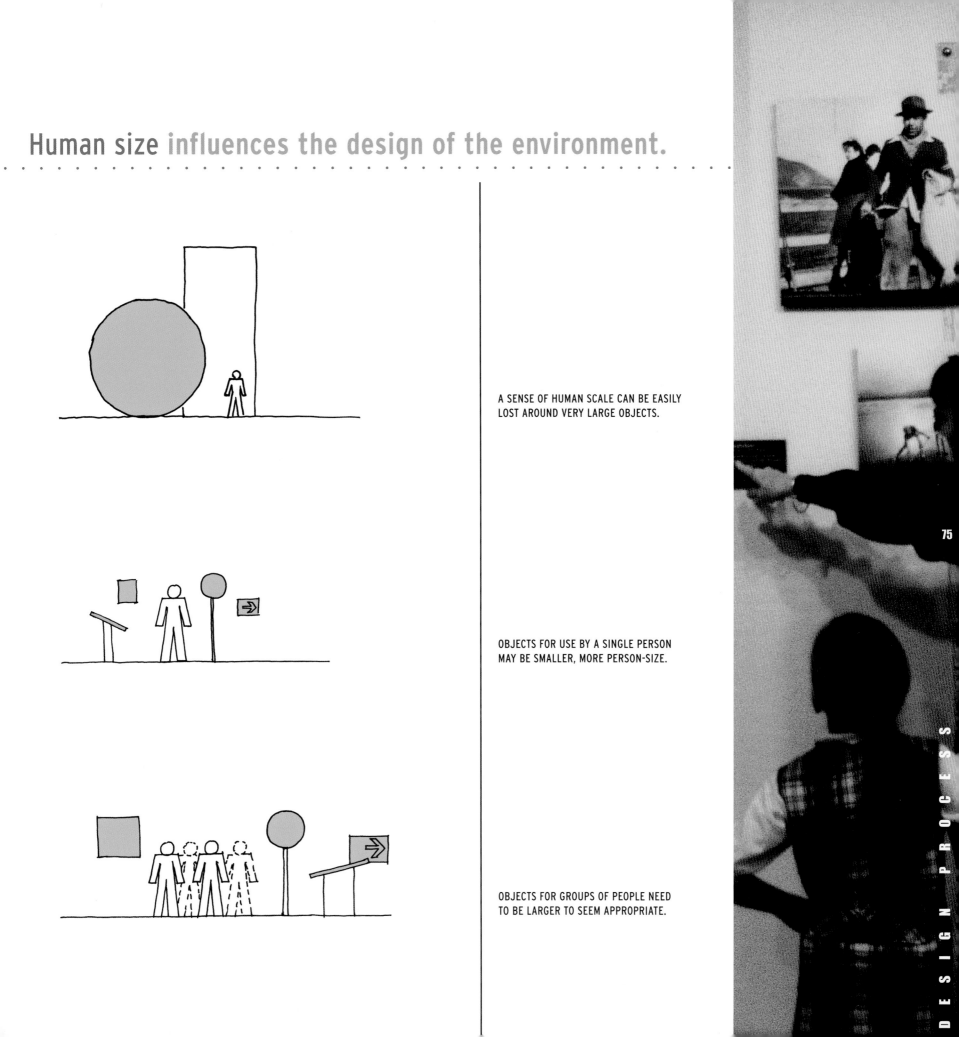

A SENSE OF HUMAN SCALE CAN BE EASILY
LOST AROUND VERY LARGE OBJECTS.

OBJECTS FOR USE BY A SINGLE PERSON
MAY BE SMALLER, MORE PERSON-SIZE.

OBJECTS FOR GROUPS OF PEOPLE NEED
TO BE LARGER TO SEEM APPROPRIATE.

HUMAN FACTORS in Perceiving the Environment

Creating effective graphics has much to do with the way people see, move, and relate physically to the environment. The upright stance of the human body and the location of the eyes in our head control the amount of information that we see and take in at any one time. Because our natural field of vision is centered on the horizon or straight ahead, things directly in front of us are seen most easily. Conversely, objects or information not "on center" are less visible and less important. The farther away from the center of this narrow cone of vision, the less we notice them.

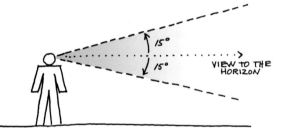

THE COMFORTABLE CONE OF VISION—APPROXIMATELY 15° ABOVE AND BELOW THE DIRECT LINE OF SIGHT.

EFFECTIVE SIGNS ARE USUALLY SIZED AND PLACED WITHIN THE USER'S CONE OF VISION.

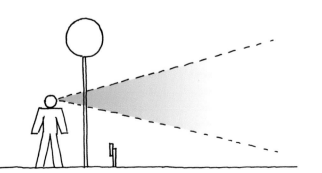

OBJECTS PLACED OUTSIDE OF THE CONE OF VISION ARE MUCH LESS EFFECTIVE (AND LESS MEANINGFUL).

The **physiology of vision** determines what and how we see.

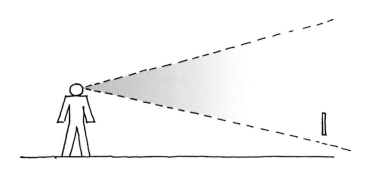

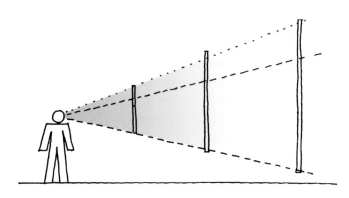

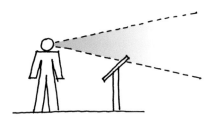

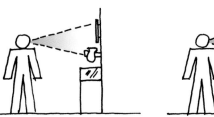

AS AN OBJECT'S SIZE DECREASES RELATIVE TO THE CONE OF VISION, IT BECOMES LESS IMPORTANT TO THE EYE.

EXCEPTIONS TO THE CONE OF VISION ARE BEST DONE ON THE HIGH SIDE.

VIEWING AND READING BELOW 30° IS UNCOMFORTABLE, UNLESS THE INFORMATION IS ANGLED UP TOWARD THE VIEWER.

OR, IF ABOVE 30° IT SHOULD BE ANGLED DOWN TOWARD THE VIEWER, AS SEEN IN INSTRUMENT DISPLAYS AND CONTROL ROOMS.

THE SAME PRINCIPLES APPLY TO EXHIBIT INFORMATION AND RETAIL DISPLAY.

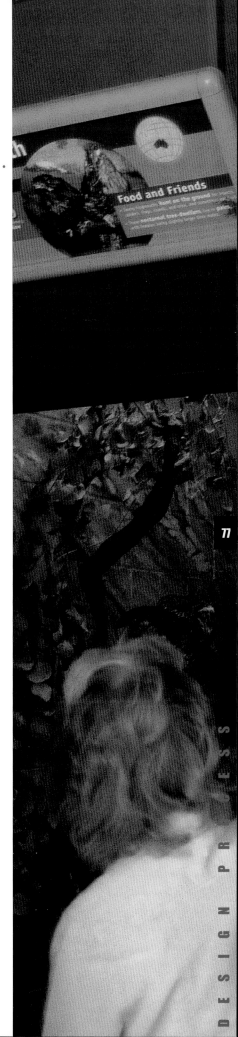

DESIGN PROCESS

Scale and Design in CHILDREN'S ENVIRONMENTS

Children are not simply small adults. While many human-scale design principles apply, other environmental interaction attributes come into play. Being much less verbal and not word oriented, kids are especially responsive to physical design qualities. Also, their natural energy and animation make it more comfortable for them to interact with and value visual stimulation outside of their cone of vision.

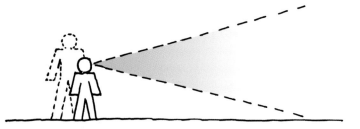

CHILDREN HAVE THEIR OWN CONE OF VISION, BUT MOST OF THE SAME PRINCIPLES APPLY AS WITH ADULTS.

CHILDREN ARE MORE FLEXIBLE IN USE OF THE CONE OF VISION THAN ADULTS.

KIDS RESPOND AND RELATE TO THINGS LARGER THAN THEMSELVES.

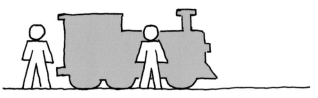

CUTOUT SHAPES AND DIMENSIONAL OBJECTS ARE ESPECIALLY APPEALING TO CHILDREN.

Kids' environments require the human scale approach, **but at a reduced size.**

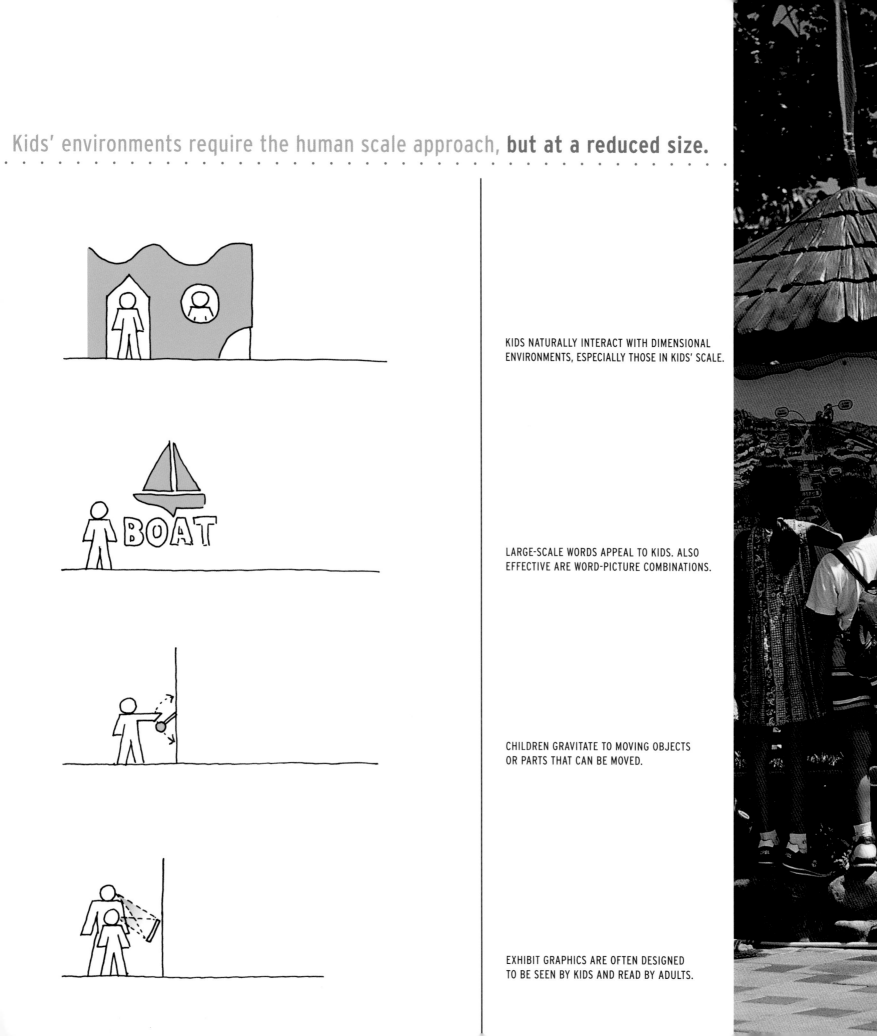

KIDS NATURALLY INTERACT WITH DIMENSIONAL
ENVIRONMENTS, ESPECIALLY THOSE IN KIDS' SCALE.

BOAT

LARGE-SCALE WORDS APPEAL TO KIDS. ALSO
EFFECTIVE ARE WORD-PICTURE COMBINATIONS.

CHILDREN GRAVITATE TO MOVING OBJECTS
OR PARTS THAT CAN BE MOVED.

EXHIBIT GRAPHICS ARE OFTEN DESIGNED
TO BE SEEN BY KIDS AND READ BY ADULTS.

DESIGN PROCESS

ARCHITECTURAL Scale

Because signs and graphics are usually part of buildings, places, or spaces, a sense of architectural scale is important. And just as important is the awareness of the key role signage can play in altering the perception of scale in a building. Because a sign is mounted on a building but is designed for a person, it is a natural scale-transition element.

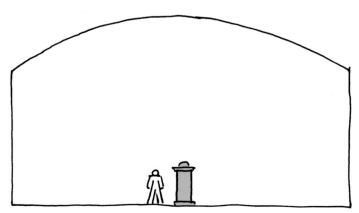

COMFORTABLE OBJECT/PERSON/SPACE SCALE.

THE SAME OBJECT IN A LARGER SPACE TENDS TO LOOK SMALLER.

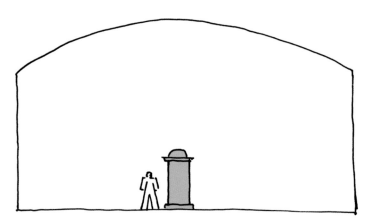

ENLARGING THE OBJECT RETURNS THE COMFORTABLE SCALE RELATIONSHIP.

The size of buildings and architectural components influences the design of environmental graphics.

ARCHITECTURAL ENVIRONMENTS CAN OFTEN BE "SCALE-LESS."

SIGNS AND GRAPHICS HELP "SCALE DOWN" LARGE OBJECTS (BUILDINGS) INTO HUMAN SCALE. THE SIZE, QUANTITY, AND PLACEMENT OF SIGNAGE AND OTHER ELEMENTS AFFECT THE PERCEPTION OF SCALE.

Counseling

Assessment Center

DESIGN PROCESS

OUTDOOR and Urban Scale

Moving to the outdoor environment, the rules of scale change once again. Things that look huge indoors suddenly appear to shrink once outside. Scale is, by definition, relative. For scale reference outside, we depend on natural things such as trees or the man-made elements of buildings and streets. But because signage and graphics are for use by people, scaling the designs to the outdoor or urban setting is paramount.

ENVIRONMENTS WITHOUT SCALE REFERENCES ARE NOT COMFORTABLE; PEOPLE NEED TO BE AROUND THINGS.

LANDSCAPE AND OTHER ELEMENTS "SCALE DOWN" THE OUTDOORS.

OUTDOOR SPACES REQUIRE EVEN LARGER OBJECTS THAN ARCHITECTURAL SPACES.

Elements designed for outdoors have even **larger scale issues.**

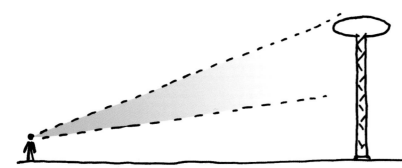

LARGE OBJECTS HAVE THE MOST VALUE WHEN VIEWED FROM A DISTANCE.

SMALL-SCALE DETAIL IS NEEDED FOR CLOSE VIEWING OF LARGE OBJECTS.

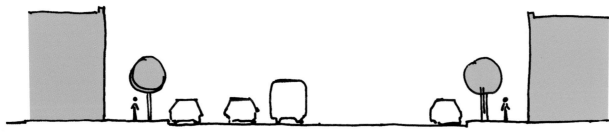

THE OVERLY WIDE STREETS OF WESTERN U.S. CITIES PRESENT CHALLENGES TO HUMAN SCALE.

THE ELEMENTS OF URBAN DESIGN:
LIGHTING, SIGNAGE, AND FURNITURE
CREATE THE REAL SCALE TRANSITION
BETWEEN BUILDINGS AND PEOPLE.

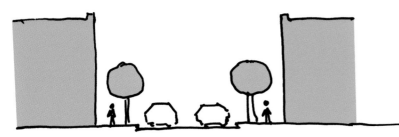

THE NARROW STREETS OF EUROPE PROVIDE A MORE HUMAN-SCALE EXPERIENCE.

VEHICULAR Environments

Moving from being a pedestrian to being a driver also changes one's scale relationships. Detail and human scale are no longer relevant; large simple forms and clarity of information are paramount. Viewing the world while in motion challenges our ability to differentiate letters and words and drastically reduces the time needed to sort content and comprehend meaning. And while the relative scale of road signs to the environment is important, their real scale success is based on vehicle speed and contrast with other signs.

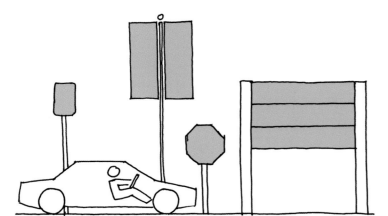

VEHICULAR ENVIRONMENTS REQUIRE VERY LARGE OBJECTS.

TRUCK ENVIRONMENTS NEED EVEN LARGER OBJECTS.

Motion and car size change the rules of scale.

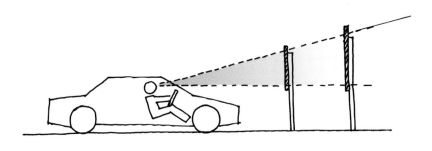

DRIVERS TEND TO RESPOND TO AND READ ONLY IN THE UPPER HALF OF THE CONE OF VISION.

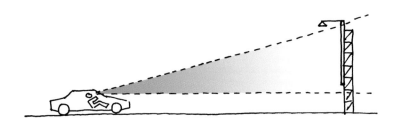

THE LONGER THE VIEWING DISTANCE, THE LARGER THE OBJECT MUST BE WITHIN THE CONE OF VISION.

VIEWING THROUGH A WINDSHIELD FURTHER LIMITS UNDERSTANDING OF THE ENVIRONMENT.

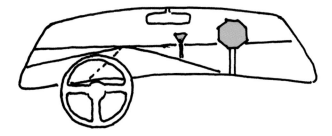

UNIQUE SHAPES AID RECOGNITION.

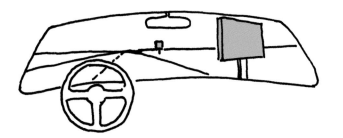

ROAD SIGNS SHOULD BE WIDELY SPACED ON HIGH-SPEED ROADWAYS.

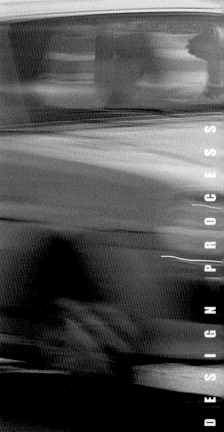

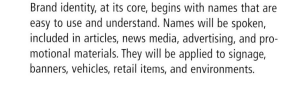

Brand identity, at its core, begins with names that are easy to use and understand. Names will be spoken, included in articles, news media, advertising, and promotional materials. They will be applied to signage, banners, vehicles, retail items, and environments.

Environmental signage develops and reinforces brand identity persuasively. Whether in a city, campus, park, or heritage area, the presence of a well-designed sign system is a tangible symbol of a welcoming environment and good management.

The process for achieving an effective and memorable environmental brand identity depends on creating a balance between image and function. Achieving the right image begins with a thoughtful search for the most interesting, appropriate, and "image-able" assets. All towns and cities have unique qualities that should be celebrated. Understanding the history, goals, and plans of the community—coupled with a visual audit of the physical environment—should be the first step.

A sketch and modeling process that explores how to interpret these assets should follow. Many elements are studied: form, hardware, use of logo/logotype, typography, color, and site location. The Richmond Riverfront has a unique juxtaposition of historic residential and industrial architecture and trestle structures, so finding an appropriate balance of expression for that system was key.

environmental identity

A **name** functions in multiple ways.
Identification: It lets the public know that the place exists; it puts it "on the map."
Image: It evokes a feeling about the place.
Uniqueness: It clarifies how this place differs from similar attractions.
Destination: It helps people get from the highway to the destination.

As part of its identity development for the City of Richmond's waterfront, Thinkframe developed the name "Richmond Riverfront" to identify the project to the public, then developed the name "Canal Walk" for one of the destinations on the Riverfront.

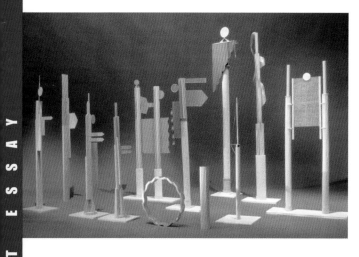

Study models explore functionality, changeability, material, and scale. They also look at different ways of reflecting Richmond's significant history, manufacturing roots, and location on the James River.

Tredegar Iron Works	Haxall East
Visitor Center	Reynolds Locks
Footbridge to Belle Isle	Shockoe Turning Basin
	Triple Cross
	City Dock
	Great Ship Lock

Key to any orientation device or information totem is a sense of site identity, changeability, and multidirectional information and map orientation to the larger context. Together, these tools confirm where you are and assist in getting you where you need to go.

EXPERT ESSAY

Finished models help with the resolution of design details and the selection of final materials, details, and colors. They also provide the client with something more tangible to examine and understand.

Functional aspects are investigated simultaneously and greatly inform the design process, including: wayfinding strategy, nomenclature, information hierarchy, ADA considerations, changeability, placement, sequence, modularity, materials, lettering technologies, fabrication methods, maintenance, and cost.

Virginia Gehshan and Jerome Cloud, two of the principals at Thinkframe, based in Philadelphia.

Thinkframe is an enterprise founded on our belief that when creative people of many kinds are brought together with a common goal, they will achieve remarkable results. Our staff includes professionals of widely ranging talents and backgrounds—those who tell stories in words, and those who employ images; those who shape experiences in print or on the Web, and those who communicate in the three-dimensional world.

This unusual range of perspectives enables our team to frame problems in clear new terms and find original and unexpected solutions.

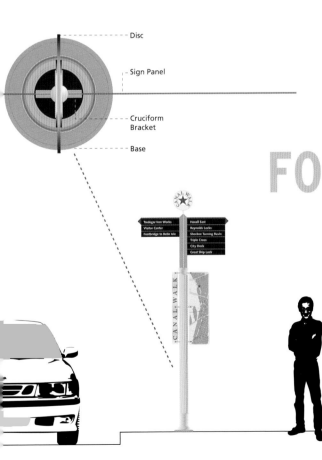

Disc

Sign Panel

Cruciform Bracket

Base

FORM message hardware location

Pedestrian Directional and Orientation Map

Map Directory

Building Identification

Pedestrian Gateway Identification

communicate pride

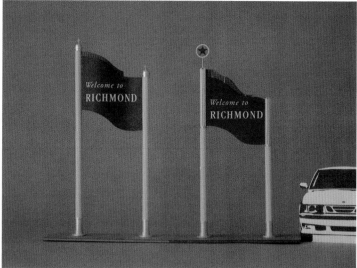

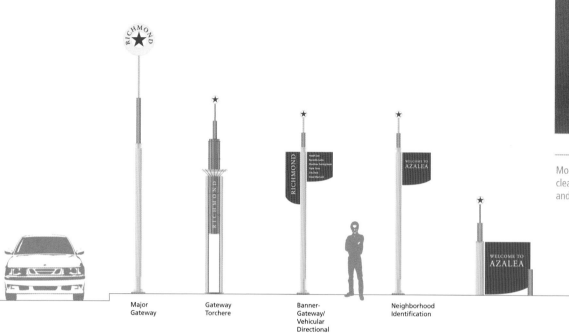

| Major Gateway | Gateway Torchere | Banner-Gateway/ Vehicular Directional | Neighborhood Identification |

Models showing varying details communicate options clearly to the client, help refine the system's aesthetics, and are useful in obtaining pricing.

Phase two of the sign system extended to the city and neighborhood gateways, as well as vehicular directional signage. The design process included studies for a series of gateway torchères which are to be located downtown; they signal arrival and help to activate and illuminate the streetscape. Neighborhood district markers also communicate a sense of identity and pride within the individual communities.

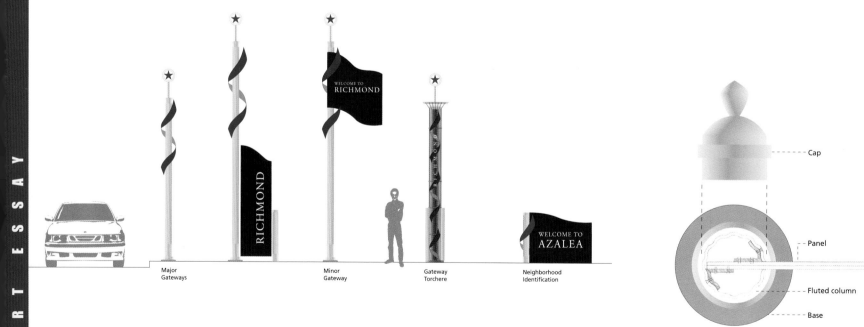

| Major Gateways | Minor Gateway | Gateway Torchere | Neighborhood Identification |

- Cap
- Panel
- Fluted column
- Base

Newly installed aluminum banners are located throughout the city.

ACTIVATE the streetscape

RICHMOND
Gem on the James

Welcome to RICHMOND

Welcome to MCGUIRE

← Science Museum of Virginia

→ Virginia Historical Society

↑ Virginia Museum of Fine Arts

Banners line major entry points to the city. Made of integral-color nylon fabric with appliquéd lettering, they can last anywhere from nine months to one year depending upon wind and weather conditions. Frequently banners can be taken down, cleaned, repaired, and reused.

Banner

Major Gateway

Vehicular Directional

less is more

Developing a successful signage and interpretive system can be as much about forming good relationships as it is about coming up with the right concepts and realizing the final system. That was certainly the case when Thinkframe was hired by Philadelphia's Fairmount Park Commission to develop a directional and interpretive signage system for a six-mile recreational path nestled in the park's Wissahickon Valley.

The Wissahickon Valley is a spectacular 1,800-acre forested gorge that is a much-treasured part of Philadelphia's Fairmount Park, a system of neighborhood parks that comprises one-tenth of the land in the city. "Forbidden Drive," so named since it was closed to vehicular traffic in the early 1900s, is a peaceful, tree-lined pathway frequented by runners, walkers, bicyclists, equestrians, and cross-country skiers. A strong sense of community ownership in the area created special challenges for the team.

Less is more, lower is better: despite the generally agreed-upon need for new signage, there was much concern by users that the signs not result in "visual pollution"—to destroy the illusion of the valley's wilderness would certainly not add to the user experience. Thinkframe succeeded by listening to the stakeholders and creating a signage system that complements its natural surrounding without overwhelming it, and by reducing the number of signs in the park from ninety-three to seventy-two. Low-profile signs do not obstruct the natural vistas and views. The signs are accessible but not intrusive; they are visible for those who need and want them, but they do not dominate.

Sketches of etched granite markers placed at half-mile increments along the drive.

Parking-lot signs carry the name and lot number so that police and emergency personnel can easily locate people calling in distress.

Park map helps visitors locate points of interest, interpretive sites, parking, restrooms, bridges, and park trails.

WISSAHICKON VALLEY PARK

lower is better

le Marker	Parking Identification	Trail Directional	Animal Regulatory Panel	Vehicular Regulatory	Park Regulatory & Map Panels	

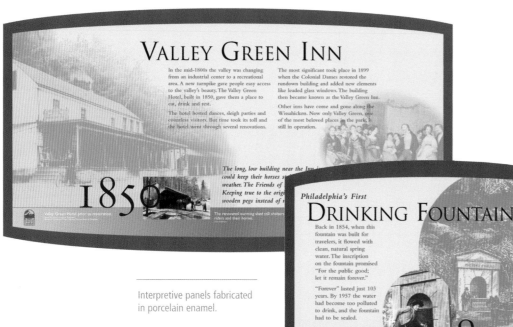

Interpretive panels fabricated
in porcelain enamel.

Interpretive signs

Relatively few users of the Wissahickon Valley know its history or importance. Forbidden Drive has seen changes that cover the full continuum of American history, from its first use as a route for Indian migration through European settlement and the American Revolution. The Wissahickon Creek was later host to more than twenty-seven mills during the height of its growth as an industrial center.

According to Dommert Phillips, Thinkframe's interpretive consultant on the project, knowledge about a park's resources, ecology, and history is a key means of promoting stewardship for the environment. Inspirational messages, such as writing, poetry, or quotes by famous people who have a close association with the area, can become powerful tools for creating an emotional connection with the park. Interpretive signs should be permanent and should not rely on visitors having brochure information in hand.

Things to be considered

1. Anticipated audiences/special characteristics/
    reading level
2. Audience knowledge about the area/common
    myths or misconceptions
3. Mission/purpose of the interpretive signs
4. Take-home messages
5. Define the "voice" to deliver the content
6. Characteristics of the writing style
7. Single perspective vs. multiple perspectives on
    a portrayed topic or issue
8. Content to be timeless vs. representative of
    current attitudes/approaches

Small Interpretive Display

Large Interpretive Display

Additional examples of large interpretive panels.

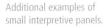

Additional examples of small interpretive panels.

Model-building is essential to the design resolution of complex organic forms like these.

Full-size demonstration mock-ups created out of temporary materials were used in focus group exercises to test the form and content of messages.

Mission of the interpretive signage

To educate users of Forbidden Drive about the natural, cultural, and historical importance of the Wissahickon Valley Park.

To inform park users about the unique balance necessary for the park to remain healthy and the ongoing restoration efforts needed to insure its long-term health.

To tell the stories of individuals who have made personal contributions to the Wissahickon Valley Park so that the park can be sustained and thus continue enhancing the lives of Philadelphians and visitors to the area.

To inspire users of the park to become better stewards by increasing their respect for the natural and man-made features of the park.

Final interpretive structures were fabricated out of stainless steel with a powder-coated paint finish. Final interpretive panels were made in full-color porcelain enamel.

promote environmental stewardship

THREE-Dimensional Typography

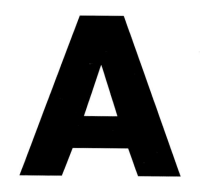

Two-dimensional letterforms can be expressed in three dimensions

Typographic characters are essentially two-dimensional. Even though there are hundreds of typefaces that offer almost endless variety in personality, expression, and style, letters and numbers on a printed page remain flat. They have no thickness, cast no shadow, and express no literal texture. And while the best graphic designers can create implied depth, virtual physicality, and visual texture, their work is, in the end, still flat.

However, the physical world allows environmental graphic designers to add real, tangible depth to the already interesting qualities of typography. All of the rich and sculptural aspects of three-dimensional design can be applied to letterforms.

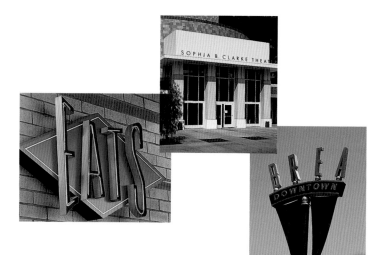

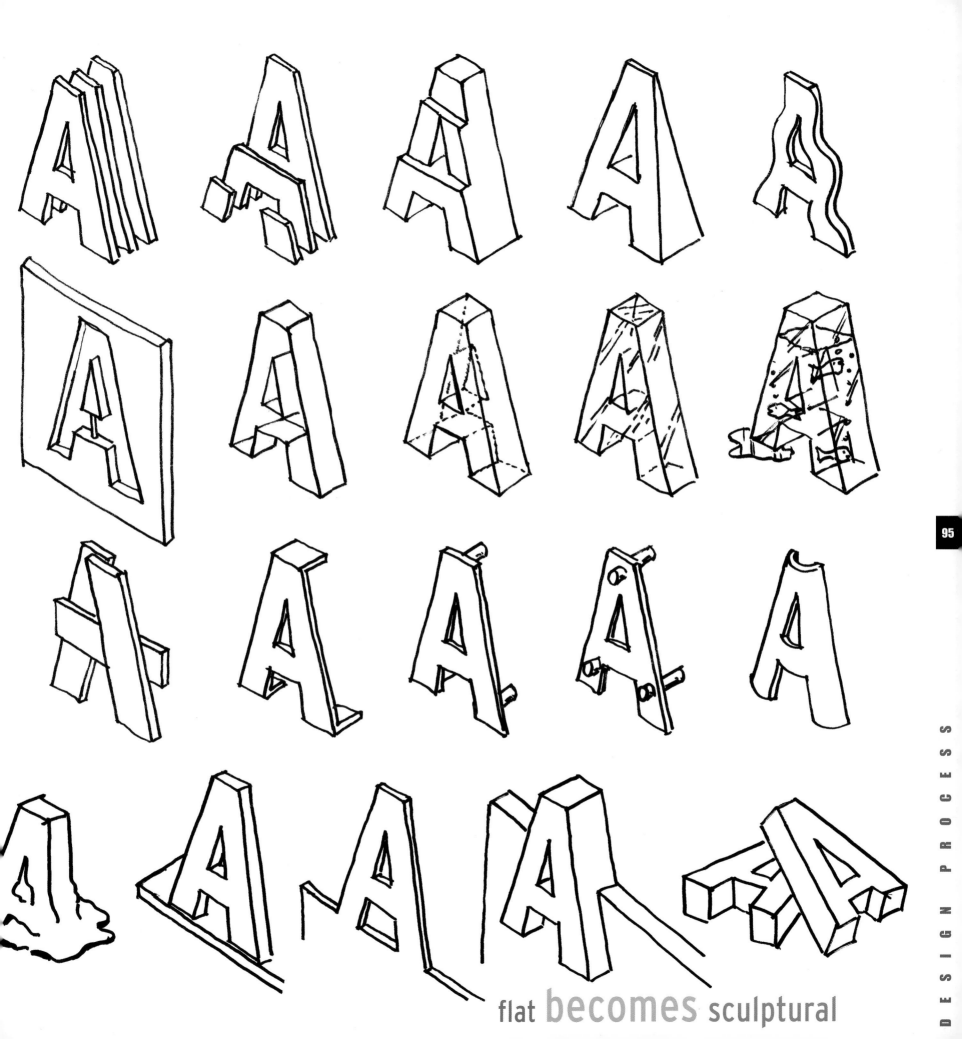

flat **becomes** sculptural

PHYSICAL Composition

Much of environmental graphics involves the shaping of individual components and their combination into interesting, stable, and appropriate signage elements. A typical issue is the joining of a sign panel with a base: information needs to be placed up, within the cone of vision, but many signs are ground mounted—hence the need for an integrated, dimensional design.

The classic post-and-panel sign is only one of dozens of design challenges and opportunities in sign design configuration. These sketches show just a few of the virtually limitless compositions possible.

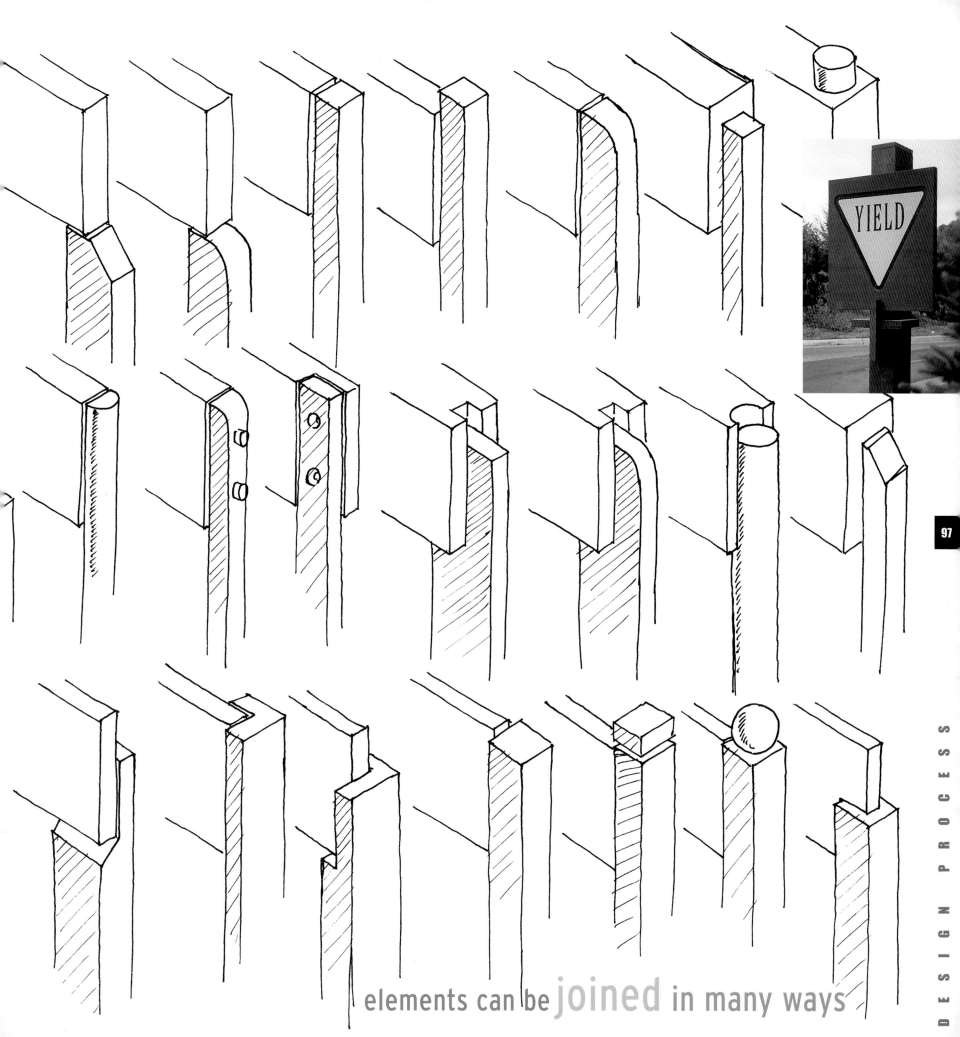

elements can be joined in many ways

BALANCE and Visual Interest

Balance in design concerns the "visual correctness" or even the psychological effect of how something is composed. Designers can manipulate and manage balance, creating symmetrical designs or asymmetrical compositions that look balanced.

THIS SIGN CAN BE BUILT TO STAND SAFELY, BUT IT LOOKS SPINDLY AND OUT OF BALANCE. ENLARGING THE BASE PROVIDES BALANCE AND VISUAL COMFORT.

THIS CANTILEVERED SIGN LOOKS UNSTABLE. THE SAME PANEL ON A FULL-HEIGHT POST LOOKS BETTER.

THIS CONFIGURATION APPEARS TO BE UNSTABLE. EXTENDING THE POST ABOVE THE PANEL VISUALLY STRENGTHENS THE VERTICAL LINE AND RESTORES BALANCE.

OBJECTS COMPOSED OF EQUAL-
SIZED COMPONENTS ARE NOT
ALWAYS INTERESTING.

USING ASYMMETRICAL ELEMENTS
IN COMPOSITION ADDS INTEREST.

relative **proportion** is important

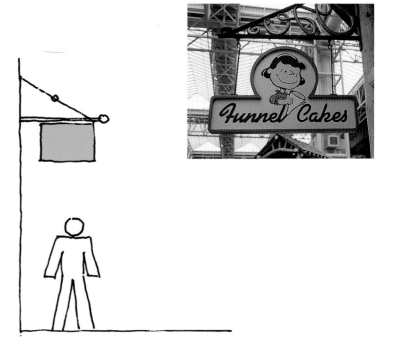

THIS BLADE SIGN LOOKS UNSTABLE,
EVEN THOUGH THE POLE CAN
SUPPORT IT. ADDING EVEN A
MODEST TRIANGULAR SUPPORT
MEETS OUR PSYCHOLOGICAL NEEDS
FOR VISUAL STRENGTH.

DESIGN PROCESS

ARROWS

Pointing the way is the whole point

Directional signs make up a large part of wayfinding programs, and each has an arrow form of some kind. From the nineteenth-century drawings of a pointing finger to today's optically corrected Helvetica arrow, designers have explored countless ways to simply point the way.

Two schools of design thought exist on the design and selection of arrows. More traditional designers view the arrow as a unit of typography and prefer arrow forms that mimic or relate to the sign's type style. A more contemporary method is to establish contrast with the typography, either with unique designs or by enclosing arrows in circles or other shapes. This approach is dominant on vehicular signs, where quick sorting of messages is important.

Recreational environments, such as theme parks and hotels, offer opportunities for arrow forms to play a decorative role in signage design.

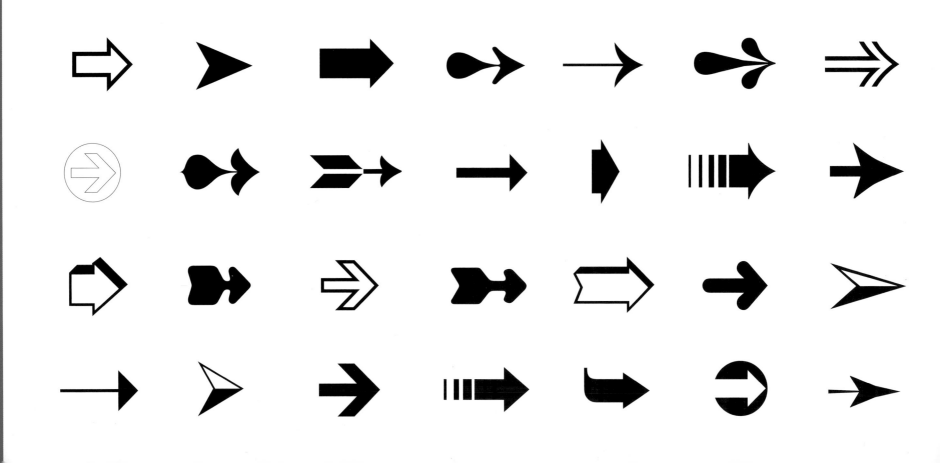

DESIGN PROCESS

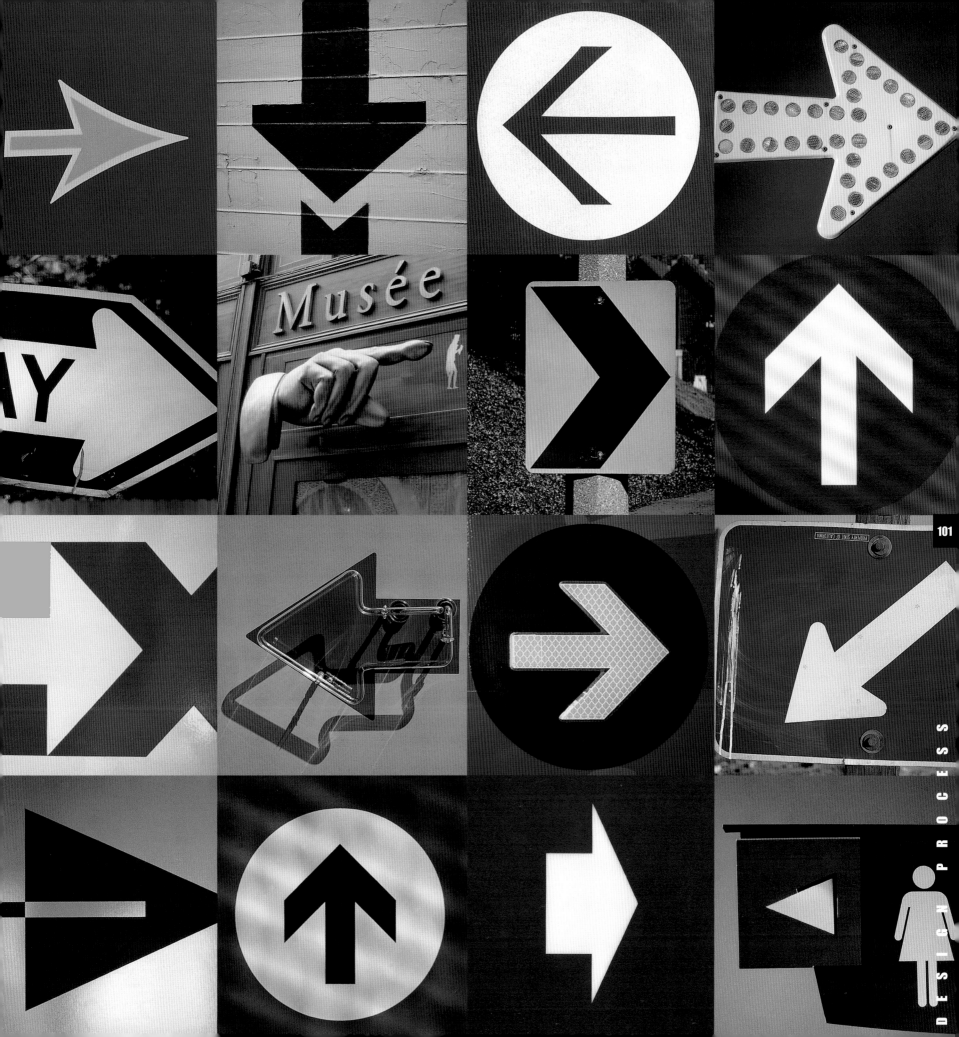

Large letters establish this food court's nature theme and serve as a landmark and identification. The engaging sign is visible from the far end of the mall and parking lot.

Good placemaking is **second nature**

I don't know how much our clients learn from us, but we definitely learn a lot from them. Two of the visionaries of retail design and development as we know it today were the late James W. Rouse, founder of the Rouse Company, a pioneering mall developer, and the late John Krantz, director of design at the Mills Corporation, originators of the idiosyncratic "Mills concept" of shopping environments.

Jim Rouse stressed the importance of designing places that were "warm and human," whether they were enclosed malls, outdoor shopping environments, or new planned communities. He believed that the quality of our surroundings has an enormous effect on how we feel and relate to each other and that it is the responsibility of all who are involved in the building process to contribute positively to the places we design.

John Krantz helped transform the idea of the shopping mall into a shopping machine—a giant but artful machine. With structures almost a mile long and originally in a "train wreck" or "racetrack" configuration, artfulness came in the form of sculpture, murals, animation, and every other type of graphics—graphics as architecture and lots of it! Both of these innovators understood the immense value of graphics in these specialized environments, as well as the intrinsic bond between the graphics and the architecture which is required for success.

THE FOUNDATION

Some things we need to always consider as we lay the foundation of our designs:

Community pride

The graphics component of every project works with and supplements the architecture to bring a human scale to the built environment. By creating a shared experience and community pride, the project can mirror people's sense of themselves. Researching the community, its history, its people, the things they make and do allows us to gain an understanding of what is meaningful to the community in order to reflect an artful interpretation of what we've learned. Customers recognize and appreciate the effort to customize their mall…to make it truly theirs.

Retail graphics are for **frequent** visitors.

Digital prints allow repetition of imagery for a cohesive look.

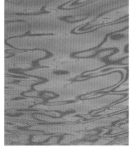

Patterns from nature are used for tabletops in the food court, contributing to the "landscape."

Native fish—their heroic scale shows their beauty.

The outdoors is important in this area of Northern California where fishing is a top activity. Identification is unnecessary—everyone already knows the difference between a bull trout and a brook trout.

SCALE
Artful, integrated FORM AND IMAGE...
CREATING LANDMARKS

Ann established her design office, Dudrow/Design, in Los Angeles in 1998 after a long career working for architects and developers.

She began in New York with a BFA in illustration from Rhode Island School of Design and a desire to create children's books, but she soon migrated to Baltimore where, billed as a "New York designer," she was hired by the Rouse Company. It was there that an initial immersion in retail graphic design—"in those days we designed every tenant storefront and every tenant sign"—led to a lifetime in the field.

When Ann landed at RTKL Associates, the idea of graphics as a component of retail architecture was only just beginning to gel, and she helped transform that practice with the philosophy that a mall without graphics is like a day without sunshine.

Ann is active in the Society of Environmental Graphic Design, where she has served on the board of directors, and she was named a Fellow of the organization in 1993. She also is an occasional instructor of environmental graphics at Art Center College of Design in Pasadena, California.

Photography:
 Dudrow/Design
 RTKL/Whitcomb

This entry feature recalls the great agricultural heritage of Texas as it orients shoppers coming and going.

The banners boast in superlatives as did the famed "Thrilla in Manila" heavyweight bout hosted on this site.

Involvement

We are always trying to find new ways to involve the shopper. The more distinctive the graphics, the more people pay attention to them. It is advantageous to draw people in, to give them a continuing sense of discovery, to elicit a second and third and fourth take. Some ways of doing this are:

1. With words: quotations, rhymes, words, puns—on the walls, in the floor, on the tabletops, etc.
2. With motion: animatronics, electronic, and dynamic signs such as Trivision, LED displays, and simple motor-driven features or images projected in light—the options for animated imagery are growing constantly.
3. With scale: surprising juxtapositions of large and small objects.
4. With art: images in 2-D or 3-D, painting, photography, or sculpture invite shoppers to stop and look.
5. With ambiguity, metaphor, and symbolism.
6. With sound.
7. With lighting.
8. With drama.

104

EXPERT ESSAY

Sculptural arrows entice people to the upper levels at Lalaport Shopping Center, Tokyo.

Demographics

It is essential to understand who your shoppers are. Is it a young community with many children? An older, upper-middle-class part of town? What is the ethnic mix? The souci-economic mix? The designer also needs to recognize that the mall population changes significantly throughout the day: early morning is for the mall walkers, usually retired people getting their exercise; at midmorning, retirees gather with friends at the food court. At lunch, there are office workers; in the late morning or early afternoon, mothers shop with small children. By late afternoon to early evening the mall might be dominated by teens just hanging out. So is there a place where everyone feels comfortable? Is there a special children's area or feature? Have potential vandalism or graffiti problems been considered?

One of a series of watercolors that were translated into murals for a food court. Visitors did a double take as they noticed the food in the landscape.

2.0 m

9.45 m

3.75 m

Letters

Banner

Gateway

Truly landmarks—these day-and-night orbs enhance the shopping experience by adding to Reston Town Center the kind of elements typical in long-established cities.

MOTION

METAPHOR...

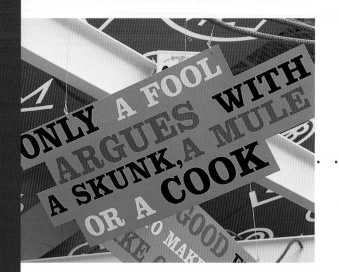

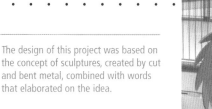

The design of this project was based on the concept of sculptures, created by cut and bent metal, combined with words that elaborated on the idea.

Suspended over the escalator leading up to the food court, this sign announces the food court, the LRT, and the cinemas. Though consisting of four separate parts, they visually combine as you ride up the escalator.

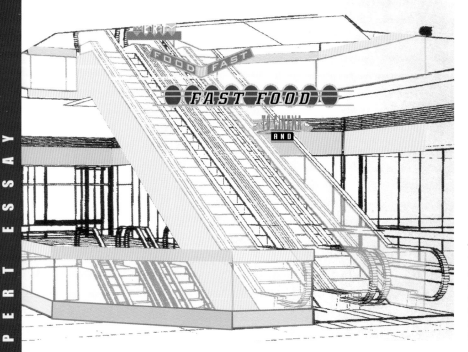

The theme for this mall is a celebration of celebrations. In the food court, the signage takes on the character of Manila jeepneys, a kind of stretch jeep that serves as public transportation. Each is individually painted and adorned in an attempt to outdo the competition.

The Process
Every project begins something like this

1. Decide on the big idea, the design brief, the concept, the attitude, the story, the theme, or whatever you want to call the thing that will inform the design from start to finish. The idea could be visual and based on a look, a style, or a set of imagery. It could be literary, based on poetry, historical references, folklore, quotations, etc.; it could be tied to physical or cultural aspects of the location or the community; it could be serious or playful, spare or ornate.

2. As the idea is established, the look, tone, texture, and palette are decided. Will this be an upper-end mall with subtle colors, neutrals, or metallics? Or is it really about color? Is the intent to melt into the architecture or to jump out from it? Will you be using a palette of traditional materials, such as mosaics or hand-painted murals, or will you be using LED displays and digital imagery? Will the graphics take on a folk-art look or a traditional one? Southwestern or Asian? Edgy and modern, or classic and understated?

A basic graphic motif can be applied to myriad applications: banners, trailblazing signage, murals, partitions, counter fronts, countertops, and tables. The more ways the basic idea is applied, the more meaningful the shoppers' experiences will be. The goal is to create interest, not just awareness.

The green area is planting; the rest is paving.

Always viewed from different angles—on it, from above, through the floor openings, from the bridzges—the floor provides the greatest opportunity for color and pattern. The history of the Coliseum is laid out underfoot as incised lettering recalls forty years of events.

Even interruptions for planted areas can work within the overall geometry. Round shapes define one end of the mall, rectilinear shapes the other. They meet here in the middle: the thrill's in Manila!

defining PLACES
and positioning them within the whole

3. As you work simultaneously with plans, sections, and elevations—usually when the architecture is in the schematic design phase—a general approach to, applying the graphics emerges. Are spaces to melt into each other, or are they intended to be distinct? Where do we use the floor or the handrails; where do graphics elements complete the spaces and where are they used to demarcate areas? Do the graphics reinforce the edges of the spaces or help to fill them? Is there a variety of elements to use in the horizontal plane of the floor, the horizontal plane overhead, the plane perpendicular to travel, and the plane parallel to the line of travel (don't forget that this is a three-dimensional design opportunity)?

4. Do the items that support the main idea exist separately as graphic elements or are they integrated with light poles, planters, fountains, or benches? And should they really be graphic elements at all or would the idea be better served as a lighting installation? And speaking of lighting, this is the time to work with the project's lighting consultant to be sure that the lighting concept works with the graphics.

When people are hungry, they say, "Let's eat"—a great way to identify a food court. The graphics program is supplemented by words—lots of words: cooking words at the food stalls, eating words at the tables, plenty for people to read while their mouths are full.

Why and where?

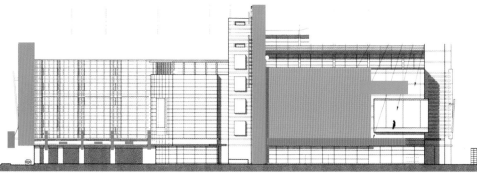

The why and where

In most shopping centers, especially one-level developments, there are very few walls to work with and ceilings may be too high, too low, or nonexistent, leaving columns, handrails, floors, bulkheads, or trusses as our only canvas—our only opportunity—to put the philosophies of Rouse and Krantz into action.

Graphics in retail environments are placed where they are for several reasons:
1. To call attention to important junctures, such as where two arcades cross.
2. To call attention to or announce venues on upper (or lower) floors.
3. To name or differentiate different zones or functional areas of the mall. This can be done with a change in color, a change in name, use of symbolic icons, upgrading or downgrading the perceived quality of materials, or altering the amount of visual noise, to name a few. The important thing is that the differentiation is felt in a significant way.
4. To provide visibility: for example, blade signs can be used for tenants whose storefronts lack visibility from down the mall.
5. To emphasize a sense of transition from one space to another.
6. To ornament.
7. To distract from awkward architectural features.

Hierarchy of Signage

1. Main project identification (glowing element)

1a. Supporting graphic (nature image)

2. Anchor ID signage

3. Mini-anchor ID signage (electronic)

4. Directional signage

Looking up, the floating ceiling at the food court level becomes a feature, with patterns and images projected in white and/or colored light.

This elevation, with its formal entryway and the food court glowing visibly above, provides opportunities for using the entire façade to reinforce the idea behind the project identity. The building becomes part of the natural environment, with a mural of glazed tile providing a focus.

Columns of light resemble folded paper shades and visually connect the sunken garden, ground, and second levels.

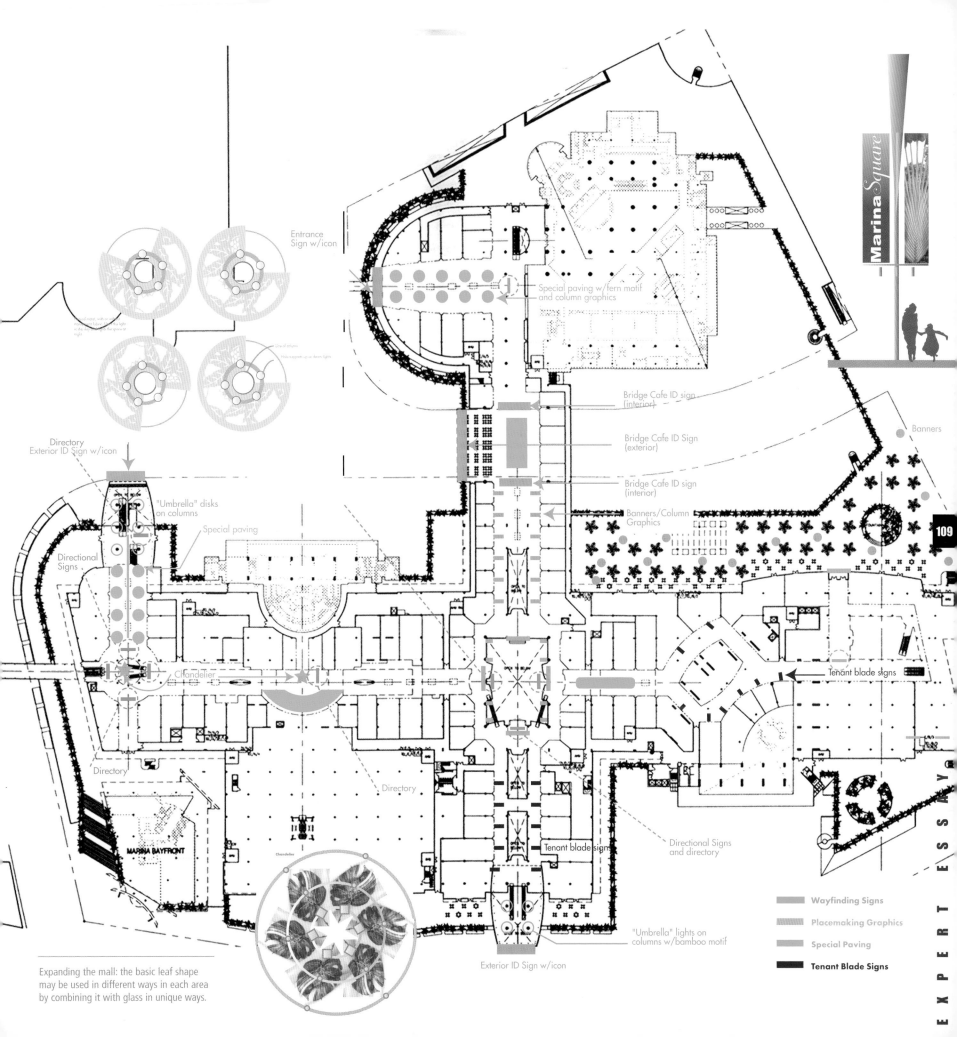

Entrance
Sign w/icon

Special paving w/fern motif
and column graphics

Bridge Cafe ID sign
(interior)

Bridge Cafe ID Sign
(exterior)

Bridge Cafe ID sign
(interior)

Banners/Column
Graphics

Banners

Directory
Exterior ID Sign w/icon

"Umbrella" disks
on columns

Special paving

Directional
Signs

Chandelier

Tenant blade signs

Directory

Directory

Directional Signs
and directory

MARINA BAYFRONT

Chandelier

Tenant blade signs

"Umbrella" lights on
columns w/bamboo motif

Exterior ID Sign w/icon

Expanding the mall: the basic leaf shape
may be used in different ways in each area
by combining it with glass in unique ways.

	Wayfinding Signs
	Placemaking Graphics
	Special Paving
	Tenant Blade Signs

PLACEMAKING PROJECTS

Environmental graphics that define buildings, places, and spaces

NORTH END at Northridge

A fun addition to a formal shopping center

After the suburban Los Angeles–area Northridge Fashion Center was devastated in an earthquake, it was rebuilt as a sleek high-tech mall featuring apparel and upscale stores. But even though successful, its all-indoor configuration soon became dated as competing centers added exciting outdoor areas to feature entertainment and to lure younger shoppers. Usually based around movie theaters, these new developments often are designed as a streetscape of shops and restaurants.

The center's owner, General Growth Management, made plans for a 150,000-square-foot outdoor expansion to be built around a ten-screen theater complex. To establish a complete and unique visitor environment, the architect designed an intimate walkway of stores and restaurants with tasteful lighting and hardscape details. What was needed was a way to distinguish the interesting addition from the massive mall, as well as a method to guide shoppers into it.

The center already had a strong and effective identity and signage program; establishing a secondary and parallel image would be a challenge. Consultant Hunt Design suggested that the expansion needed not only a unique look, but its own name as well.

The addition would be positioned as an attraction within the main mall or as a discreet component of it. To signal its northerly orientation on the property and to reinforce it as a distinct place, Hunt created the name "North End at Northridge." The name, easy to pronounce and recall, led easily to graphic interpretation in logos and signage.

While signage in the expansion is minimal, signage about North End at Northridge in the main mall and around the massive property is not. The graphic designers went to great lengths to integrate large, iconic pieces into the public spaces of the mall, not an easy task in a finished building. Also challenging was the parking area wayfinding, where a thorough and distinctive sign program was already in place. The solution was an independent set of signs designed to coexist with the existing program.

A completely new identity was needed to distinguish the new shopping center from the older portion of the mall.

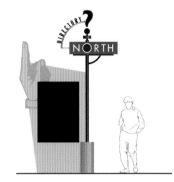

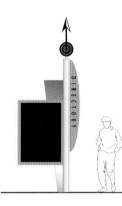

113

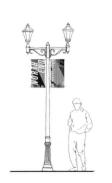

Photo-illustrations helped evaluate how the new
graphics would look in the existing building.

Three equal but distinct design
schemes were considered.

Early ideas to integrate a large gateway element into an existing bookstore building proved unsuccessful.

The design theme, selected from three preliminary concepts, is based on an abstraction of a compass or weather vane and features a dimensional letter "N." All of the twelve sign types present the letter in some form. The designs were given a casual, eccentric look to work with the expansion's entertainment concept and to contrast with the signage in the mall. Asymmetrical compositions and skewed forms are dominant.

A substantial challenge was the implementation of a series of major North End pieces into the main mall to help draw shoppers to the new area. The solution was overhead "marquees" mounted to fascias above the escalators and exit doors. These pieces are intentionally nonmassive and "transparent" to preserve views to the existing architecture.

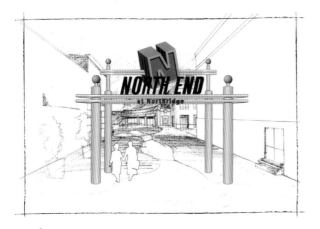

fun
FUNKY
quirky

Studies based on a freestanding gateway show compositional variations of basic "logo" components.

Design **Analysis**

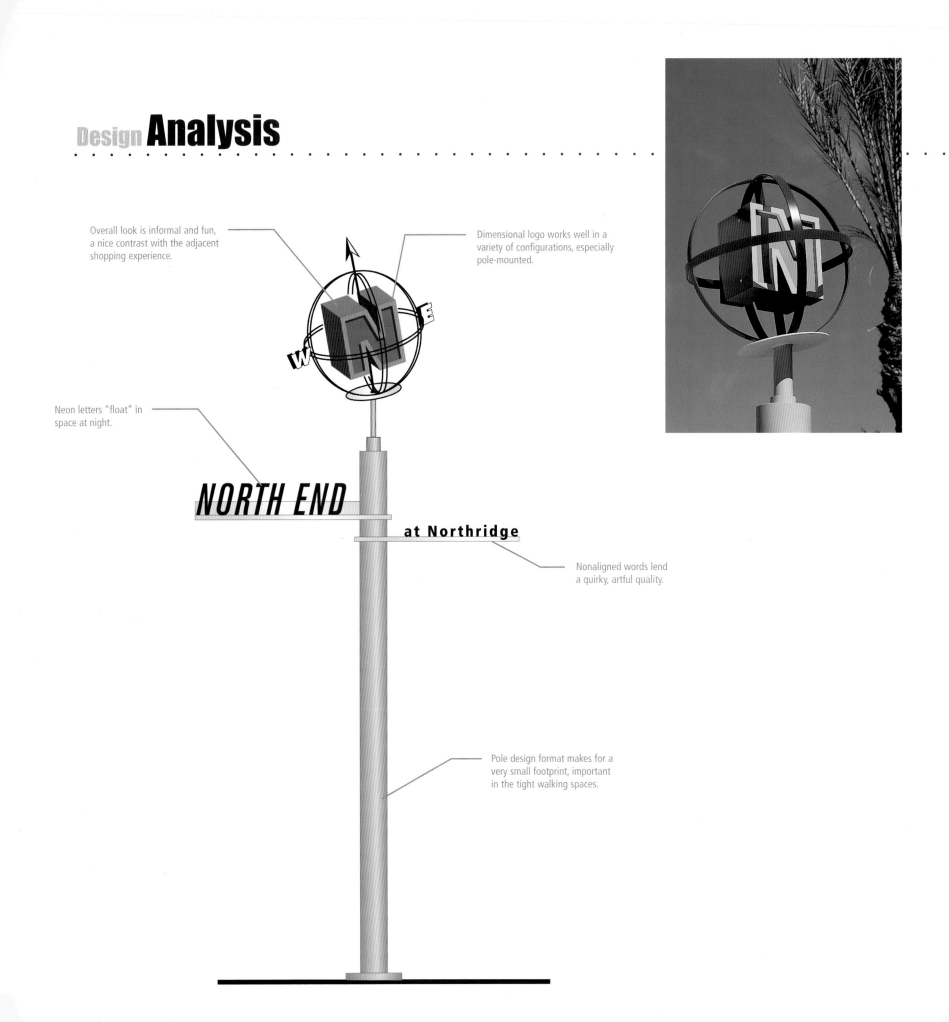

Overall look is informal and fun, a nice contrast with the adjacent shopping experience.

Dimensional logo works well in a variety of configurations, especially pole-mounted.

Neon letters "float" in space at night.

NORTH END

at Northridge

Nonaligned words lend a quirky, artful quality.

Pole design format makes for a very small footprint, important in the tight walking spaces.

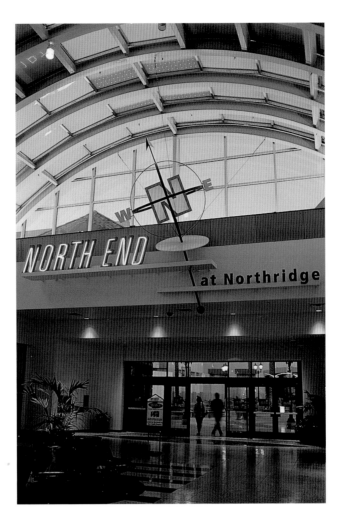

arrowhead.
finish.

The final installation inside the
existing mall is remarkably like
the original sketches.

11"

1'-9"

2 1/2"   2 1/2"

en face aluminum
nnel letter with
mm single tube
n. Fabricated
minum raceway
h painted
sh.

7"   4 1/2"

1" 4" 1"

3 1/2"

1" thick flat
cut out alum.
plate w/ painted
finish. (typ.)

m bar stock framing.
interior w/ painted finish.

abricated aluminum
abinets with front
nged access doors.
ainted finish.

uorescent lamps
ith wireways as per
.L. standards. Lamp
s per even illumination.

/16" thick (min.) clear
exan cover.

/4" thick clear acrylic
raphic panel with
igital color translucent
verlay.

d aluminum
el mounting
rt frame.

solid aluminum
/ painted finish.

2'-4"

lass sphere with
t fill. Painted finish.
pre-position pole
phere prior to

B DETAIL SECTIO

3/4"

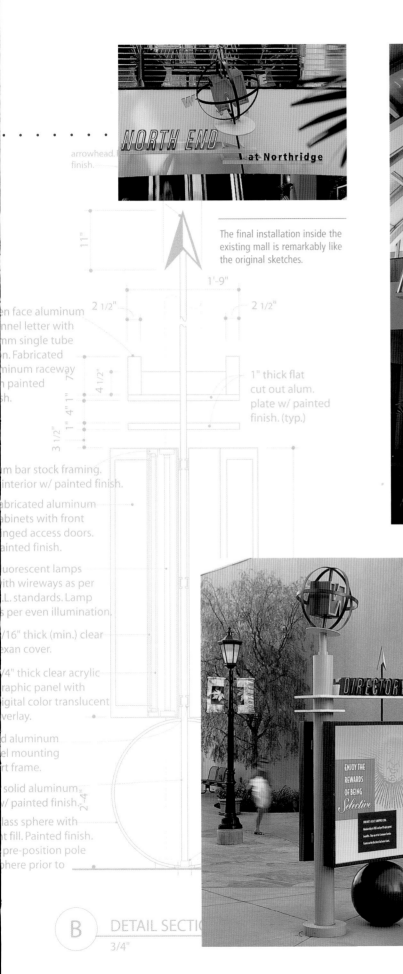

Mall directories are important
focal points for shoppers—this
one is no exception.

PROJECT OVERVIEW
Graphics program for an entertainment
addition to an upscale shopping center.

PROJECT FACTS
Client:
    General Growth Management
Graphic Design Team:
    Hunt Design:
    Christina Allen, Dinnis Lee,
    Wayne Hunt, Perry Shimoji,
    John Temple
Sign Company:
    AHR Ampersand
Schedule:
    One year
Photography:
    Jim Simmons (Del Zoppo Simmons)

MATERIALS & TECHNIQUES
Aluminum posts and letters; exposed
neon, inner-illuminated channel letters.

UNIQUE ASPECTS
New graphics had to coexist with,
but complement, an existing signage
program.

117

The all-aluminum design under
construction at the sign company.

PARIS Las Vegas

Thematic signage and graphics for a Parisian environment

Today's gaming projects are some of the most complex building types imaginable. Part theme park, huge hotel, conference center, restaurant row, entertainment center, resort, and of course, casino, they rely on the coordinated efforts of more than a dozen design disciplines to plan, design, and build. And increasingly, graphic designers play major roles in establishing the look and personality of these destination developments. Hunt Design was pleased to be one of the signage-and-graphics consultants selected to create the prewar Parisian ambience in this dynamic gaming property.

Consisting of 2,900 hotel rooms, multiple restaurants, a Parisian shopping street, and a massive conference center, Paris Las Vegas is the product of Park Place Entertainment, a major gaming company and owners of Caesar's Palace, the Flamingo, and other major properties. The charge from Park Place from the outset was to design the best themed casino yet. The innovative New York New York hotel, opened two years earlier, had set the standard for casinos designed around a single theme, and Paris Las Vegas was meant to exceed even its design and detail.

Creating a believable Parisian environment requires the right mix of period architecture, romantic streetscape, elegant lighting, and appropriate graphics. Signage is the final layer of design in a themed environment, and when well executed, it can make all the difference in credibly establishing a theme. Here, the sheer quantity of graphic images and details probably exceeds those of any casino property yet opened. Hunt's team alone created more than three hundred graphic designs for the interior spaces; other designers added dozens more, many expressed in fine detail in the elegant Rue de la Paix shopping street.

After a detailed programming phase that determined the locations and wording for most of the graphic elements, an intensive research phase was begun. The "script" called for a "prewar" Paris aesthetic, so accurate reference material was essential. The designers pored over Paris tour guides, French architecture books, and stacks of photographs provided by the client.

Composite photographs of the architect's model were for sign planning.

The owner and interior designer composed a detailed scrapbook of Parisian images for reference by the entire design team.

period streetscape

Multiple, highly rendered designs were done for each finished sign.

RACE & SPORTS BOOK

LE JARDIN

LES TOILETTES

Les Desserts

Eiffel TOUR

LE CABARET

Eiffel TOUR

Eiffel TOUR

Eiffel TOUR

The design work was organized into the broad signage categories of exterior/site, parking, casino
wayfinding, casino marquees (large or illuminated
signs), theme or enhancement, gaming, and code
signs. Later, a layer of small decorative graphic
enhancements was added to the scope. Each category
was programmed, designed, revised, and developed
as a separate bid package. Close coordination with
the project's two architects and interior designer was
especially important because of the complex circulation plan and the richly detailed façades. Also, as in
most large casino resort properties, the many department heads and area managers had special needs
and requests. For example, the slots manager wanted
highly themed but brightly illuminated gaming signs,
a request that ran counter to the prewar look.

each element
UNIQUE
and individually designed

Care was used to find and use
period typefaces where practical.

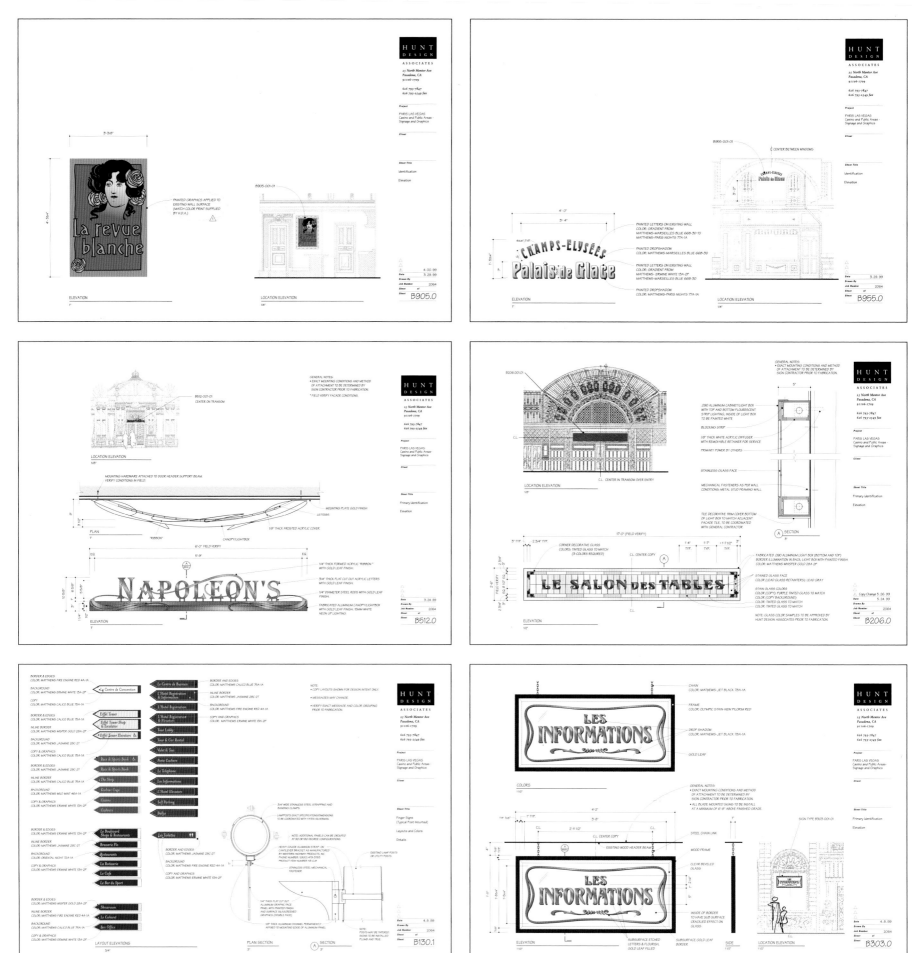

BURGUNDY

NORMANDY

LES TOILETTES

Telephone

Dames WOMEN   LE THEATRE d'ARTS

LE CENTRE DE CONVENTION
LES INFORMATIONS

Cashier

125

NAPOLEON'S

Le Club PARIS

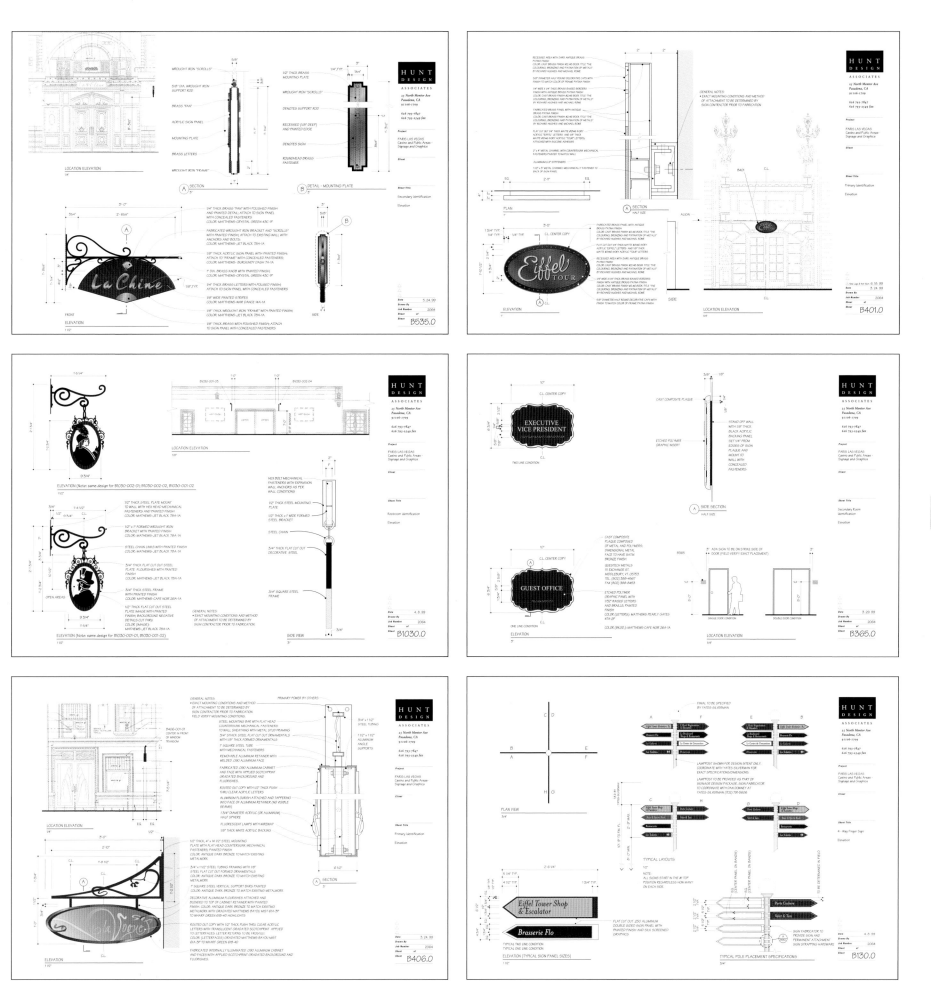

PROJECTS

Design **Analysis**

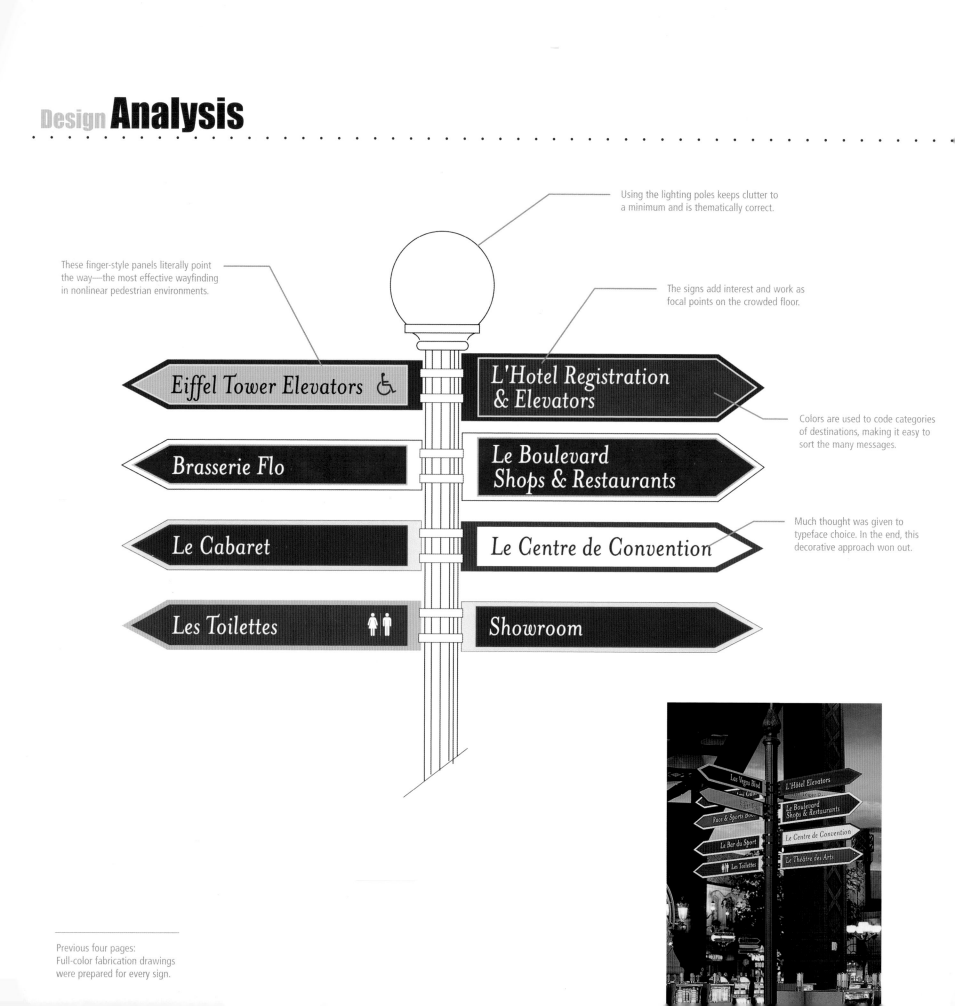

Using the lighting poles keeps clutter to a minimum and is thematically correct.

These finger-style panels literally point the way—the most effective wayfinding in nonlinear pedestrian environments.

The signs add interest and work as focal points on the crowded floor.

Eiffel Tower Elevators

L'Hotel Registration & Elevators

Colors are used to code categories of destinations, making it easy to sort the many messages.

Brasserie Flo

Le Boulevard Shops & Restaurants

Le Cabaret

Le Centre de Convention

Much thought was given to typeface choice. In the end, this decorative approach won out.

Les Toilettes

Showroom

Previous four pages:
Full-color fabrication drawings were prepared for every sign.

Wayfinding design in the colorful facility

The casino's eighty-foot ceilings precluded the use of hanging directional signs, the type seen in most casinos. The solution came from Paris itself: a series of "street"-mounted (floor-mounted) pointer or finger signs with message slats that literally point the way to each destination. Color-coding was used to help differentiate the messages for quick reading and understanding: red signs indicated amenities, blue signs shops and restaurants, white signs for convention center, etc. Instead of the typical map directories, the designers added the property map to the Paris-style poster kiosks that had been selected for thematic enhancement.

Parking garage communications, always a challenge for Las Vegas operators, was solved by assigning Parisian landmarks to each level and creating a color-based sign system. Exterior signage is also highly themed and features Art Nouveau forms with faux-copper details.

A program of faux-copper signs greets drivers.

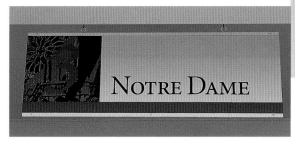

Digital prints are used for backgrounds on all parking signs.

PROJECT OVERVIEW
Wayfinding and themed graphics for a resort hotel, including casino, pool, convention center, parking, and site.

PROJECT FACTS
Client:
    Park Place Entertainment
Graphic Design Team:
    Hunt Design:
    Christina Allen, Karen Aseltine, Jennifer Bressler, Esteban Hernandez, Wayne Hunt, In Sung Kim, Dinnis Lee, Sharon Persovski, Perry Shimoji
Sign Companies:
    Federal Signs, Studio Arts & Letters, YESCO
Schedule:
    Three years
Photography:
    Jim Simmons (Del Zoppo Simmons)

MATERIALS & TECHNIQUES
The complex project made use of nearly every sign-making technique.

UNIQUE ASPECTS
Very complex creative team with two architects, four design firms, and a complicated site and facilities program.

129

theme: inside and out, front to back

MEASURE Y Construction Sign

Big results from a small budget

When supporters of a school improvements bond issue, Measure Y, won a hard-fought victory at the polls, there was concern that many of the resulting small, nonglamorous construction projects might go unnoticed. Voters tend to imagine large new construction as the primary use of bond funds; they often don't realize that dozens of minor, or "hidden," improvements are happening right in their own neighborhoods.

To help signify that projects were, in fact, underway on multiple school sites, the Pasadena Unified School District called on Hunt Design to create a design for an inexpensive construction marker. The design brief called for a low-cost freestanding sign that could be quickly installed in any site conditions and that would last for up to six months.

To keep the unit cost under $300, the designers started with the idea that a standard four-by-eight-foot sheet of plywood could be decorated and easily installed on four-by-four posts. After developing several designs based on a flat painted panel, a concept featuring a cutout letter "Y" was put forward. This "transparent" design immediately captured the fancy of the client; it allowed viewers to see through the sign to the construction work while still delivering the key message.

An additional benefit to the cutout symmetrical solution was that it could be installed in any orientation—perpendicular or parallel to the street—and still be legible from two sides. And the background, whether trees or building features, played a role in the total design.

Several design options were explored before the final version was selected.

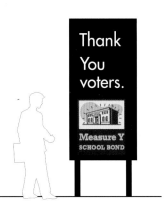

Seeing through the sign to the construction projects made it especially interesting.

"transparent" design

PROJECT OVERVIEW
Fifty easy-to-install construction signs.

PROJECT FACTS
Client:
    Pasadena Unified School District
Graphic Design Team:
    Hunt Design:
    Jennifer Bressler, Felicia Lee
Sign Company:
    Curcio Enterprises, Inc.
Schedule:
    Eight weeks

MATERIALS & TECHNIQUES
Painted and screened plywood;
wood posts.

UNIQUE ASPECTS
Designed as a very low-cost,
temporary program.

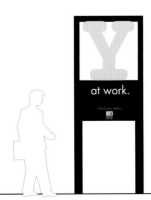

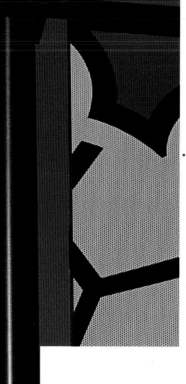

TURTLE BAY Exploration Park

Colorful identity and signage for a special collection of attractions

The Northern California city of Redding has an interesting mix of cultural attractions, and in 1998 they merged their separate trustee boards to form a single dynamic civic destination. Originally comprising an arboretum, art museum, trail system, summer camp, and butterfly zoo, the new organization set out to develop the combined property into the premier nature-oriented attraction in the region. A master plan was completed which called for a state-of-the-art visitor center and two interpretive buildings, one on each side of the Sacramento River (the three-hundred-foot-wide waterway bisects the facility).

At the same time, world-renowned architect and bridge designer Santiago Calatrava was selected to design a dramatic footbridge to be built across the river. The unique and eclectic destination was on its way to fulfilling its role as a major regional asset.

Needed now was a new name—and an all-new, unified identity. Operating under the awkward moniker "Turtle Bay Museums and Arboretum on the River" was difficult, and there was a clear need to move

toward a cohesive description free of the "listing of attractions" approach. Selected to design the visual identity, Hunt Design suggested that the words "Turtle Bay" could still work, but with a new secondary phrase, "Exploration Park." Dozens of logo designs were created for review, and a colorful, boldly drawn turtle image was chosen.

To express the new identity, the designers began work on a signage plan for the multiacre property. Again, color was the order of the day. In contrast to many nature-based attractions, Turtle Bay management wanted to avoid the drab "park service" look and use colorful graphics to unify the huge site.

Sign types were developed for everything from major monuments to restroom signage. In addition to the bright colors, the turtle image was used as a background on many signs, even on the glass entry doors to the visitor center. Rigid banners of perforated metal define the parking edges, and modest directional signs mark the paths between attractions.

The fanciful entrance monument displays all of the elements of the colorful identity program.

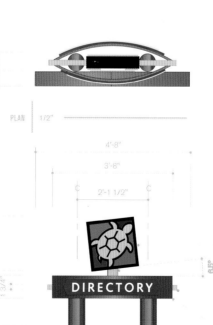

PLAN 1/2"

4'-8"

3'-8"

2'-1 1/2"

DIRECTORY

Double sided fabricated .090 aluminum logo cabinet with floating flat cut out 1/2" thick acrylic "turtle" with halo illumination; cabinet and "turtle" with painted finish.

3 1/2" and 1 3/4" square steel support tubing with welded closed ends and painted finish.

Double sided non-illuminated formed .125 aluminum panels with 1/2" thick flat cut out acrylic letters; panels and letters with painted finish.

Double sided internally illuminated fabricated .090 aluminum cabinet with directory panel and back lit duratrans transparency; Cabinet to have hinged glass doors with cylinder locks.

More than one hundred sketches preceded
selection of the final logo. Multiple client
reviews led to a more colorful approach.

LOOK LEARN TOUCH EXPLORE

TURTLE BAY

TURTLE BAY
EXPERIENCES

Turtle Bay
experiences

133

express *identity* with color

PROJECTS

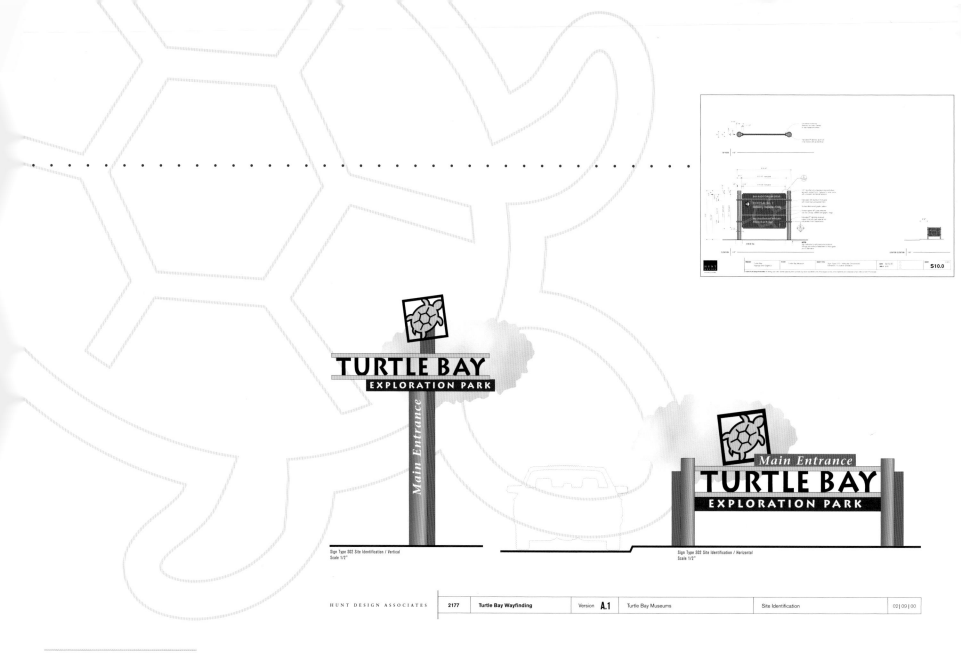

Sign Type S02 Site Identification / Vertical
Scale 1/2"

Sign Type S02 Site Identification / Horizontal
Scale 1/2"

An outline interpretation of the turtle from the logo frequently appears as decorative background.

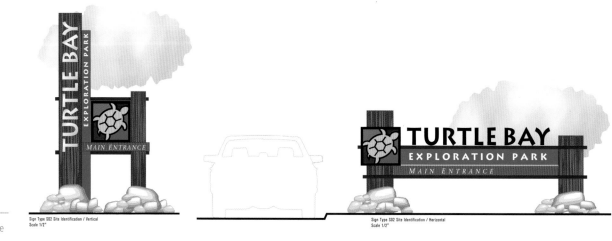

Early design studies for the entrance monument.

Sign Type S02 Site Identification / Vertical
Scale 1/2"

Sign Type S02 Site Identification / Horizontal
Scale 1/2"

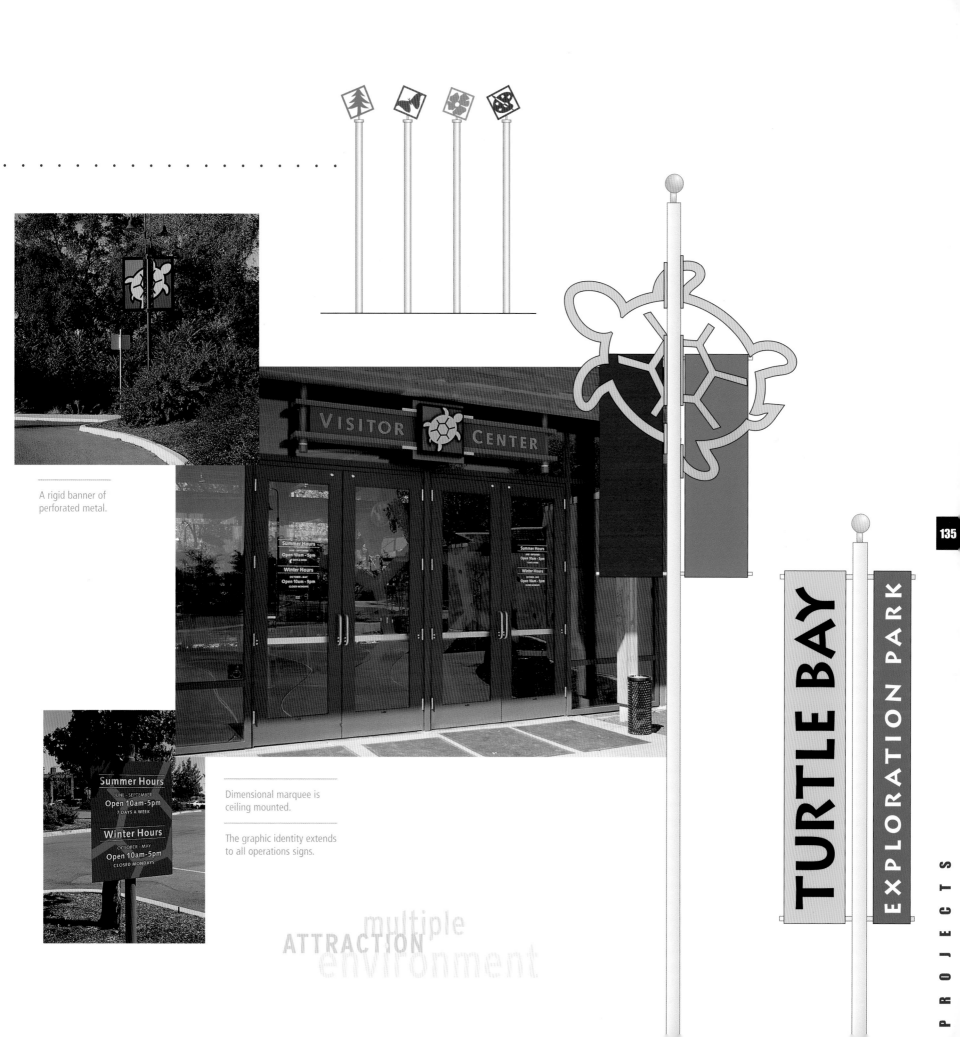

A rigid banner of
perforated metal.

VISITOR 🐢 CENTER

Summer Hours
JUNE – SEPTEMBER
Open 10am-5pm
7 DAYS A WEEK

Winter Hours
OCTOBER – MAY
Open 10am-5pm
CLOSED MONDAYS

Dimensional marquee is
ceiling mounted.

The graphic identity extends
to all operations signs.

TURTLE BAY

EXPLORATION PARK

multiple
ATTRACTION
environment

135

PROJECTS

Multiple colors suggest the multiple attractions of Turtle Bay.

Good logos often have a "picture" of something—here it's the first word in the name.

Design was drawn to separate colors for easy reproduction.

Hexagonal graphic form is a scientific reference and works well as a separate decorative device.

Typography is playful but bold, and kept black to contrast with the logo.

Bright colors translate easily to retail product design, an important consideration.

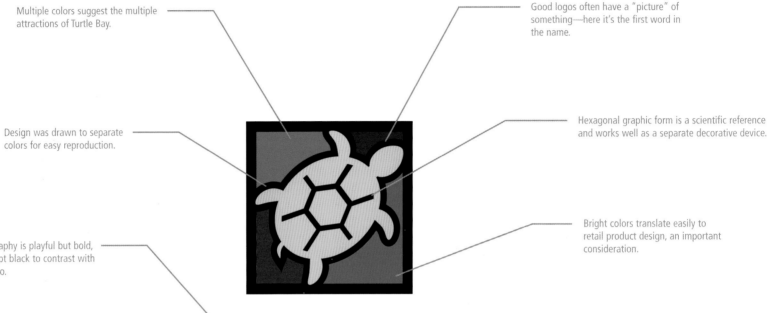

TURTLE BAY
EXPLORATION PARK ™

The colorful logo makes a bright "highlight" wherever it is applied.

All exterior signs on the huge site feature bold use of the logo colors.

Interior signs have a softer, monochromatic appearance.

details count

PROJECT OVERVIEW
Graphics program to unite diverse museum and nature attractions.

PROJECT FACTS
Client:
    Turtle Bay Exploration Park
Graphic Design Team:
    Hunt Design:
    Karen Aseltine, Jennifer Bressler, Rick Chavez, Esteban Hernandez, Wayne Hunt, Dinnis Lee, Heather Watson
Sign Company:
    Wiedner Architectural Signage
Schedule:
    Two years (first phase).

MATERIALS & TECHNIQUES
Aluminum sign structures with screened graphics; fabric banners.

UNIQUE ASPECTS
The sprawling wooded site and diverse attractions called for bold, colorful designs.

13

CAL STATE UNIVERSITY Los Angeles

Cafeteria and bookstore in a design-driven building

This new auxiliary services building establishes new standards for architecture and design for a 175-acre university campus located on a hilltop 10 minutes from downtown L.A., at the edge of the San Gabriel Valley. The building was designed to feature a Barnes and Noble bookstore, among other campus services that include a credit union, conference center, university club, and cafeteria. To encourage use by students and invite circulation, the architectural concept is shaped around a curved promenade, making the building's program components viewable and easily accessible.

The design architect, Tate Snyder Kimsey, called on frequent collaborator Hunt Design to support the unique building with a wayfinding and identity sign program. But instead of traditional architectural signs, the graphics designers, inspired by the building's retail mall-like format, recommended a bolder, more dramatic approach.

Hunt proposed a series of bladelike rigid banners to herald, from a distance, the existence of the destinations within the building. These retail-like designs preclude the need for directional signs and lend an active, animated quality to the environment. At the actual entrances, or storefronts, more formal signs in stainless-steel letters greet visitors. Overhead are smaller signs identifying building amenities, such as restrooms.

The designers also proposed that a sleek freestanding directory be installed in the new hardscape around the structure, linking the dramatic building to the rest of the Cal State L.A. campus. Although the campus employs a graphics standard for signs, in this case building-specific signage was considered appropriate to match the dramatic architecture of the new facility.

The building's unique shape influenced the signage design.

Sign location plan shows the arcade space at ground level.

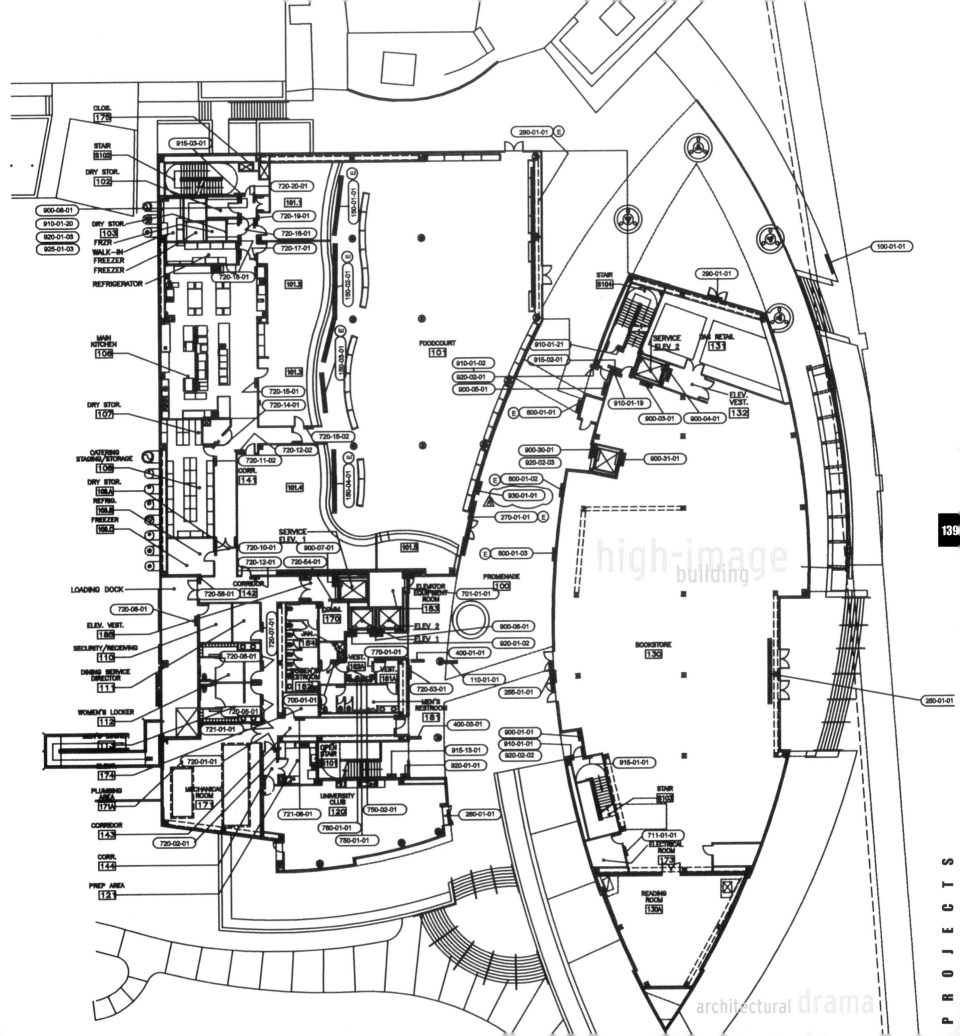

CLOS.
175

STAIR
S102

DRY STOR.
102

915-03-01

720-20-01

900-08-01
910-01-20
920-02-03
925-01-03

DRY STOR.
103
FRZR
WALK-IN
FREEZER
FREEZER
REFRIGERATOR

101.1

720-19-01

720-18-01

720-17-01

720-16-01

101.3

101.3

MAIN
KITCHEN
106

150-01-01

150-02-01

150-03-01

720-15-01

720-14-01

DRY STOR.
107

280-01-01 E

FOODCOURT
101

910-01-21

915-02-01

920-02-01

900-05-01

910-01-19

900-03-01 900-04-01

STAIR
S104

290-01-01

SERVICE
ELEV 2

RETAIL
131

ELEV.
VEST.
132

100-01-01

CATERING
STAGING/STORAGE
108

DRY STOR.
108A
REFRIG.
108B
FREEZER
108C

720-15-02

720-12-02

720-11-02

CORR.
141

101.4

150-04-01 E

900-30-01

920-02-03

E 600-01-01

E 600-01-02

930-01-01

270-01-01 E

900-31-01

SERVICE
ELEV. 1

720-10-01

720-12-01 720-54-01

900-07-01

101.5

E 600-01-03

high-image
building

LOADING DOCK

720-58-01

CORRIDOR
142

720-08-01

ELEV. VEST.
185

SECURITY/RECEIVING
110

DINING SERVICE
DIRECTOR
111

WOMEN'S LOCKER
112

720-08-01

720-07-01

720-05-01

ROOM
170

JAN.
184

VEST.
183A

KITCHEN
RESTROOM
182

VEST.
181A

ELEVATOR
EQUIPMENT
ROOM
183

ELEV 2

ELEV 1

770-01-01

PROMENADE
100

701-01-01

900-06-01

920-01-02

400-01-01

110-01-01

720-53-01

MEN'S
RESTROOM
181

255-01-01

BOOKSTORE
130

250-01-01

MEN'S LOCKER
113

ELEV.
174

721-01-01

700-01-01

400-03-01

915-13-01

920-01-01

900-01-01
910-01-01
920-02-02

PLUMBING
AREA
171A

720-01-01

MECHANICAL
ROOM
171

OPEN
STAIR
S101

915-01-01

STAIR
S103

CORRIDOR
143

720-02-01

UNIVERSITY
CLUB
120

721-08-01

780-01-01

750-02-01

750-01-01

280-01-01

711-01-01
ELECTRICAL
ROOM
173

CORR.
144

PREP AREA
121

READING
ROOM
130A

architectural drama

139

pedestrian-friendly **SPACE**

Close cooperation with the architect allowed
sign concepts to be incorporated in renderings.

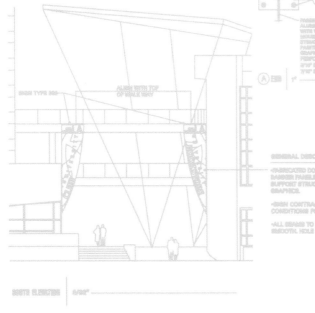

Finished project differs little from
the original drawing.

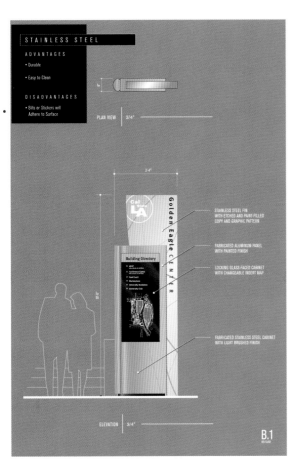

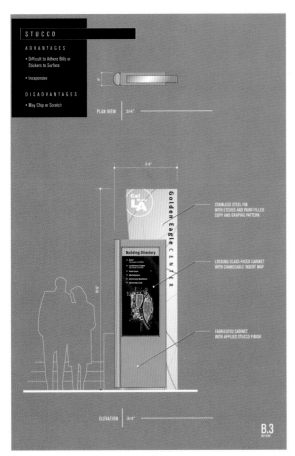

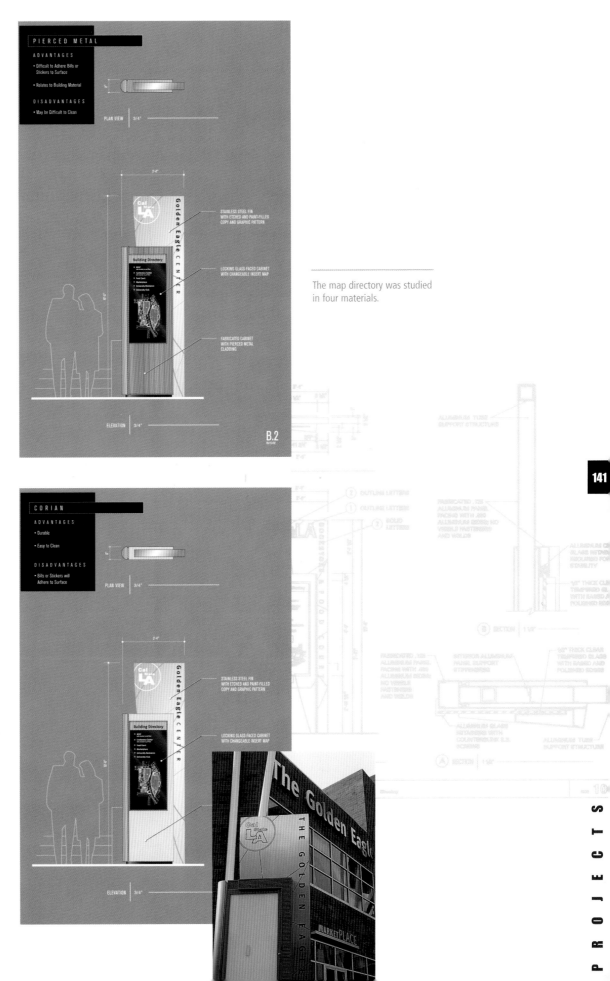

The map directory was studied
in four materials.

141

PROJECTS

Design **Analysis**

Blade sign solution provides visibility from entrance.

University logo is worked into all primary sign elements.

Eclectic typography and graphic illustrations lend important detail. and interest.

Freestanding stainless steel letters reflect traditional campus signage.

Colors are drawn from the architect's palette, but brighter.

Sign shapes lead the eye downward toward the doorways.

The design-driven graphics complement the contemporary architecture.

Minor signs have curved forms.

PROJECT OVERVIEW
An integrated signage program for a new student services building.

PROJECT FACTS
Client:
    California State University,
    Los Angeles
Graphic Design Team:
    Hunt Design:
    Dinnis Lee, Perry Shimoji,
    John Temple
Sign Company:
    AHR Ampersand
Schedule:
    Eighteen months
Photography:
    Jim Simmons (Del Zoppo Simmons)

UNIQUE ASPECTS
Unique building design led to exception from the campus sign program.

143

WILMINGTON Trust

Signage as part of rebranding

As Wilmington Trust, a venerable East Coast financial services company, evolved into a global wealth-management company, a new personality and upscale look emerged. Branding consultant Boyd Communications was chosen to create elements of the enhanced brand to appeal to the changing marketplace. Everything from letterheads to Web sites was evaluated and redesigned to help reposition Wilmington Trust as a sophisticated and trusted choice for wealth management services.

As part of the comprehensive rebranding project, the powerful medium of signage was identified as an important way to communicate changes to customers at diverse branch locations. Boyd brought in frequent collaborator Hunt Design to assist in interpreting the new branding look into signage applications. The firms had worked together on numerous projects, including the successful branding/signage program for Sanwa Bank of California.

Establishing effective brand statements in diverse urban and suburban environments is not easy. Eclectic branch architectural styles, varying site plans, and landscape conflicts present challenges for brand

designers. Intense competition for drivers' attention from existing roadside signs also complicates matters; today retail and consumer financial companies are reaching out with colorful and engaging signage presentations along roadways.

The designers developed several design options, each projecting an upscale image with elegant forms, dark colors, and a broad use of silver paint. The aesthetics of the proposals related well to the lifestyle design present in the daily lives of Wilmington Trust's customers. Major influences were the sleek, understated images of youth-oriented luxury cars and high-tech consumer products. This jewellike look was in stark contrast to the often-generic suburban architecture of the branch buildings.

The final design features a slim silver pylon sign tower with cantilevered dark-blue curved-face graphic panels. Pushthrough, edge-lit letters are used for the name and logo and add an elegant touch. Secondary and wall-mounted signs share details with the pylon. The creative use of materials, color, and form signaled positive changes while providing high visibility and recognition.

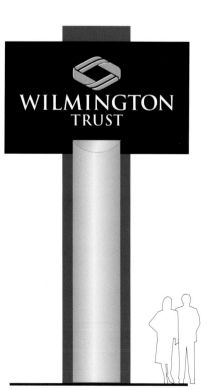

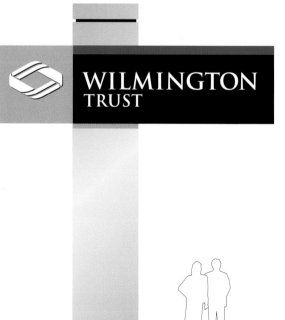

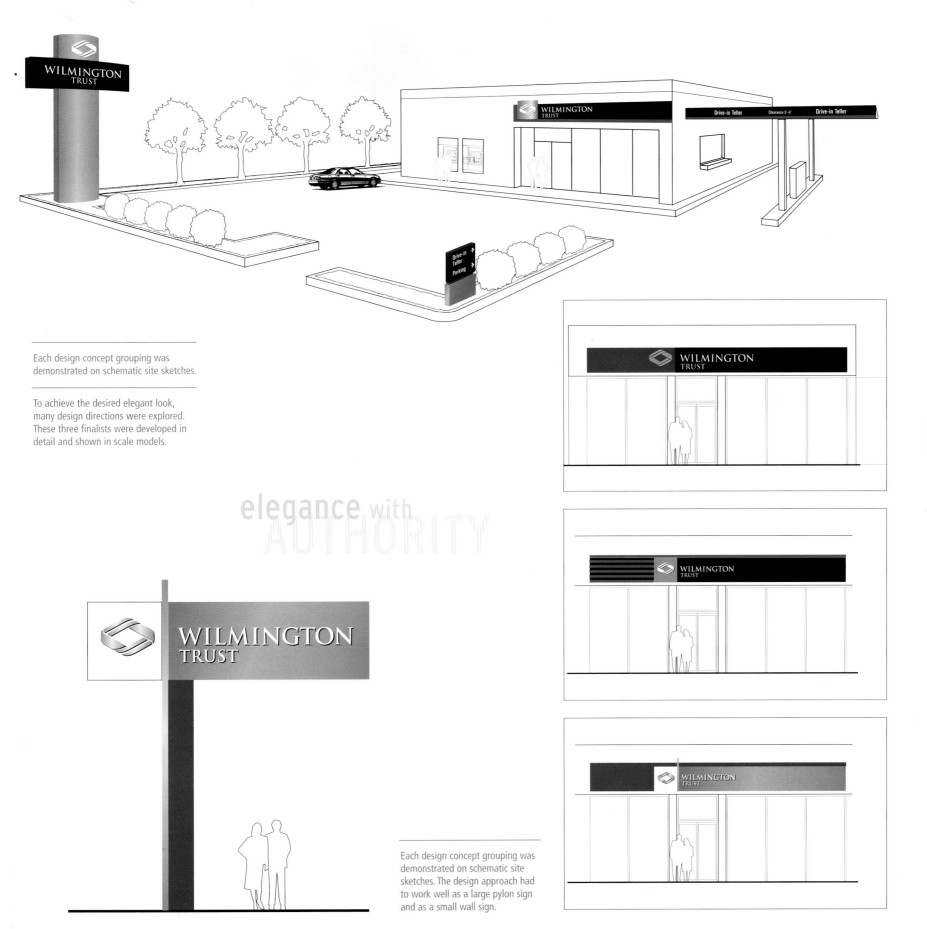

Each design concept grouping was demonstrated on schematic site sketches.

To achieve the desired elegant look, many design directions were explored. These three finalists were developed in detail and shown in scale models.

Each design concept grouping was demonstrated on schematic site sketches. The design approach had to work well as a large pylon sign and as a small wall sign.

WILMINGTON
TRUST

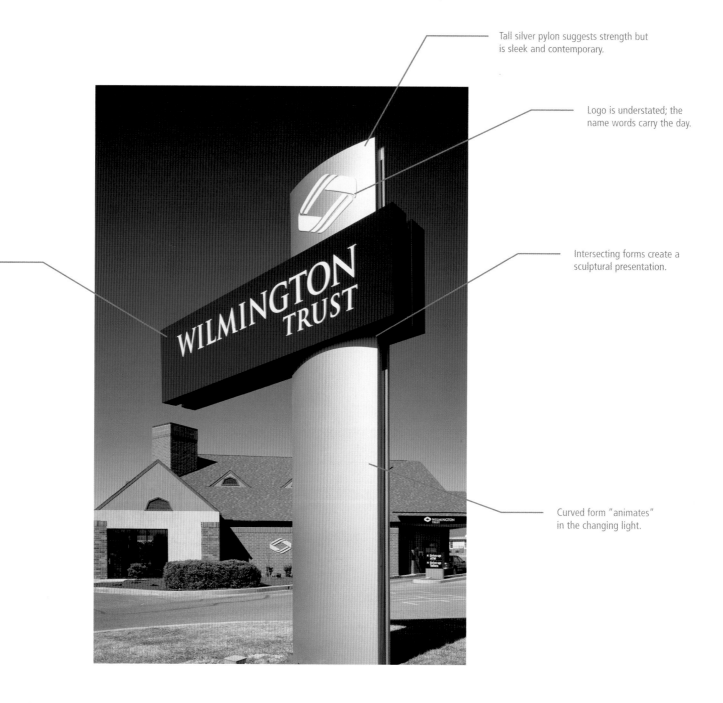

Tall silver pylon suggests strength but is sleek and contemporary.

Logo is understated; the name words carry the day.

Cantilevered asymmetrical design is unusual for the financial business.

Intersecting forms create a sculptural presentation.

Curved form "animates" in the changing light.

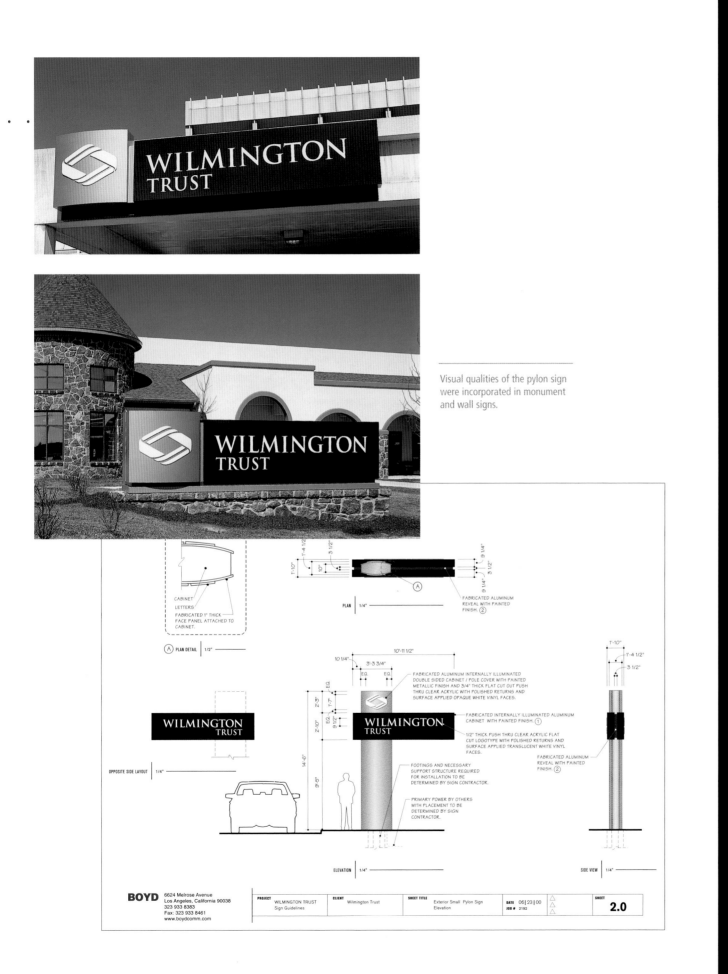

Visual qualities of the pylon sign
were incorporated in monument
and wall signs.

PROJECT OVERVIEW
Multiple location site signage program.

PROJECT FACTS
Client:
    Wilmington Trust
Branding Design Team:
    Boyd Communications;
    Signage Design:
    Hunt Design:
    Dinnis Lee, Perry Shimoji,
    John Temple
Sign Company:
    Philadelphia Sign Company
Schedule:
    One year

UNIQUE ASPECTS
The design solutions grew out of a
two-dimensional branding program.

14

WILMINGTON
TRUST

WILMINGTON
TRUST

WILMINGTON
TRUST

CABINET
LETTERS
FABRICATED 1" THICK
FACE PANEL ATTACHED TO
CABINET.

PLAN 1/4"

FABRICATED ALUMINUM
REVEAL WITH PAINTED
FINISH. (2)

(A) PLAN DETAIL 1/2"

OPPOSITE SIDE LAYOUT 1/4"

10'-11 1/2"

10 1/4"

3'-3 3/4"

EQ.   EQ.

FABRICATED ALUMINUM INTERNALLY ILLUMINATED
DOUBLE SIDED CABINET / POLE COVER WITH PAINTED
METALLIC FINISH AND 3/4" THICK FLAT CUT OUT PUSH
THRU CLEAR ACRYLIC WITH POLISHED RETURNS AND
SURFACE APPLIED OPAQUE WHITE VINYL FACES.

FABRICATED INTERNALLY ILLUMINATED ALUMINUM
CABINET WITH PAINTED FINISH. (1)

1/2" THICK PUSH THRU CLEAR ACRYLIC FLAT
CUT LOGOTYPE WITH POLISHED RETURNS AND
SURFACE APPLIED TRANSLUCENT WHITE VINYL
FACES.

FABRICATED ALUMINUM
REVEAL WITH PAINTED
FINISH. (2)

FOOTINGS AND NECESSARY
SUPPORT STRUCTURE REQUIRED
FOR INSTALLATION TO BE
DETERMINED BY SIGN CONTRACTOR.

PRIMARY POWER BY OTHERS
WITH PLACEMENT TO BE
DETERMINED BY SIGN
CONTRACTOR.

ELEVATION 1/4"

SIDE VIEW 1/4"

BOYD   6624 Melrose Avenue
       Los Angeles, California 90038
       323 933 8383
       Fax: 323 933 8461
       www.boydcomm.com

PROJECT	WILMINGTON TRUST Sign Guidelines	CLIENT	Wilmington Trust	SHEET TITLE	Exterior Small Pylon Sign Elevation	DATE	06|23|00		SHEET
						JOB #	2192		2.0

ROSE BOWL

A graphics face-lift for a famous venue

Built in 1922, the Rose Bowl is a beloved, multiuse stadium set in Pasadena's beautiful Arroyo Seco. As the site of the annual Rose Bowl game and home to UCLA football, the 103,000-seat facility also has hosted three NFL Super Bowls, soccer's World Cup, as well as concerts and events as diverse as the Rolling Stones and Billy Graham. But because of the venue's age and all-concrete structure, efficient circulation is difficult for large crowds. The 2002 Bowl Championship Series (BCS) championship game provided the right incentive and funding to update the signage in and around the stadium. Hunt Design took on the design assignment and the challenge of a rush schedule—four months from concept to installation.

Most important to the client was improving the appearance of the Rose Bowl's eight entrance gates, the point of first impression for visitors. These framed turnstile enclosures would set the tone for the entire graphics program. In addition, a "traditional stadium" look was important; the Rose Bowl needed to reestablish its own identity, free from any one tenant's aesthetics.

Starting with a selection of sign types from the property, the designers prepared a series of alternate design schemes, including one featuring backgrounds of large digital graphics of roses. The Rose Bowl and its prime tenant strongly preferred a more neutral "stadium green" appearance in which bright colors were used only as accents.

Working with the very old building proved challenging. Sight lines to logical sign locations were limited, and there were few placement opportunities for new signs. The building's all-concrete construction posed mounting problems, and new sign lighting required surface-mounted conduit. And because blending in with the rough concrete surfaces was impractical, the designers decided to use the more than one hundred sign elements to help establish a new visual identity.

The resulting designs are targetlike, with a circular outline used for emphasis and as a continuity device. Typography is boldly stated and reflects a sports sensibility. To contrast with the green sign backgrounds, the designers specified a strong palette of red, yellow, and white for the words and numbers. Great care was used in the design of the many regulatory signs that often present a negative greeting and add a cluttered appearance at sports venue entrances.

The design program extended out into the vast parking areas and also included off-site directional signs along area roads. In addition, a program of temporary signs was developed for use when the adjacent golf course is used for parking.

All-new signage welcomes fans to the Bowl Championship Series game.

Several color options were considered, including one with a motif of digital rose petals.

25

traditional but bold

Kit **5** option B

isometric of gateway identity sign

LOCATION ELEVATION 1/8"

HUNT DESIGN ASSOCIATES | 2270 | Rose Bowl | Kit 5 | Stadium Gate OPTION B | 09 | 30 | 01

Kit **5** option B

isometric of gateway identity sign

LOCATION ELEVATION 1/8"

HUNT DESIGN ASSOCIATES | 2270 | Rose Bowl | Kit 5 | Stadium Gate A, OPTION B without banners | 09 | 15 | 01

FREEWAYS

210 WEST | 210 | 134 | 110 | 210 to 134 110 EAST

LAYOUT 1/8" Outbound

ROSE BOWL
General Parking / ♿ / Passes
↓ BOTH LANES ↓

In a parallel project, a program of temporary overhead banner signs was developed to direct game-day traffic in and out of the constricted site.

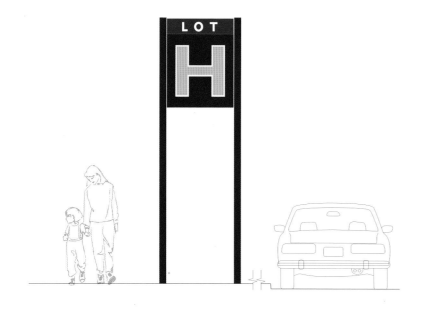

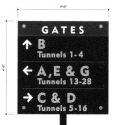

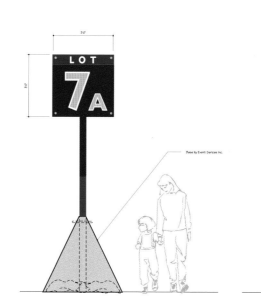

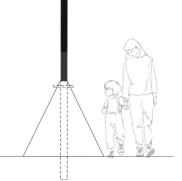

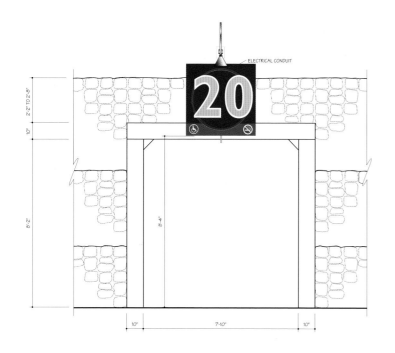

Scaled sketches of the final designs show the color theme: green background, red band, yellow letters and numerals.

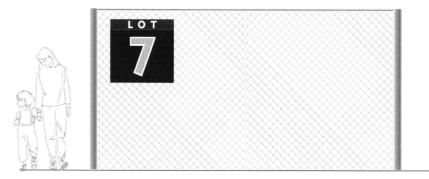

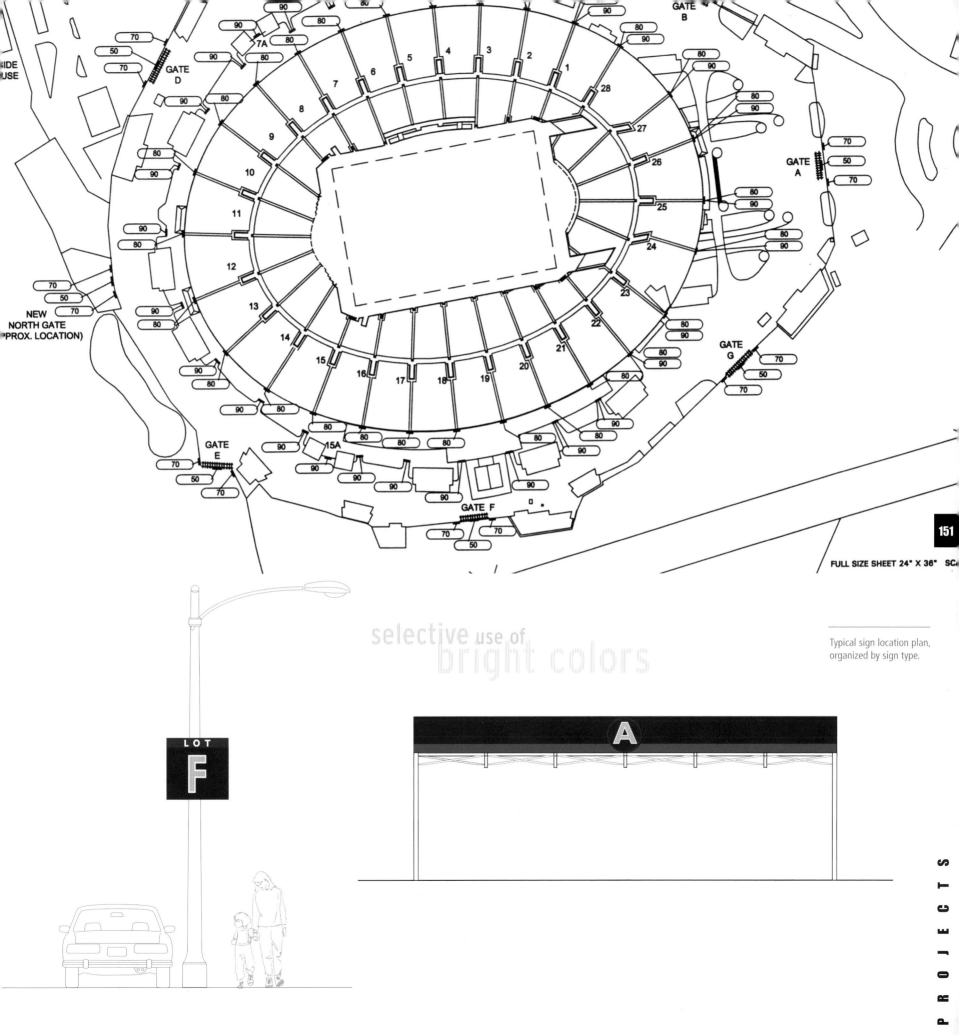

90 90 80 80 90 GATE B 80 90

70 50 70

GATE D

90 80 7A 80 90 6 5 4 3 2 1 28 80 90

80 90 7 80 90

8 27 70 50 70 GATE A

9 26 80 90

10 25 80 90

11 24 80 90

90 80 12 23

70 50 70

NEW NORTH GATE (PROX. LOCATION)

13 22 80 90

90 80 14 21 GATE G 70 50 70

15 20 80 90

90 80 16 17 18 19 80 90

90 80 7A 80

80 80 80

GATE E 90 80 15A 80 80 90

70 50 70 90 90 80 90

90 90

GATE F

70 70

50

151

FULL SIZE SHEET 24" X 36" SC

selective use of
bright colors

Typical sign location plan,
organized by sign type.

LOT
F

A

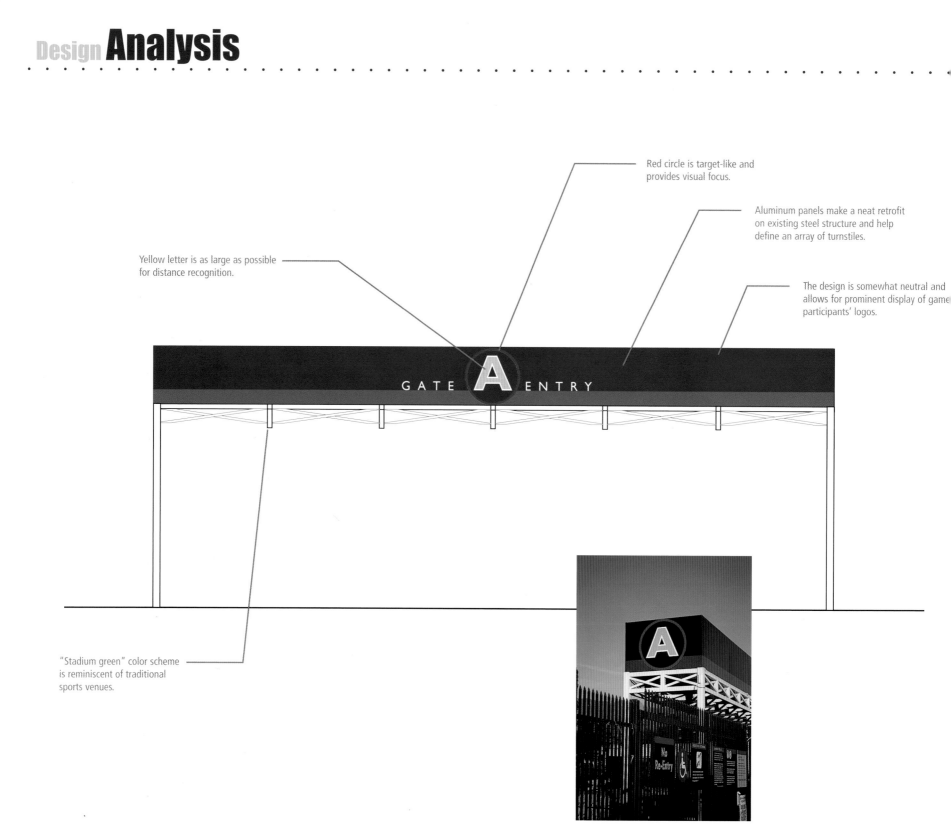

Red circle is target-like and provides visual focus.

Aluminum panels make a neat retrofit on existing steel structure and help define an array of turnstiles.

Yellow letter is as large as possible for distance recognition.

The design is somewhat neutral and allows for prominent display of game participants' logos.

GATE A ENTRY

"Stadium green" color scheme is reminiscent of traditional sports venues.

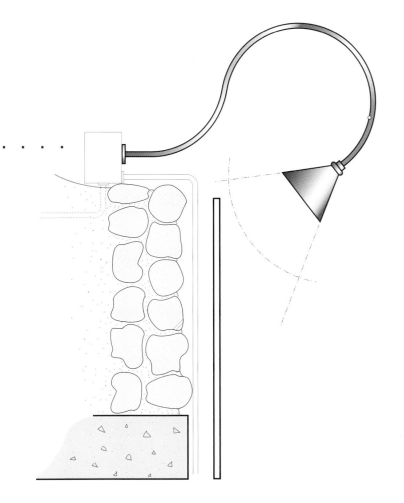

LIGHT DETAIL | 1/2"

stadiums: information-rich
environments

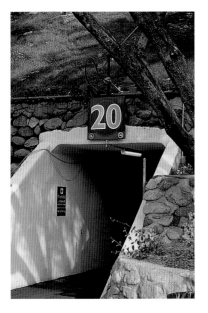

The finished signs demonstrate how color is used to both stand out (red) and blend in (green).

Great care was given to the organization and positive presentation of the many rules and regulations.

PROJECT OVERVIEW
New wayfinding and identity signage for the Rose Bowl.

PROJECT FACTS
Client:
    The Rose Bowl;
    Pasadena Tournament of Roses
Graphic Design Team:
    Hunt Design:
    Karen Aseltine, Rick Chavez,
    Wayne Hunt, Dinnis Lee, Perry Shimoji,
    John Temple, Heather Watson
Sign Company:
    AHR Ampersand
Schedule:
    Four months

MATERIALS & TECHNIQUES
Aluminum sign panels with painted, vinyl, and screened graphics; vinyl banners.

UNIQUE ASPECTS
The century-old facility posed difficult implementation challenges.

15

PROJECT FACTS

Jan Lorenc on EXHIBIT DESIGN AND PROGRAMMING

When planning an exhibit, most clients have defined an overall message they wish to convey and have determined a need to communicate it to "their" public. When we begin to program and design such a project, one of the guiding principles that sustains the process, start to finish, is the "story," our extended interpretation of the message. It is essential for us to develop a broad and deep understanding of the client, its mission, and the potential visitor. The exhibit, when brought to physical form, must communicate this understanding in a well-organized format in order to effectively tell the story.

Exhibit projects tend to be more complex, yet more focused, than wayfinding or visual identification programs, but they are similar in that an essential design concept must be established to serve as the "guiding light" throughout the programming and design process. Further, the concept is conveyed in a logical, sequential physical arrangement in the resulting built-out exhibit. Greater complexity and focus require a concept more flexible and more capable of evolving during the design process.

Conducting thorough and meaningful advance research reveals the narrative, which is key to understanding the essential message of the exhibit. The design process then methodically transforms the narrative into a sculpted three-dimensional space, bringing the story to life for each visitor. Just as in architectural and interior design disciplines, the space must be organized into a sequence that relates the space to the story, and the story to the visitors. Typically, a sequence of experiences arranged around a timeline theme or a hierarchical theme—in the same way that a verbal story would be told—will communicate in a logical and comfortable

manner. We provide experiences one after another, allowing the visitor to build up the whole story but never allowing him to see or experience the whole story at once. Revealing the story step by step is a key factor in engaging the visitor.

Collaboration with a large team of specialists, including client, project architect, interior designer, lighting consultant, audiovisual consultant, acoustic consultant, and interactive computer hardware and content consultants is a routine requirement for producing a complex exhibit environment. We must work closely with the overall team to effectively bring the narrative through the process. The team will have concern for the entire exhibit space as well as the spaces surrounding, especially those that form an approach sequence, including the vehicular approach to the site, the pedestrian approach, the building entry sequence, and the transition into the exhibit space. This entire sequence affects a visitor's impression of the story. Clearly, the exhibit narrative helps establish the overall guiding principles, but all of the other disciplines have contributions to make to assure the success of the exhibit and the entire visitor experience.

The designer must appreciate the aspirations of the exhibit, its functional criteria and goals. As a team we pursue the design concept, design development, and implementation of the overall program. Sensitivity to all aspects of design, including coordination with all design team members, budget requirements, calendar schedules, and spatial allowances, must be included. All aspects of the exhibit, from overall concept down to tiny details for connections, graphics, and finishes, must be coordinated.

Concept elevation sketch and finished theater space.

Bible Focus   Introduction   Life without the Bible   Language Portal   Theatre

Rich and varied materials establish a warm, inviting environment.

Flow diagram shows visitor circulation sequence and choices.

welcome desk

lobby sculpture

Involvement

partnerships

Children's corner Storytelling

Theatre

Chapel

changing Exhibit/or expansion space

vision & mission

The Bible, Central Exhibit

Jaars

media resource center

Missionary Life

The scope & the need

Language The Beauty & the Challenge

The Wycliffe Story

outdoor garden

Language & Culture   modern translation   Involvement Y2025

Jan holds a bachelor of science degree in Industrial Design, a master of science in Visual Design, both from the Institute of Design in Chicago, and a master of science in Architecture from Georgia Tech. He was selected to jury the SEGD Competition in 1996, and in 2001 he was the jury Chairman. He is on the Advisory Board for the Georgia Tech College of Architecture Industrial Design Department and is a frequent speaker at design schools and conferences. He helped establish the Allied Design Council in Atlanta, which promotes dialogue among various design disciplines.

In 1978 Jan established Jan Lorenc Design in Chicago and then moved the firm to Atlanta in 1981. He relocated again in 2000, to historic Roswell, Georgia, and at the same time renamed the firm Lorenc+Yoo Design (LYD), acknowledging his partnership with Chung Youl Yoo. The firm includes a multidisciplinary team of twelve designers with broad experience in industrial design, architecture, interior design, graphic design, furniture design, and journalism, all collaborating in crafting a narrative for each client and each project which is then realized through the design of various complex environments.

LYD undertakes projects of varying complexity and magnitude involving museum planning and design, visitor center design, trade show exhibits, and a variety of environmental graphics programs. Our mission in our projects is the unification of the arts where all of the images and spaces and details of each project are coordinated seamlessly into a complete design statement, imparting a singular narrative specific to the project goals.

An exhibit must tell a well-organized story

When conducting advance research for the programming phase, the designer must carefully listen to the client and to other people who influence or affect the client's business, activities, or organization. We gather every conceivable type of information relating to the message from the client and other sources. Further, we must understand opportunities embedded in the exhibit message. This might include "reading between the lines." It is important to understand the client and the message beyond the factual information gathered.

Once the message is understood, the process of producing a narrative version of the message must begin. This complex process involves breaking the message into segments according to the anticipated needs of the visitor. It is important to research and understand the variety of visitors with whom we must communicate effectively. The message segments then evolve into a physical space with attributes that address basic human ergonomics, circulation, and graphic and sensory elements. In essence, the designer must arrive at an architectural definition of the nature of the overall exhibit space.

The exhibit design process

The process helps organize the overall execution of the goals defined by the client and the design team. The traditional architecturally based process of conceptual design, design development, fabrication documentation, and construction administration helps to establish a basic organization for the design effort. The process benefits greatly from continual feedback and response from the client, focus groups, or other study measures to ensure that the design communicates effectively and comfortably with the intended visitors.

Materials and graphics must be supportive of the story. If the story is speaking of the future and high technology, the design should reflect those values. If the story is more grounded in history, then aspects or artifacts from the time period should be considered without resulting in trite or condescending messages.

The segments of the narrative must be communicated effectively and may be further broken into elements of primary focus, secondary focus, sidebar or supporting information, or additional categories. This communication should be tailored to the intended visitor types—those familiar with the subject, those unfamiliar with the subject, children, visually focused, auditory focused, and sensory focused. Further, the information must be meaningful when experienced briefly or with greater scrutiny.

Once the segments are known and the degree of detail is determined, the designer must determine the physical means of communication. This area of effort invites enormous creativity since the communication may occur through an almost endless variety of means, including: visual, auditory, touch, interaction, technology, color, light, vibration, mechanical devices, and so on. As the method of communication is determined, the segment of the narrative defined, and the narrative sequence maintained, a well-organized, meaningful exhibit experience will begin to emerge.

"Rendered" elevations are easy to prepare, and very informative for clients.

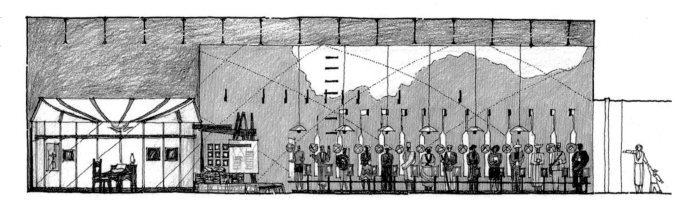

Study model and installed show—it's always gratifying when the finish fulfills the model's intent.

COMMUNICATE
beyond the visual into the **sensorial**

Involvement V2025   modern translation.   Language and Culture

Simple perspective sketches remain powerful design tools.

THE STORY
provides the opportunity to **learn** beyond
one's own immediate life **experience**

The Bible: Its Power & History
Conceptual Sketch.

Exhibit design principles

1. Foster an environment that nurtures the mission and vision.
2. Invite and motivate the visitors to share in the mission.
3. Maximize the storyline communication. Install a clear and compelling message that informs, educates, and engages the visitor.
4. Create a memorable exhibit experience that captures the imagination of the visitor. Inspire, motivate, and stimulate the heart and mind to greater understanding and awareness.
5. Assist self-guided flow and circulation through the exhibit. Allow for a sequential story but allow random browsing.
6. Develop strategies to allow for expansion and flexibility where required. Consider the needs for further expansion in a master plan.
7. Create a variety of exhibit displays within an organizing scheme. Look at the big-picture ideas together with the component details.
   a. Provide places to pause and reflect along with places for active integration.
   b. Accommodate a wide range of visitor groups of different ages, different backgrounds, different degrees of familiarity and education.
   c. Utilize a combination of electronic, mechanical, 2-D/3-D displays of varying complexity to engage the casual or active visitor.
   d. Provide a solution that will accommodate groups of various sizes.
8. Assist the client in designing a cost-effective solution that presents the story and overall quality goals.
9. Communicate the narrative in a creative, imaginative, and visually appealing way, but in no way allow exhibit design features to overwhelm the message.

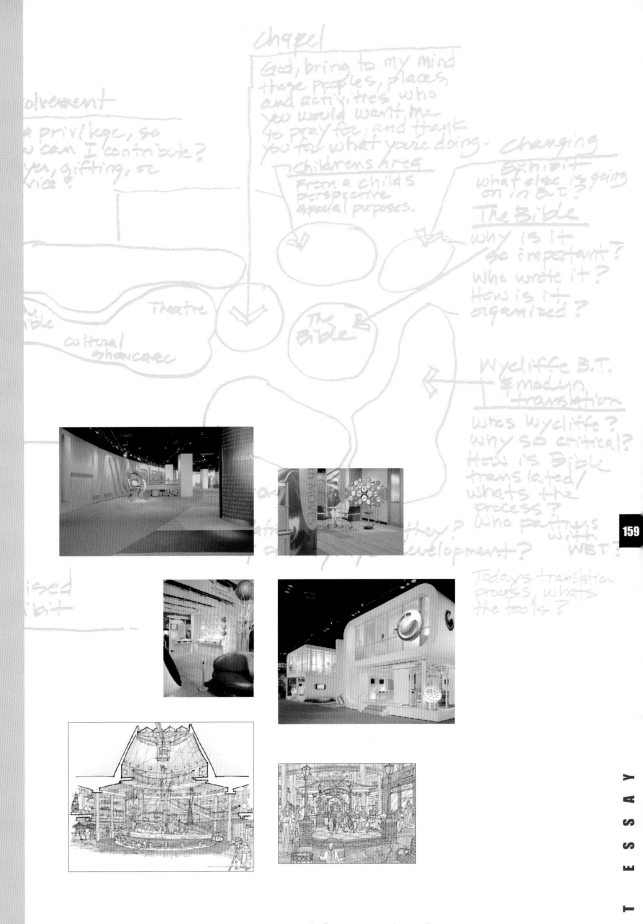

159

Engage and stimulate the visitor

SATURN V
MORE POWERFUL THAN...

EIGHT THOUSAND DAYTONA 500 STARTING FIELDS

The Saturn V's first stage alone generated approximately 160,000,000 horsepower. That makes it over eight thousand times more powerful than all of the race cars in this year's Daytona 500 combined.

ELECTRICITY TO NYC FOR 1-1/4 HOURS

The Saturn V's first two stages together generated enough energy to have supplied electricity to New York City for over one hour and fifteen minutes.

OVER TWO HUNDRED F-18 JET FIGHTERS

The five F-1 engines in the rocket's first stage together generated over 7.5 million pounds of thrust, a force larger than the thrust produced by two hundred thirteen F-18 jet fighters.

A MATTER OF THRUST

LIFTOFF

Since a fully loaded Saturn V weighed 6.2 million pounds, a force at least that large was required to launch the vehicle. The first stage's five F-1 engines did more than just lift the vehicle off the ground, they accelerated it to a speed of over 5,000 miles per hour.

ESCAPING EARTH'S GRAVITY

The thrust required to accelerate the vehicle decreased as it consumed large amounts of its weight in fuel and as the Earth's gravitational pull upon it weakened. The one J-2 engine in the rocket's third stage produced only 225,000 pounds of thrust, but it was able to propel the spacecraft out of Earth's orbit by accelerating it to a speed of over 24,000 miles per hour.

HOW BIG IS

THE ENGINE THAT COULD

The mighty F-1 was the world's largest and most powerful liquid-fueled rocket engine. The five F-1's located at the base of the Saturn V's first stage together generated over 7.5 million pounds of thrust. As they lifted the rocket 40 miles above Earth in 2.5 minutes, the engines consumed more than 534,000 gallons of fuel.

100% RELIABLE

Ending its Apollo career with a flawless record, the F-1 proved itself immensely powerful and 100% reliable.

ROCKET PROPULSION

Liquid Rocket Engines

Liquid rocket engines generate thrust when a liquid fuel is ignited in the presence of an oxidizer, an agent that supplies oxygen to the combustion process. Energy is produced in the form of hot gases under pressure. When the gases are expelled, they create a reaction force that propels the rocket.

Combustion Chamber

Nozzle

The F-1 at Work

The F-1 engines were fueled by a form of kerosene known as RP-1 and the oxidizer LOX, or liquid oxygen. The propellants were stored in the Saturn V's first stage and were driven to the F-1's combustion chamber by a 3,000 pound turbopump assembly.

As the two propellants entered the combustion chamber, four small pre-burners caused them to ignite. The gases produced during the process were expelled from the chamber into the engine's nozzle at a rate of 1 million cubic feet per second.

Length
Maximum Diameter
Weight
Thrust
Propellants

FUEL

The propellants in an Apollo/Saturn V vehicle weighed 5,625,000 pounds and accounted for roughly 91% of its total weight. In contrast, a 1969 Corvette, the preferred automobile of the Apollo astronauts, was 96% static mass and 4% fuel.

HYPERGOLIC PROPELLANTS

Fueling an Apollo/Saturn V vehicle was a complex process that took several days to complete. The Apollo Spacecraft's hypergolic propellants, liquids that ignite when combined, were the first to be loaded.

CRYOGENIC PROPELLANTS

The Saturn V's cryogenic propellants, gases that turn into liquids at low temperatures, were the last to be loaded. The use of cryogenic propellants was vital to the Apollo program. Had all of the propellants been left in a gaseous state, the huge tanks required to contain them would have made the construction of the Saturn V impossible.

ROCKET FUEL SUPREME

DESIGN & TESTING

The development of the F-1 engine was one of the most significant engineering achievements of the Apollo program. Built by Rocketdyne, a division of the company now known as Rockwell International, the F-1 required innovative construction techniques and testing methods.

INTERPRETIVE PROJECTS
Environmental graphics that educate, enlighten, and entertain

Sears Tower SKYDECK

A visitor center 103 floors up

Once the tallest building in the world, the Sears Tower remains a major Chicago tourist destination. In addition to the spectacular views of "America's second city" from the 103rd floor, today's visitors expect and deserve more for the price of admission. Opened in the early nineties, the observation deck had, over the years, become dated and uninteresting to viewers. Also, with as many as one hundred bad weather days, when the view is less than wonderful, a new attraction that had appeal independent of the weather was needed. The property owner contracted with a multidisciplined design team to renovate the glass-enclosed space. In addition to the concept design firm and architect, Hunt Design was picked to design the graphic exhibits.

Based on Chicago stories, the exhibit is a linear interpretive experience designed to circulate guests counterclockwise around the building's elevator/service core. High traffic and near-capacity crowds make constant visitor flow important. The project's architect suggested that the display walls be curved to contrast with the rectilinear windows and to add a dynamic quality to the space. The resulting separate, curved portions provided a logical means to organize the stories and images. The perpendicular walls between the curved wall segments are filled to the edges with large backlit transparencies.

High visitor capacity and lack of floor width led to a design consisting largely of two-dimensional media. However, the designers created insets and shadow-boxes where possible and established a rhythm at the tops of the walls by setting some title headers back and moving others forward. Dramatic carpeting and heightened lighting add much to the look of the open floor, even in full daylight.

As a design counterpoint, two concave walls were included to feature two of Chicago's most important and interesting stories: sports and architecture. These rich mini-spaces provide topical focus and spatial contrast. A custom carpet design presents a large compass star as a complement to the presentation on the city's great architects.

An interesting facet of the design solution is the parallel children's story line called "Knee-High Chicago." Here, special copywriting and visuals are placed along all of the display walls at a lower height and signaled by a continuous, curving, dotted line.

Early sketches illustrate dimensional wall effect.

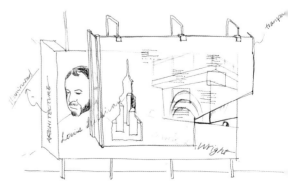

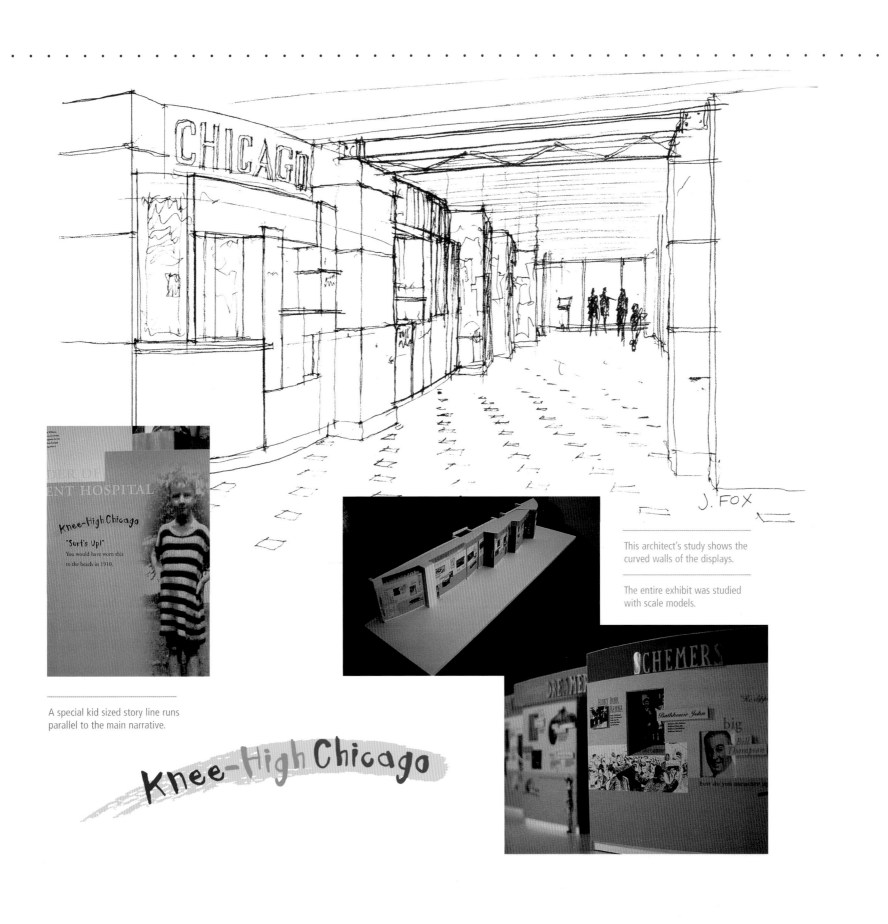

J. FOX

Knee-High Chicago

"Surf's Up!"
You would have worn this
to the beach in 1910.

This architect's study shows the curved walls of the displays.

The entire exhibit was studied with scale models.

A special kid sized story line runs parallel to the main narrative.

Knee-High Chicago

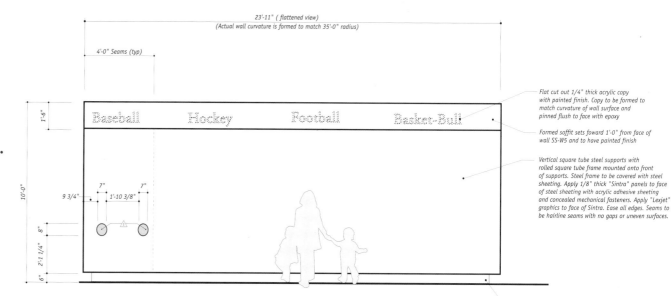

23'-11" (flattened view)
(Actual wall curvature is formed to match 35'-0" radius)

4'-0" Seams (typ)

1'-6"

10'-0"

9 3/4"

7"   1'-10 3/8"   7"

8"

2'-1 1/4"

6"

Baseball   Hockey   Football   Basket-Ball

Flat cut out 1/4" thick acrylic copy
with painted finish. Copy to be formed to
match curvature of wall surface and
pinned flush to face with epoxy

Formed soffit sets forward 1'-0" from face of
wall SS-W5 and to have painted finish

Vertical square tube steel supports with
rolled square tube frame mounted onto front
of supports. Steel frame to be covered with steel
sheeting. Apply 1/8" thick "Sintra" panels to face
of steel sheeting with acrylic adhesive sheeting
and concealed mechanical fasteners. Apply "Lexjet"
graphics to face of Sintra. Ease all edges. Seams to
be hairline seams with no gaps or uneven surfaces.

4" recessed toe-kick with painted finish
NOTE: Low voltage strip lighting recessed
into concealed area of toe-kick for down
lighting of toe-kick area.

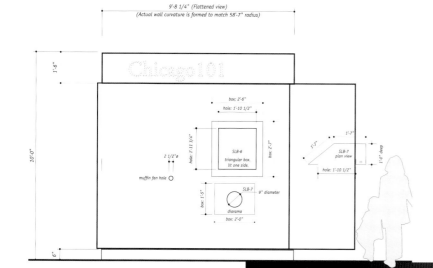

9'-8 1/4" (Flattened view)
(Actual wall curvature is formed to match 58'-7" radius)

1'-6"

10'-0"

6"

Chicago 101

box: 2'-6"
hole: 1'-10 1/2"

hole: 1'-11 3/4"

SLB-6
triangular box,
lit one side.

box: 2'-7"

2 1/2"ø

muffin fan hole ○

SLB-7
plan view

1'-7"

1'-7"

1'-0" deep

hole: 1'-10 1/2"

box: 1'-5"

SLB-7
diarama

9" diameter

box: 2'-0"

Knee-High Chicago

Hold onto your dreams...   ...and make them come true

One of the few interactives:
the narrow space and high
traffic led to a graphics-
dominant design solution.

Here a special wind effect
surprises visitors.

Concept design, construction
drawing, and finished installation
of the "Chicago Architects" section.

30'-1/8" (Flattened view)
(Actual wall curvature is formed to match 10'-0" radius)

Flat cut out 1/4" thick acrylic copy
with painted finish. Copy to be formed to
match curvature of wall surface and pinned flush
to face with epoxy

Formed soffit set back 6" from face of wall SS-E1
and to have painted finish.
NOTE: Low voltage strip lighting recessed
into concealed area of soffit for up-lighting
of soffit area

4" recessed toe-kick with painted finish

NOTE: Low voltage strip lighting recessed
into concealed area of toe-kick for down
lighting of toe-kick area.

Vertical square tube steel supports with rolled square tube
frame mounted onto front of supports. Steel frame to be covered
with steel sheeting. Apply 1/8" thick "Sintra" panels to face of
steel sheeting with acrylic adhesive sheeting and concealed mechanical
fasteners. Apply "Lexjet" graphics to face of Sintra. Ease all edges.
Seams to be hairline seams with no gaps or uneven surfaces.

linear storytelling

Design **Analysis**

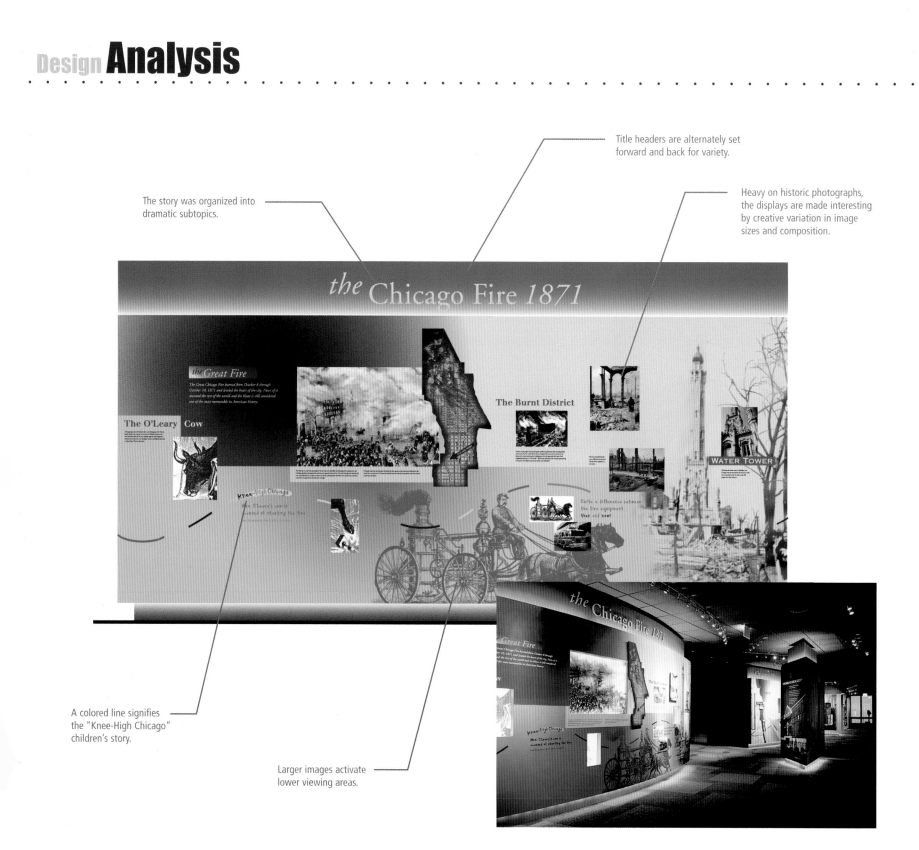

Title headers are alternately set forward and back for variety.

The story was organized into dramatic subtopics.

Heavy on historic photographs, the displays are made interesting by creative variation in image sizes and composition.

A colored line signifies the "Knee-High Chicago" children's story.

Larger images activate lower viewing areas.

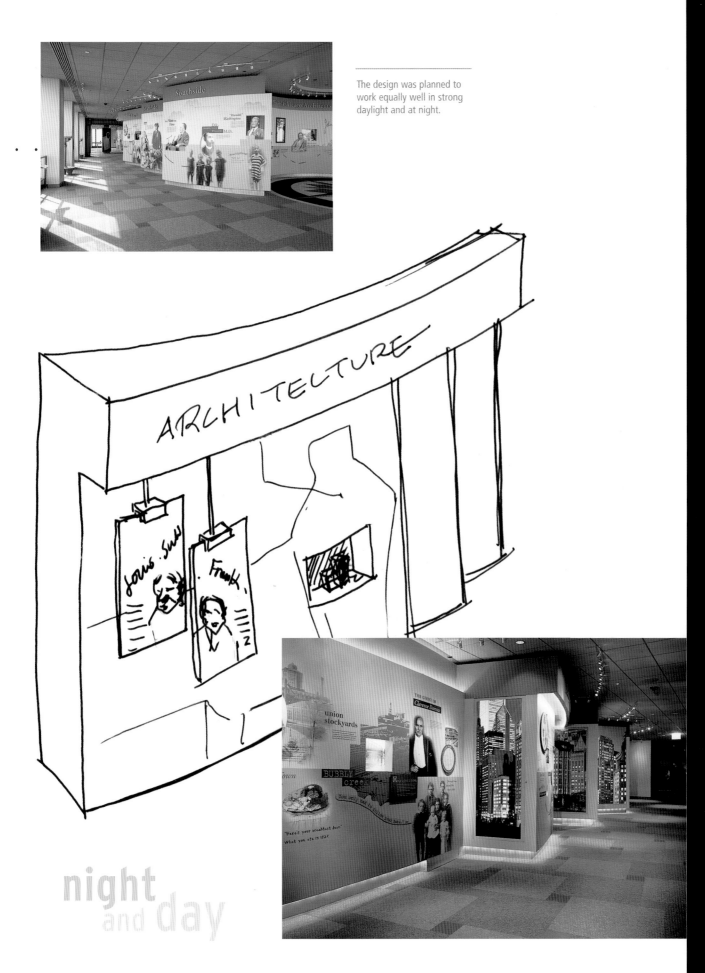

The design was planned to
work equally well in strong
daylight and at night.

night
and day

16

PROJECT OVERVIEW
An intense, graphics-oriented exhibit as
part of a major building's observation
deck and visitor experience.

PROJECT FACTS
Client:
    TrizecHahn Office Properties
Design and Production Firm:
    Dellmont Leisure Design
Graphic Design Team:
    Hunt Design:
    Jennifer Bressler, Wayne Hunt
Concept Consultant:
    Michael Devine
Project Photographer:
    Evan Mower
Architect:
    James Fox
Graphics Production Company:
    Williams Graphics
Schedule:
    One year

MATERIALS & TECHNIQUES
The graphics were digitally printed on
the reverse side of .005 Lexan and
installed in vertical four-foot pieces.

UNIQUE ASPECTS
The design had to compete with and
complement the spectacular views of
Chicago and work in daylight and night-
time for thousands of daily visitors.

CHICANO NOW American Expressions

A lively exhibit brings to life the experience of a unique culture

Traveling exhibits, shared by major museums, are becoming an important part of the changing landscape at many of our nation's cultural institutions. No longer is it always possible for a single museum to author, finance, and install complex topical exhibitions. Increasingly, independent exhibit production companies identify specific subjects of national interest and "presell" an exhibit concept to two, three, or more institutions.

Unlike permanent installations, a traveling show needs to be freestanding and somewhat portable. The floor plan must allow flexibility for differing conditions in each museum, and ceiling heights are often limited. Major set pieces have to break down for shipping, and components tend to be light in weight. All of these parameters often lead to shows that are more graphic in execution, and graphic designers often play a bigger role than they would otherwise.

In this colorful example, actor and art collector Cheech Marin collaborated with Clear Channel Entertainment Exhibitions, Inc., to create a five-thousand-square-foot multimedia show that will travel to fifteen cities in five years. To plan and script the exhibit, entertainment design firm Wyatt Design Group was selected; they in turn engaged Hunt Design to create the graphic look of the show and to design the dozens of walls and interpretive graphics. Wyatt and Hunt had teamed before, and the creative staffs of the two firms worked as a unified team to achieve the richly layered final results.

The rich-looking exhibit consists of six displays, each meant to inspire appreciation of Chicano artistic, scholastic, and cultural achievements. Included in the program are original art, three-dimensional environments, film and video presentations, music, history, and artifacts. The designers created dynamic information panels for each display, capturing the unique Chicano style by layering background imagery behind descriptive typography and original artwork.

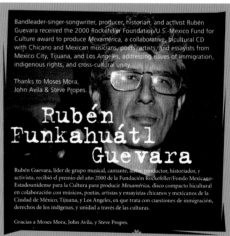

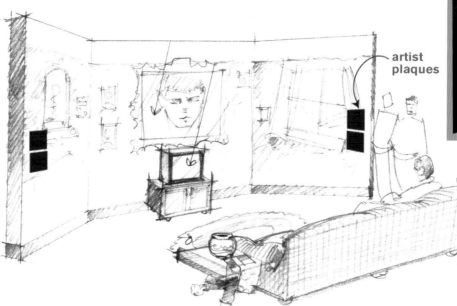

artist plaques

The exhibit is organized around artists and work commissioned for the show.

The graphic look that emerged, bright and powerful to match the spirit of the exhibit, is not what one sees in conventional interpretive exhibits. There are no plain white information plaques with easy-to-read twenty-five-word captions. While the text is readable, the narrative approach is more integrated with the artwork than is common in museums. The design team felt that the subject matter required this unique approach. The seamless integration of original scenic murals, photographs, art, and technology created an environment that invites visitors to experience the impact and joy of Chicano contributions to American culture.

A substantial challenge to the project's graphic designers was the need to speak in Spanish as well as English. Because parallel one-to-one translations often detract from the flow of visitor experience, the two languages are presented in multiple typefaces and eclectic formats.

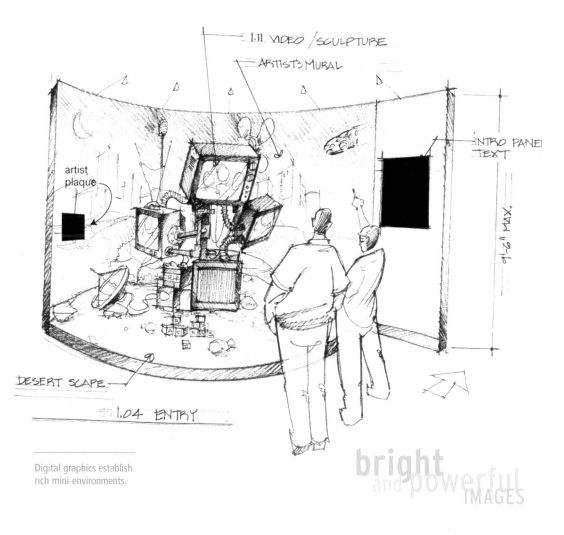

Digital graphics establish rich mini-environments.

bright
and powerful
IMAGES

THE BORDER

A Border State of Mind

The border is many borders. It is the physical border of today, the historical border of yesterday, the mythical border of everyday. It is a psychological border, always to be crossed. It is a place of convergence, interaction, creativity, transformation. For Chicanos, the border is a state of mind.

Un Estado de Animo Fronteriza

La frontera is múltiple. Es la frontera física de hoy, la frontera histórica de ayer, la frontera mítica cotidiana. Es una frontera psicológico la cual se tiene que cruzar constantemente. Es lugar de convergencia, interaccion, creatividad, transformación. Para los chicanos, la frontera es un estado de animo.

The Border

Close to a million people cross back and forth over the U.S.-Mexico border every day. Millions of dollars of goods flow back and forth every day. Culture passes back and forth and blends, as it has for thousands of years, as though there were no border at all.

La Frontera

Todos los días cerca de un millón de personas van y vienen cruzando la frontera entre México y los Estados Unidos. Millones de dólares de bienes van y vienen a diario. La cultura pasa de un lado a otro de la frontera y se mezcla, como lo ha hecho durante miles de años, como si esa frontera no existiera.

Bridge or Barrier?

The U.S.-Mexico border is 2,100 miles long. Some cross freely. Some risk their lives to cross. For some the border is a bridge; for some it is a barrier.

¿Puente o barrera?

La frontera entre Estados Unidos y México tiene una longitud de más de 3,378km. Algunos la cruzan libremente. Algunos arriesgan su vida para cruzarla. Para algunos la frontera es un puente; para otros la frontera es una barrera.

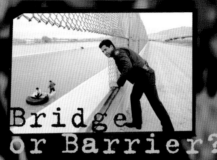

The United States of Mex

In the early 19th century, the areas of Texas, New Mexico, Arizona, California, Nevada, Utah, Oklahoma, and portions of Wyoming and Colorado were part of Mexico. Long before the U.S. absorbed the Southwest, Mexicans lived and owned land there.

Los Estados Unidos Mexicanos

A principios del siglo XIX las áreas de Texas, Nuevo México, Arizona, California, Nevada, Utah, Oklahoma y partes de Wyoming y de Colorado formaban parte de México. Mucho antes de que los Estados Unidos absorbieran el Suroeste, los mexicanos vivían y tenían tierras allí.

MEXICO.

> "The border is like an itching in the mind that simply will not go away."
>
> "La frontera es como una comezón en la mente que, simplemente, no se aliviara."
>
> –Carlos Vélez-Ibáñez, cultural anthropologist
> antropólogo cultural

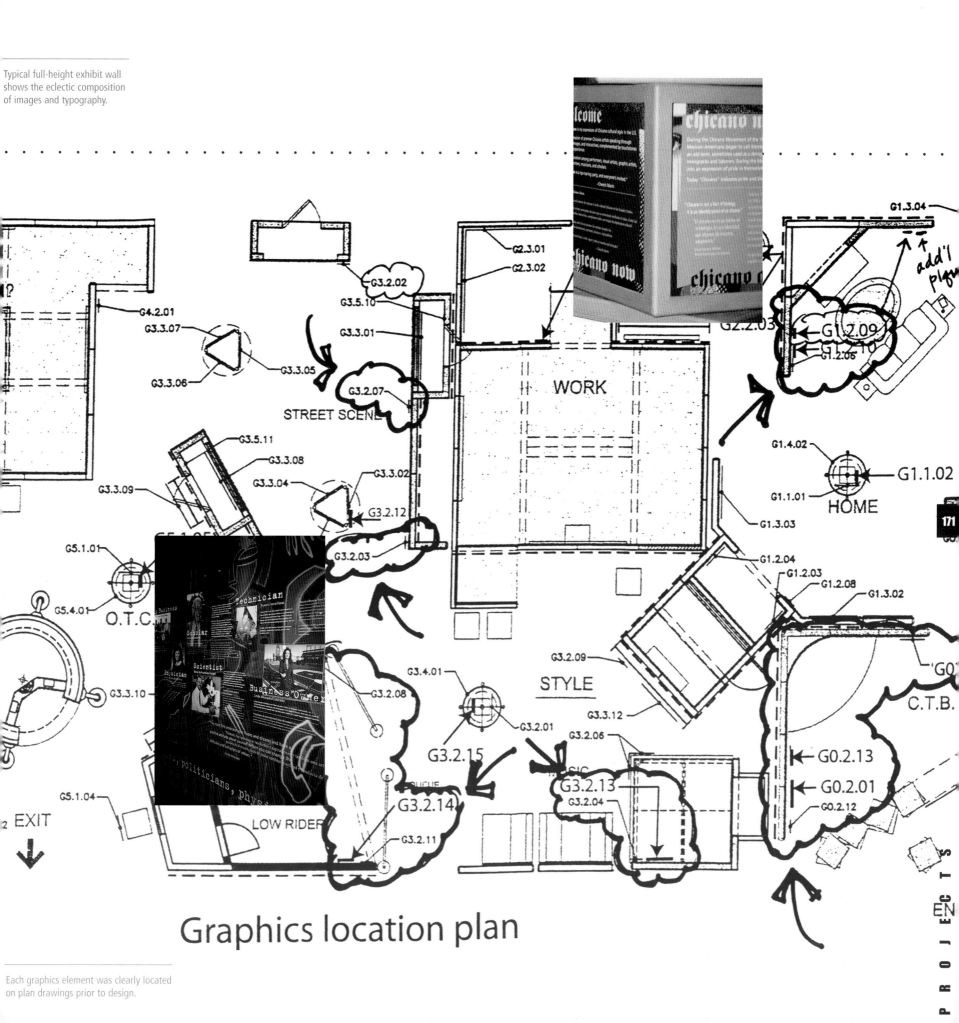

Typical full-height exhibit wall shows the eclectic composition of images and typography.

G1.3.04

G2.3.01

G2.3.02

G3.2.02

G4.2.01

G3.3.07

G3.5.10

G3.3.01

add'l plan

G1.2.09

G3.3.05

G3.3.06

G3.2.07

STREET SCENE

WORK

G1.4.02

G1.1.01

G1.1.02

G3.5.11

G3.3.08

G3.3.02

HOME

G3.3.09

G3.3.04

G1.3.03

G3.2.12

G1.2.04

G3.2.03

G1.2.03

G1.2.08

G1.3.02

G5.1.01

G5.4.01

Technician

Scholar

O.T.C.

Scientist

G3.2.09

STYLE

G3.3.10

Business "Owner"

G3.2.08

G3.4.01

G3.3.12

C.T.B.

G3.2.06

G3.2.01

G3.2.15

G0.2.13

G3.2.13

G0.2.01

G3.2.04

G5.1.04

LOW RIDER

G3.2.14

G0.2.12

EXIT

G3.2.11

Graphics location plan

Each graphics element was clearly located on plan drawings prior to design.

171

AAn "immersive" environment of imagery surrounds visitors.

The exhibit features extensive use of Spanish, but not one-to-one translations.

Layered images and text ignore traditional exhibit picture/word layouts. The effect is more like a Web site or hip magazine design.

Surprising objects, each displaying content, greet guests.

Saturated colors and dramatic lighting predominate.

DAY OF THE DEAD

Celebrating Life and Death

The Day of the Dead celebrates the cycle of life and death by remembering dead ancestors. Chicanos reinvented this traditional Mexican holiday as a means of artistic and cultural expression, often celebrating it in public places like neighborhood stores, cultural centers, and museums.

Celebración de la Vida y la Muerte

El Día de los Muertos celebra el ciclo de la vida y la muerte recordando a los antepasados fallecidos. Los chicanos reinventaron esta celebración mexicana tradicional como un medio de expresión artística y cultural, celebrándola a menudo en lugares públicos tales como las tiendas del barrio, los centros culturales y los museos.

The Aztecs dedicated the ninth and tenth months of the year to the dead. After Spain conquered the Indians' homeland in 1521, Catholic priests adapted the custom. They moved it to November 2, just after All Saints' Day. Today's Day of the Dead blends Indian and Christian elements.

Los aztecas dedicaban los meses noveno y décimo del año a los muertos. Después de que los españoles conquistaron la tierra natal de los indios en 1521, los sacerdotes católicos adoptaron esta costumbre. Esos sacerdotes pasaron esta celebración al día 2 de noviembre, justamente después del día de Todos Los Santos. Actualmente el Día de los Muertos mezcla elementos indios y cristianos.

"When you have the concept that there is no difference between life and death and that it is all part of this natural cycle, then you can believe in going back and forth."

–Tere Romo, art curator

"Cuando tienes la idea de que no hay diferencia entre la vida y la muerte y de que todo es parte de este ciclo natural, puedes creer en ir y venir."

–Tere Romo, curadora de arte

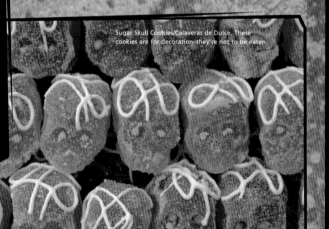

Sugar Skull Cookies/Calaveras de Dulce. These cookies are for decoration–they're not to be eaten.

Day of the Dead Bread/Pan de Muertos

"The Day of the Dead is about sharing. By sharing memories each year, the deceased can remain within the extended family."

–Mia Gonzales, art gallery owner

"El Día de los Muertos es un día de compartir. Al compartir recuerdos cada año los difuntos pueden permanecer con la familia aumentada."

–Mia Gonzales, propietaria de galería de arte

día de los muertos

PROJECT OVERVIEW
Five-thousand-square-foot traveling exhibit.

PROJECT FACTS
Client:
  Clear Channel Entertainment Exhibitions, Inc.
Design Team:
  Wyatt Design Group:
  Larry Wyatt, Eric Williams, David Woody
Graphic Design Team:
  Hunt Design:
  Jennifer Bressler, Heather Watson
  Consultant: Peter Redetsky
Exhibit Fabricator:
  Lexington Scenery; Williams Graphics
Schedule:
  Six months

MATERIALS & TECHNIQUES
Wood construction; mixed media; digitally printed vinyl laminated with satin-finish Lexan.

UNIQUE ASPECTS
A complex collaboration of two design firms, an art collector, an arts group, and a design-oriented client.

17

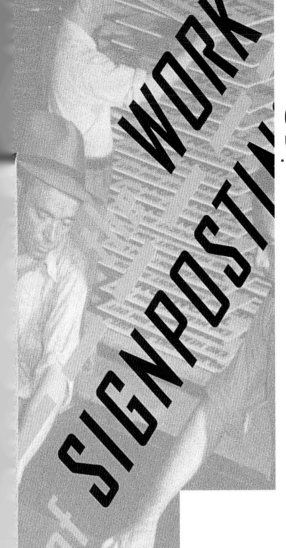

Punching out
the holes for the
reflective beads,
c. 1940.

By the earl
maintained
of standard

SIGNPOSTING Exhibit

Even small displays can be interesting assignments

The Automobile Club of Southern California operates service-oriented district offices in the Los Angeles region where members can buy insurance, plan trips, or get help with vehicle registration. Because each location serves hundreds of customers each day, opportunities exist for the club to communicate with its members about additional services and about the organization itself. In an effort to remind visitors about the rich and storied history of the Automobile Club, Hunt Design created this program of light-weight lobby exhibits.

At the turn of the last century, the Automobile Club was first to install road signs on public highways; it wasn't until after the First World War that local and state governments began to assume the role. Some of the four thousand signs the club deployed on the route between Kansas City and Los Angeles can still be seen today. And because the Automobile Club of Southern California maintains a rich photographic archive of the era, the topic of the club's historic involvement in signposting was an obvious topic for public display.

To serve the many and varied district offices, most of which had little or no display space, a modular approach was called for. The designers suggested a solution of three designs, each a different size and configuration, that could rotate through the offices in six-week cycles. A larger, freestanding unit for larger lobbies and two wall-mounted versions for smaller offices were studied and developed.

Several design themes were explored as organizing devices for laying out the varied text and photographs. The preferred concept, based on large sign arrows used as backgrounds, offered flexibility for creating large and small exhibits. The arrow shapes also lent a sculptural quality to the freestanding version and an interesting profile to the wall pieces.

Because ease of installation was important, no fasteners are needed to erect the freestanding display: the two interlocking flat pieces are held in place by gravity.

Some of the hundreds of historic photographs from the Automobile Club archive.

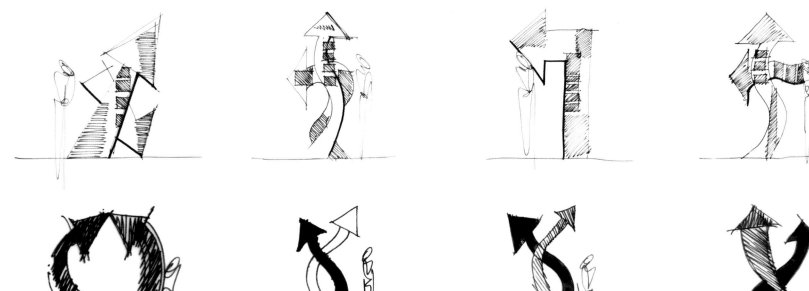

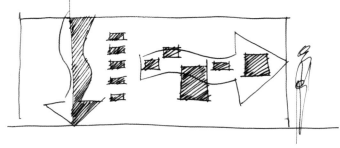

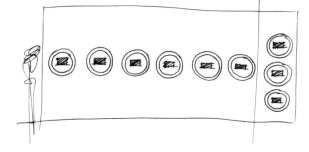

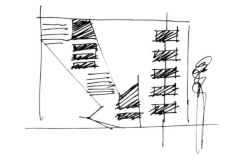

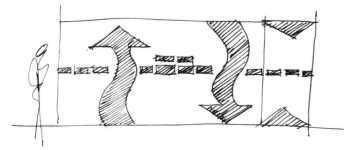

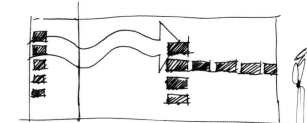

an *exhibit* about signs

Arrow forms figured in all of the initial design sketches.

Scale models aided development and helped demonstrate the knockdown design.

Many configurations were explored for the wall-mounted display.

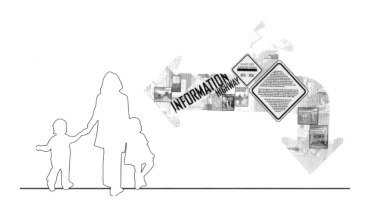

The freestanding version went through several iterations.

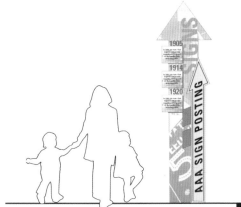

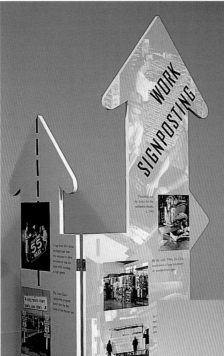

The exhibit folds flat and ships in two pieces.

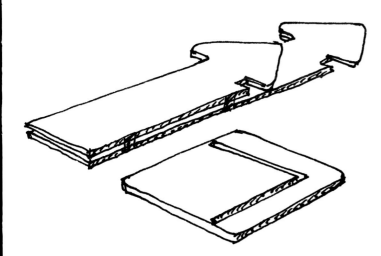

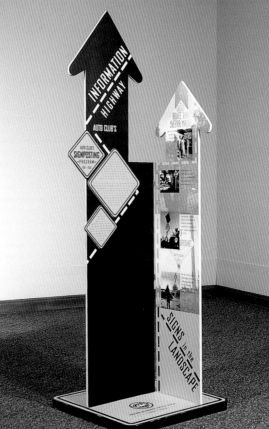

low cost, easy setup

PROJECT OVERVIEW
Lightweight, demountable history displays in three sizes.

PROJECT FACTS
Client:
    Automobile Club of Southern
    California
Graphic Design Team:
    Hunt Design:
    Jennifer Bressler, Nancy Holman,
    Wayne Hunt
Sign Company:
    Williams Graphics
Schedule:
    Six months
Photography:
    Jim Simmons (Del Zoppo Simmons)

SCHEDULE
Six months

MATERIALS & TECHNIQUES
Digital prints on Sintra.

UNIQUE ASPECTS
Low cost, easy to transport and install
(no fasteners).

APOLLO SATURN V CENTER

Exhibition design for America's Apollo Moon program

Mounted permanently in its own 400,000-square-foot building, the mammoth Saturn V rocket is said to be the largest object ever put on display indoors. Its restoration and installation as the centerpiece of a spirited exhibit marked the completion of a major expansion of the Visitor Center at Florida's Kennedy Space Center. The all-new attraction, known as the Apollo Saturn V Center, tells the exciting story of America's greatest adventure of the twentieth century—man's voyage to the moon.

To create a compelling and educational feature around the phenomenal Apollo program, NASA selected noted entertainment and attraction design firm BRC Imagination Arts. BRC's concept team proposed a three-part visitor experience: a large static exhibit designed around the 330-foot rocket flanked by two theatrical shows demonstrating a Saturn V blastoff and a dramatization of the historic Moon landing of Apollo 11. Hunt Design, a frequent collaborator of BRC, was brought in to design the exhibit for the mighty Saturn V.

Exhibit designers frequently look for a single big story to build an exhibit around. Here was the biggest single story imaginable; the challenge was how to tell it credibly in an indoor forty-five-minute experience. With the huge rocket as the dominant object in the sunlit space, the designers turned to a series of supporting stories: the rocket's power, its function and components, and its development by four hundred American companies. The stories are presented in a series of modular displays visible along the walkway beneath the rocket. Each display features a neon question mark for distance recognition, as well as a single provocative title, such as "How Big Is Big?"

The designers used exhibit elements and graphics to "scale down" the huge rocket.

178

PROJECTS

To provide order and add visual punctuation throughout the long exhibition space, each of the ten Apollo missions is presented in sequence along the rocket. The colorful mission patches of the flights were recreated in sixteen-foot-diameter banners that form a dramatic overhead procession. The segmented stages of the giant rocket are identified with flying signs, and an actual Moon lander, or LEM, hangs above the crowd. Smaller individual displays, such as Astronaut James Lovell's Apollo 13 space suit, add more detail and serve as substories.

The exhibit also works as a circulation device, attracting visitors and flowing them toward the climactic Lunar Theater at the far end of the hall. Along the way are restrooms and the Moon Rock Café, featuring an actual Moon rock on display. The designers added a sculptural blade sign for the café and a neon marquee for the theater to further aid visitor traffic flow.

Proposed designs were demonstrated on the architect's building model.

This early sketch is remarkably similar to the finished exhibit.

The design issues faced were not unlike those in any large exhibit, except one: the gigantic Saturn rocket tended to overwhelm anything placed next to it. Everything looks small in comparison, especially information and graphics planned for human scale, a requirement of most exhibits. Further complications included the expressive architecture, with its many large trusslike columns along the walls which precluded the use of wall-type displays, as well as the natural light shining in from three sides of the building—designers prefer a light-controlled environment.

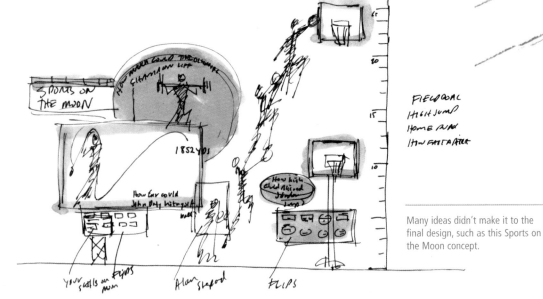

Many ideas didn't make it to the final design, such as this Sports on the Moon concept.

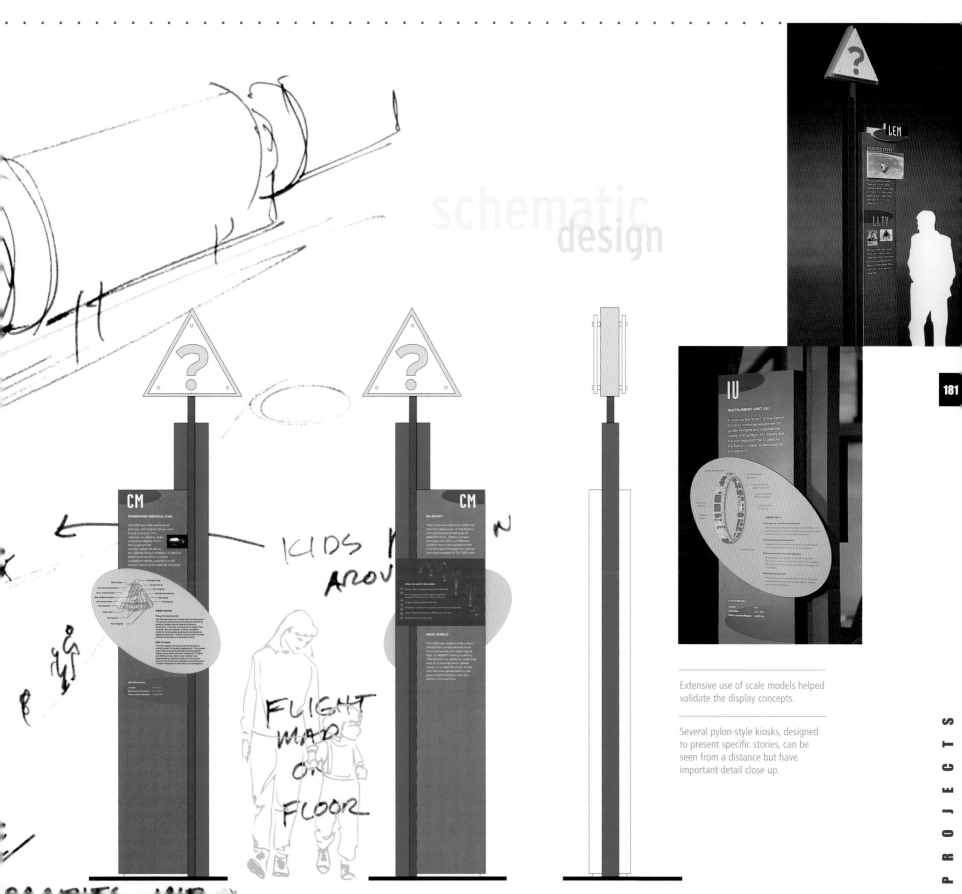

181

schematic
design

Extensive use of scale models helped
validate the display concepts.

Several pylon-style kiosks, designed
to present specific stories, can be
seen from a distance but have
important detail close up.

PROJECTS

Demonstrating a touch of humor, this food outlet sign projects out over the walkway.

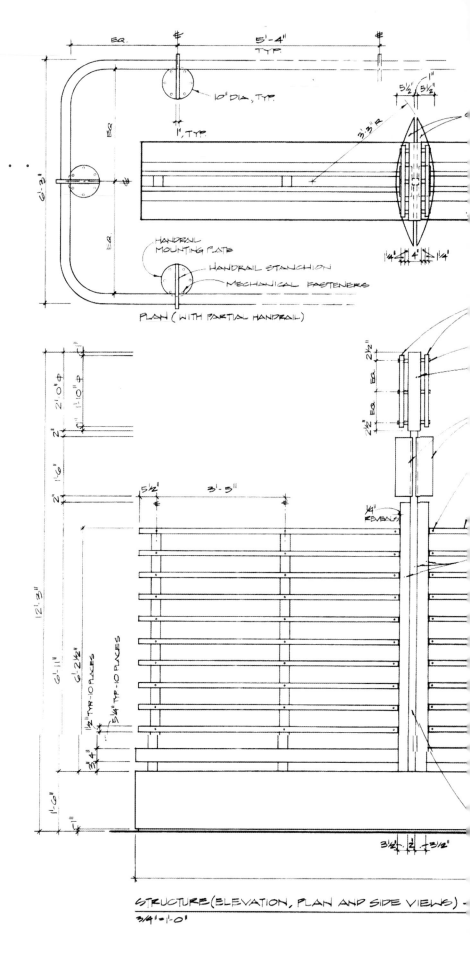

PLAN (WITH PARTIAL HANDRAIL)

HANDRAIL MOUNTING PLATE
HANDRAIL STANCHION
MECHANICAL FASTENERS

10" DIA. TYP.

STRUCTURE (ELEVATION, PLAN AND SIDE VIEWS)
3/4" = 1'-0"

"Tranquility Base here. The Eagle has landed."
— Neil Armstrong

DATE   July 16 - 24, 1969

CREW   Commander: Neil Armstrong, 38, Gemini 8
         Command Module Pilot: Michael Collins, 38, Gemini 10
         Lunar Module Pilot: Edwin "Buzz" Aldrin, 39, Gemini 12

CRAFT   Command Module: Columbia
         Lunar Module: Eagle

HIGHLIGHT

Apollo 11 achieved President Kennedy's goal of landing a man
on the Moon and returning him safely to Earth. After landing on
the Moon with only 30 seconds of fuel remaining, astronauts
Armstrong and Aldrin planted the American flag and collected
the first samples of lunar soil.

Each of the eleven Apollo missions
is featured on a graphic panel and
hanging mission patch banner.

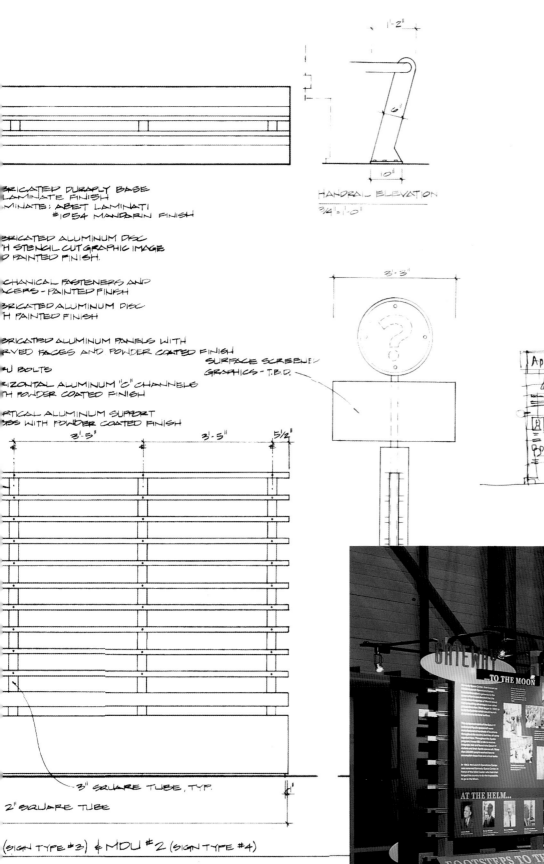

HANDRAIL ELEVATION
3/4" = 1'-0"

1'-2"

6"

10"

BRICATED DURAPLY BASE
LAMINATE FINISH
MINATE: ABET LAMINATI
        #1054 MANDARIN FINISH

BRICATED ALUMINUM DISC
TH STENCIL CUT GRAPHIC IMAGE
D PAINTED FINISH.

CHANICAL FASTENERS AND
CERS - PAINTED FINISH

BRICATED ALUMINUM DISC
TH PAINTED FINISH

BRICATED ALUMINUM PANELS WITH
RVED FACES AND POWDER COATED FINISH

U BOLTS

IZONTAL ALUMINUM "C" CHANNELS
TH POWDER COATED FINISH

RTICAL ALUMINUM SUPPORT
BES WITH POWDER COATED FINISH

3'-5"   3'-5"   5½"

3" SQUARE TUBE, TYP.

2" SQUARE TUBE

(SIGN TYPE #3) & MDU #2 (SIGN TYPE #4)

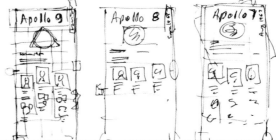

3'-3"

?

SURFACE SCREENED
GRAPHICS - T.B.D.

Apollo 9   Apollo 8   Apollo 7

183

The main Apollo stories are presented in
island-style displays along the rocket.

WHAT'S INSIDE?

APOLLO/SATURN V

SATURN V FIRST STAGE (S-IC)

SATURN V SECOND STAGE (S-II)

SATURN V THIRD STAGE (S-IVB)

EXIT TO BUSES

Design **Analysis**

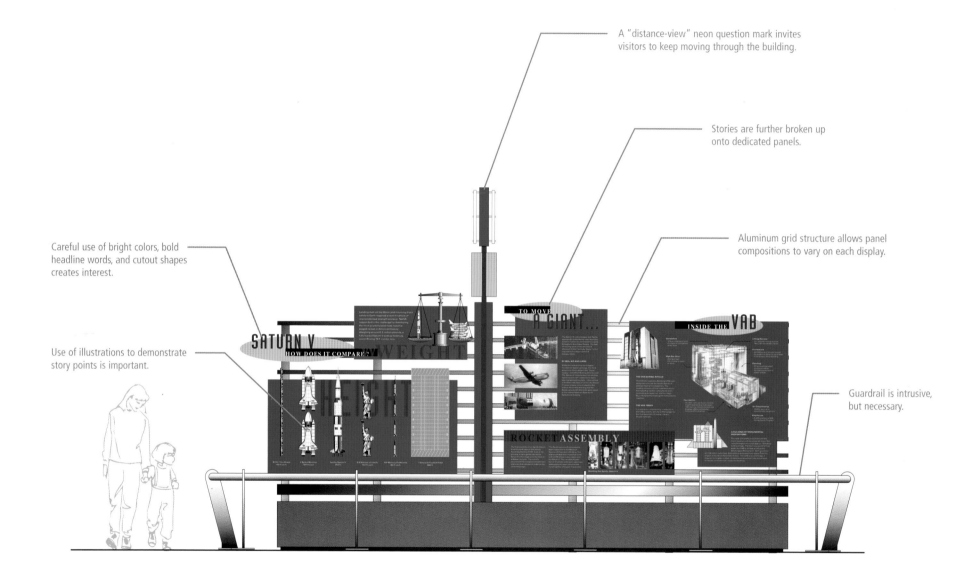

A "distance-view" neon question mark invites visitors to keep moving through the building.

Stories are further broken up onto dedicated panels.

Aluminum grid structure allows panel compositions to vary on each display.

Careful use of bright colors, bold headline words, and cutout shapes creates interest.

Use of illustrations to demonstrate story points is important.

Guardrail is intrusive, but necessary.

Large flying signs mark the Saturn rocket stages and help establish zones in the huge space.

The designers also developed the attraction logo. Here are some of the many design studies.

PROJECT OVERVIEW
Exhibit design for Apollo Space Programs as part of the Kennedy Space Center Visitor Center.

PROJECT FACTS
Client:
    NASA; Kennedy Space Center
Project Producer:
    BRC Imagination Arts
Graphic Design Team:
    Hunt Design:
    Christina Allen, Esteban Hernandez,
    Wayne Hunt, Dinnis Lee,
    Brian Memmott
Exhibit/Sign Company:
    Lexington Scenery
Schedule:
    Two years
Photography:
    Jim Simmons (Del Zoppo Simmons)

UNIQUE ASPECTS
A detailed, multistory exhibit all staged around a huge single object—the Saturn V rocket.

MATERIALS & TECHNIQUES
A wide variety of exhibit media was used, including aluminum structures with digital graphics; backlit transparencies; hand-painted canvas; neon letters; and sculptural media.

MATERIALS & TECHNIQUES
The many media of environmental graphics

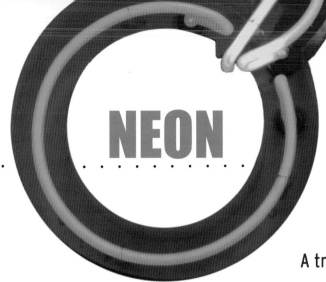

NEON

A traditional sign medium makes a splendid return after years of disrespect

Invented more than one hundred years ago, neon soon became the standard for sign illumination on our nation's streets and in its downtowns. Technically, neon is only one of several gases that, when energized by electricity in sealed glass tubes, produce vibrant concentrated colored light. This brightness of illumination, combined with the bendability of heated glass tubes, virtually made "writing with light" possible. The result is a timeless graphic and decorative medium.

After its heyday in the thirties and forties, neon fell from popularity as people came to associate the technology with bars and seedy hotels; in the sixties many cities actually banned the use of exposed neon. Today neon has been rediscovered, and its visual purity and flexibility of use have led to a major resurgence in both traditional and new applications.

A true classic—hand-painted illustration outlined in neon.

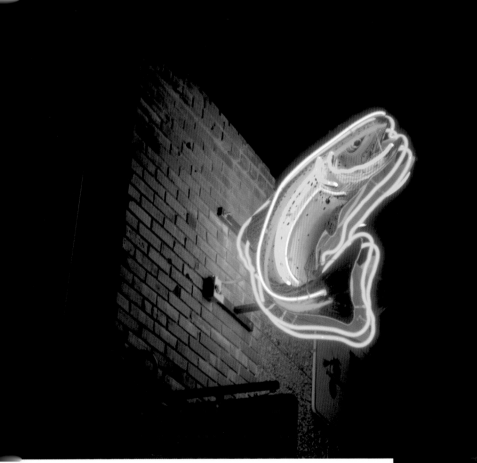

Obscure glass lens creates an interesting effect.

Neon used as an edge detail on flat cutout forms.

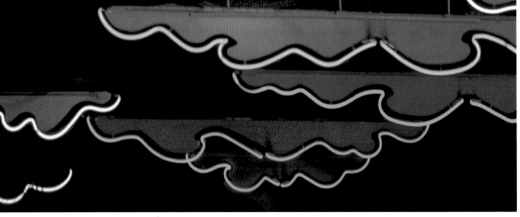

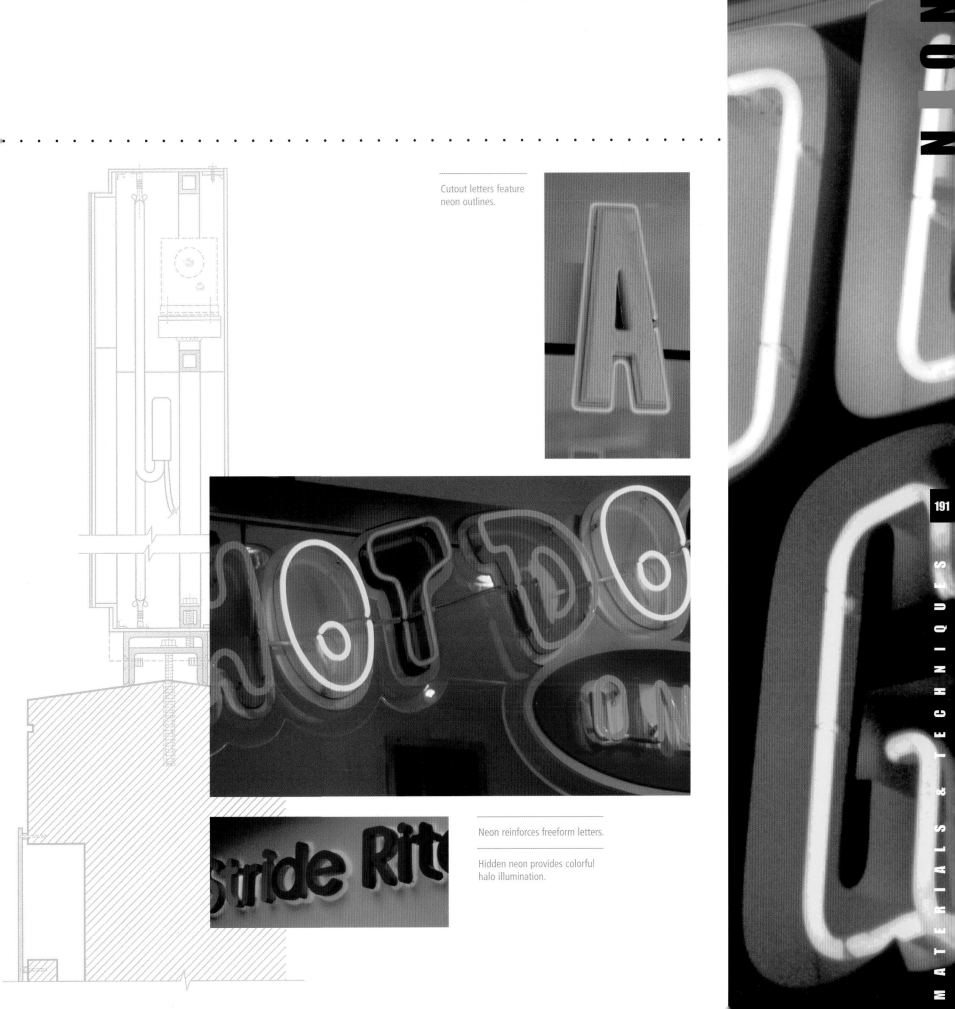

Cutout letters feature
neon outlines.

Neon reinforces freeform letters.

Hidden neon provides colorful
halo illumination.

STONE

Ornate letters cut into granite.

THE SACRED EARTH WHERE YOU NOW STAND REPRESENTS THOSE WHO HAVE GONE BEFORE US, GIVING US OUR CULTURAL HERITAGE AND TEACHING US TO BE CHEROKEE. WE PAY OUR RESPECTS TO THOSE ANCESTORS, PAST, PRESENT AND FUTURE.

4"

1 1/2"

1 1/4" typ

1" typ

2'-5"

1 1/2"

Front View

Polished bevel and face

1/4" wide x 1/16" deep "V" groove border - No infill

L.D. EDGAR

STOLEN HORSES - B

BUTCH CASSIDY C

Wyo

These words are sandblasted deep into the stone.

The first and most enduring sign material

Stone is an ancient building material and probably the first sign medium. The carving of figures and letters into stone walls predates modern man and to this day remains a major sign-making technique. Stone can be carved by hand or sandblasted; it can be fabricated into shapes, and it can be etched with acids and cut with water jets. Carved-out letterforms can be paint filled or decorated with gold leaf; stone's surface can be polished to a reflective smoothness or left rough and natural-looking.

While many kinds of rock can be used for signs, marble, limestone, and granite are the most frequently chosen. Stone's timelessness and durability make it appropriate for dignified and formal sign solutions.

10"

Countersunk stainless steel
fasteners

Fabricated aluminum cabinet with
waterproof removable face; paint
finish all exposed surfaces

Self-drilling stainless steel
concrete anchors

Letterface/star to be 1/8" thick
push-thru acrylic with back-up

Fluorescent lamps; evenly spaced

Primary power conduit stub-out
at sign location

Classic hand-carved numerals.

Chisel-cut, flat profile
letters in tiled stone.

1" conduit; run up thru concrete
to sign location (by others)

7 1/2"
typ.

A Section
1 1/2" = 1'-0"

Cast-in-place concretes:
not stone, but stone-like.

WOOD

In its dozens of varieties, wood is a favorite sign-making material

Because it requires only the lowest of technology and it does grow on trees, wood of all types has been a popular choice for sign-making for generations. And in the right hands, wood can be especially beautiful for graphics applications.

As a sign face, wood can be carved, sandblasted, or milled for a wide variety of effects. Letters can be cut, carved, and routed. Woods are also used as sign structures, delivering high strength with relatively light weight in many situations. Wood finishes are myriad, from paints and metal-leafing to transparent finishes that show off natural grain and visual texture.

Cedar panel with stencil-cut letters and acrylic.

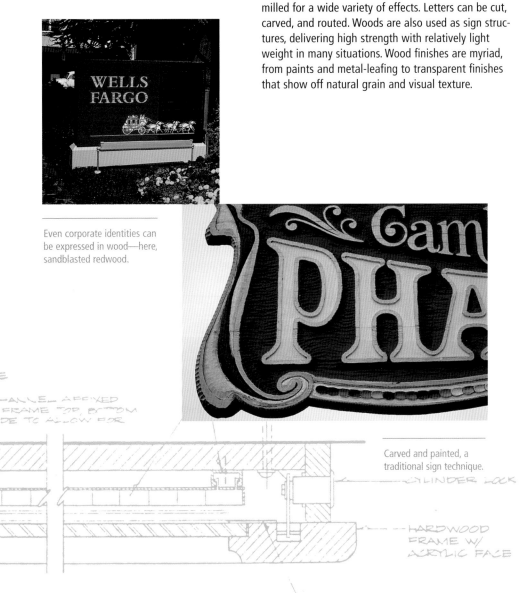

Even corporate identities can be expressed in wood—here, sandblasted redwood.

Carved and painted, a traditional sign technique.

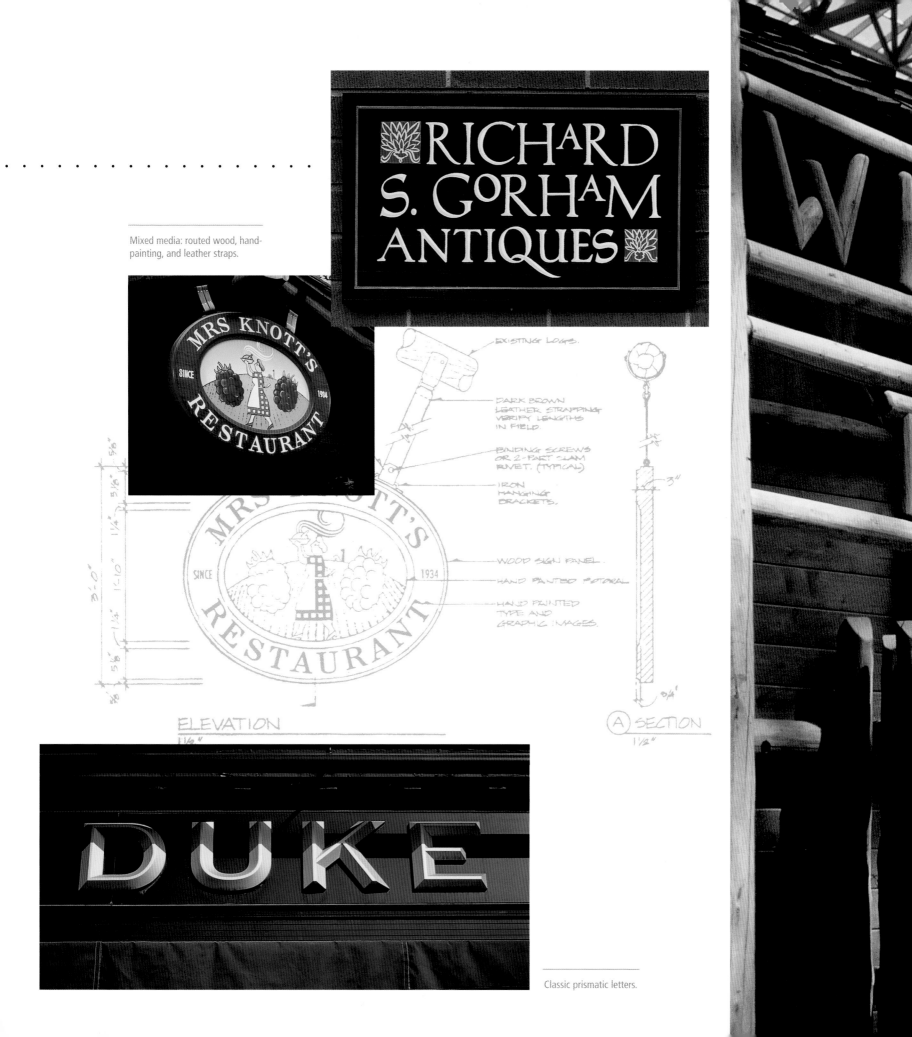

Mixed media: routed wood, hand-painting, and leather straps.

EXISTING LOGS.

DARK BROWN LEATHER STRAPPING VERIFY LENGTHS IN FIELD.

BINDING SCREWS OR 2-PART SLAM RIVET. (TYPICAL)

IRON HANGING BRACKETS.

3"

WOOD SIGN PANEL.

HAND PAINTED PICTORIAL

HAND PAINTED TYPE AND GRAPHIC IMAGES.

3/4"

5'-0"

5/8" 1'-4" 1'-10" 1/4" 5/8" 5/8"

ELEVATION
1 1/2"

A SECTION
1 1/2"

Classic prismatic letters.

195

MATERIALS & TECHNIQUES

WOOD

GLASS

Brilliant, reflective, and durable

Light-transmitting qualities and a reflective surface have made glass a popular choice for a wide variety of signage designs. From decorative window graphics to sophisticated etching techniques, glass is an appealing substrate for graphics applications. Glass is available in several quality grades and multiple thicknesses and can be acted upon by a wide variety of graphic and physical media. Glass can be fabricated, carved, sandblasted, etched, and silk-screened on either the front or back surface. It can be back lit, edge lit, or left to reflect ambient light.

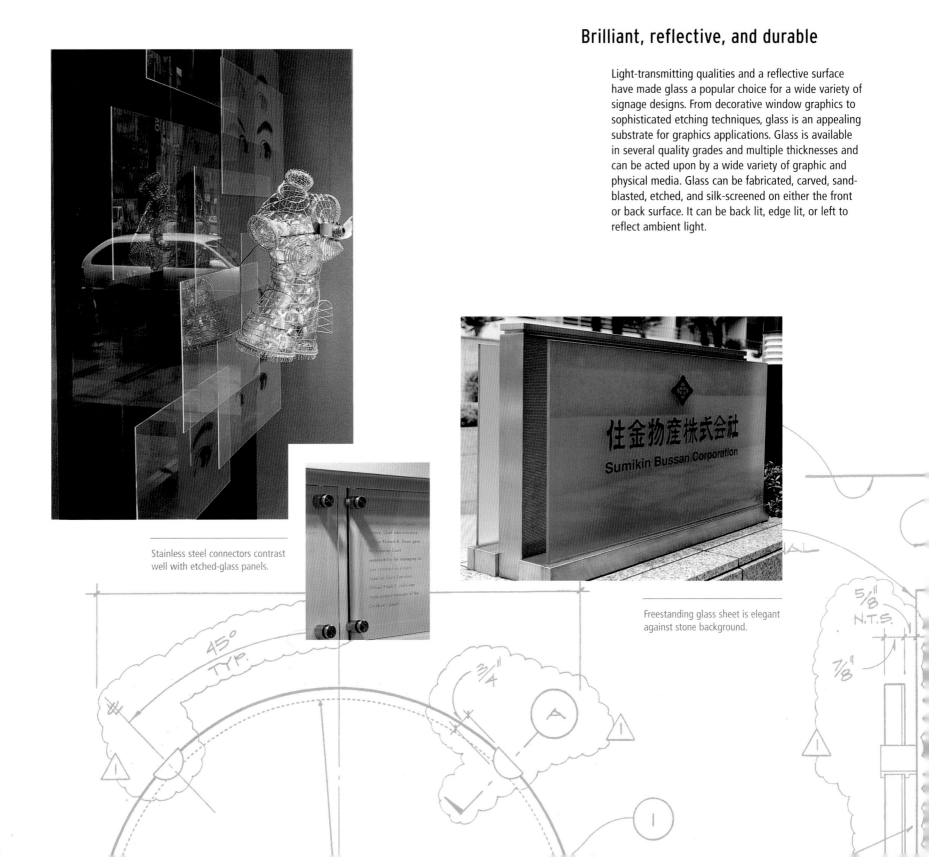

Stainless steel connectors contrast well with etched-glass panels.

Freestanding glass sheet is elegant against stone background.

Multilayered sandblasting
yields this sculptured look.

→
東展示棒
East Exhibitio
東1〜6ホ
East Halls 1-6

THICKNESS
T.B.D.

ACRYLIC
PAINTED
ALL SIDES

GLASS

3/4"

1/8

THE GREAT SEAL OF THE STATE OF
EUREKA
CALIFORNIA

SEAL LAYOUT

OUTSIDE EDGE OF
IMAGE AREA

A SECTION
FULL SIZE

197

801.802会議室 管理ロビー 高層レストラン
会議会議室 701〜703会議室
601〜610会議室
エントランスホール 連絡ブリッジ レストラン
レセプションホール 101,102会議室 レストラン

CALIFORNIA PLAZA

Sandblasted glass with laminated
stainless steel letters.

ALUMINUM

Layered aluminum panels
make up these stadium signs.

Light, strong, and workable

Emerging in the 1950s as an alternative to steel, aluminum is probably the most frequently used material for large sign faces and components. Aluminum does not rust, and with its high strength-to-weight ratio, this contemporary metal can be used for many types of sign fabrication. It can be cut, formed, welded, routed, etched, and engraved. It can be painted, powder-coated, and anodized for virtually unlimited color expression.

Aluminum can also be cast into letters, plaques, and other shapes. This "moldability" has led to this flexible metal's use in manufacturing complex, high-quality extrusions; these structural, often interlocking frame members are important in many elegant and efficient "off-the-shelf" signage products and systems.

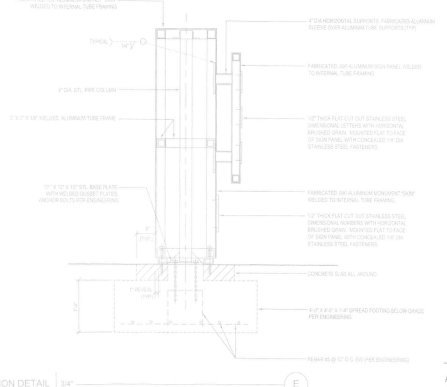

ELEVATION DETAIL | 3/4" ———————————— (E)

Aluminum is used as structure
in this airport directory sign.

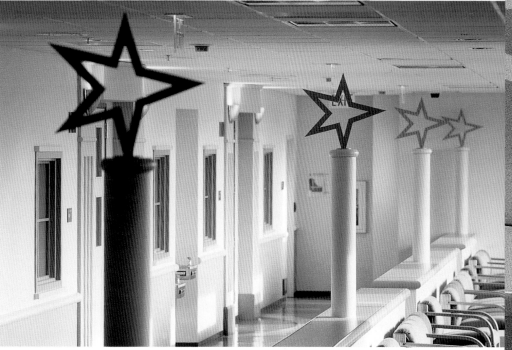

This aluminum cabinet and base hide a steel frame.

Sheet aluminum takes on a decorative quality when "captured" by vertical poles.

199

STEEL

An elegant stencil-cut sign in stainless steel plate.

Cast iron, one of the most durable sign materials.

Strength and durability keep steel in the forefront of sign-making

Displaced by aluminum as the primary material for making sign faces, steel remains the main component for large sign-making; it is frequently the hidden internal structure. And as an exposed surface material, steel has limitless possibilities. It can be cut, fabricated into shapes, welded, and torch-cut. Steel can be painted and finished any number of ways, or even left to rust for certain aesthetic effects.

Stainless steel, not really steel at all, has seen widespread use for signage, from classic individual letters to entire sign faces. Its self-finishing surface can be brushed, ground, or polished for a variety of effects.

A beautiful painted casting from Europe.

Stainless on stainless: the contrast comes from the difference in finishes.

DECORATIVE FACADE BY OTHERS
TO MATCH EXISTING FACADE.

10"

TOP SERVICE ACCESS PANELS.

INTERNALLY ILLUMINATED FABRICATED
HORIZONTAL GRAIN #4 BRUSHED STAIN
STEEL CABINET WITH LASER CUT COPY
PUSH THRU 1" THICK AMBER ACRYLIC LE
TO MATCH ADJACENT LIGHT FIXTURE; E
POLISHED.

Stainless steel base;
aluminum panels.

E SUPPO

REWAY

FFUSER
T TOP AN
S.

Mixed metals: the sign frame is welded
steel, the panels aluminum and the
logo porcelain enamel.

RAIN #4
TRUCTURAL

GLE FACED
N #4 BRUSHED
TH LASER CUT
ACRYLIC PUSH
ACENT LIGHT
1/8" THICK

7"

10"

201

EXOTIC METALS

This illustrative marker, with its bas relief effect, is likely cast aluminum.

The results of ancient metallurgy remain valid today

Metal chemistry, from the Bronze Age to today, has given us beautiful, enduring metals that excel as sign materials. Bronze, copper, brass, zinc, and other metals are specified for a wide variety of signage types. Each exotic metal has unique visual and physical qualities as well as advantages and disadvantages.

A primary appeal of exotic metals is their rich and slowly changing finishes created by aging and exposure to various environments. Copper, for example, can express not only reds and oranges, but also vivid blues and greens.

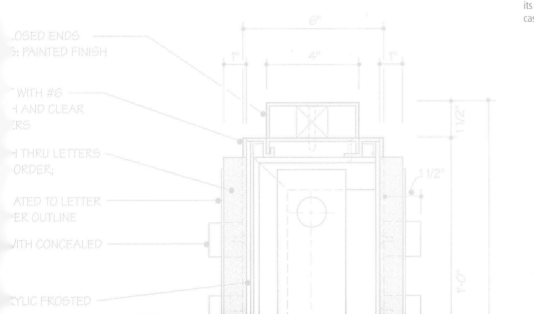

Constant foot traffic keeps this bronze piece polished.

Bronze casting with a rich patina, developed over many years.

ALNUT STREET

SE ARE SMALL SCALE SITE PLANS TO HELP THE BLIND
GET A BETTER UNDERSTANDING OF
INDEPENDENCE NATIONAL HISTORICAL PARK
KEY TO SYMBOLS

PATHS   STEPS   CROSSWALKS   ENTRANCES   TREES
GRASS   MAJOR ROUTE FOR BLIND   WALLS   BENCHES

Casting can render
significant detail.

THIS PROPERTY
HAS BEEN PLACED
ON THE

CITY OF VANCOUVER
HERITAGE
BUILDING

MARINE BUILDING
Architects: McCarter & Nairne

Once the tallest building in the British Empire, the
Marine Building enjoys a special heritage status as
an internationally acclaimed example of Art Deco
architecture. Completed in 1930, the Marine Building's
main lobby has impressive ceiling detail, ship's prows
as lighting and a marble floor with the 12 zodiac signs,
ships and whales. The Marine Building's terra cotta
exterior depicts scenic landscapes, sea life, 1920s state
of the art modes of transportation, and vessels significant
to Vancouver's business and development history.
The 1980s renovation program restored unique architectural
features and upgraded the building's operation systems.

Contemporary styling and painting
distinguish this elegant plaque.

Telephone

Restrooms

Brass frames unify the
signage in a civic building.

PORCELAIN ENAMEL

A "mural" of porcelain panels presents children's self-portraits.

A vibrant and enduring sign medium

Consisting of a layer of glass fused to a steel surface, this rich-looking sign methodology has stood the test of time for color-fast, durable signage—many porcelain enamel signs from the early 1900s still look good today. Nearly all mass-produced commercial signs from 1930 to 1960 were made using this eye-appealing technique. And until just recently, porcelain enamel was the standard on roadside highway signs. Colors are virtually fade-proof, and except for direct damage to the sign face, a porcelain sign will last forever.

Porcelain enamel signs are prevalent throughout Europe.

Porcelain's toughness is perfect for "touchable" signs.

205

Two examples of porcelain enamel's size range—from six inches to six feet.

A porcelain enamel road sign with reflective letters.

HANDCRAFTED MEDIA

Many types of signs can still be made the old-fashioned way—by hand

From timeless sign lettering to the contemporary carving of high-tech sculptural foam, appreciation of handcrafted signs and graphics has never been higher. Predating the emergence of the designer, makers of handmade signs brought not only craft and skill, but aesthetics and creativity too. Today, when a craftsperson executes a design from a designer, the result is often better than the original drawing.

Carved and painted sign foam is used for sculptural effects.

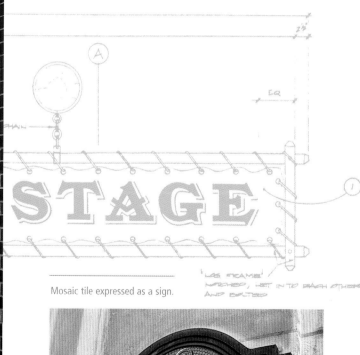

Mosaic tile expressed as a sign.

Remnants of sign painters past.

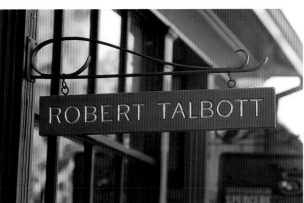

Hand-painting over masonry—
a traditional sign technique.

Authentic leaded and
stained glass.

Gold-leaf letters—a classic
sign-making method.

Carved wood remains an
appealing sign medium.

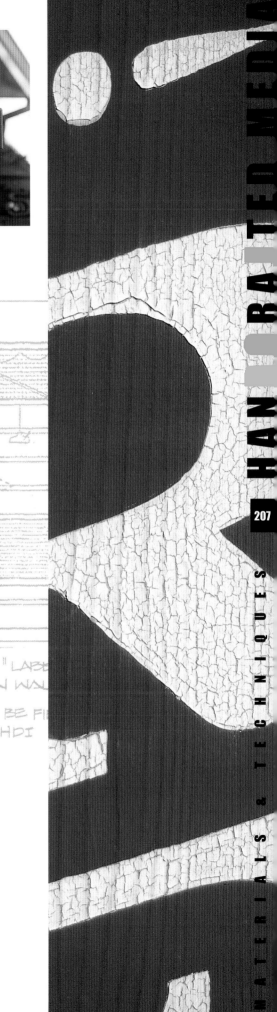

FABRIC MEDIA

Banners allow bold use of color in otherwise monochromatic environments.

Flags come alive in the breeze.

Screened letters on stretched awnings.

Digital images can be dramatic on flexible surfaces.

Signage and graphics need not always be made of rigid materials

The banner revolution is in full force. New fabrics and flexible substrates, combined with breakthroughs in digital printing and other application techniques, have made the use of banners popular for many kinds of projects. Whether screen-printed, pieced together, or digitally executed, banners and flags bring animation and color to the environment.

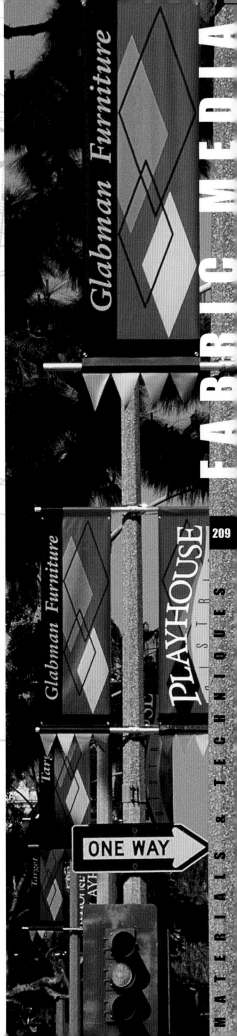

Fabric elements form a pattern high on this building.

ELEVATION   3/4"

Overhead banners and streamers animate the street.

— Banner

Sphere

DIGITAL MEDIA

Digital print on Sintr,™ a plastic substrate.

Now, any image can be presented on nearly any kind of sign

The last fifteen years have seen the continued evolution of image-making based on digital technology. Made up of small dots, or pixels, complex images have gone beyond the printed page to be displayed on countless substrates and sign materials, both permanent and temporary. One especially interesting process allows the capturing or embedding of digital images within durable layers of high-pressure laminates.

This two-block fence features large prints laminated to plywood.

Increasingly, zoos and other
attractions are specifying digital
graphics embedded in phenolic
resin laminates.

A temporary sign of digital output
on foam board.

GLOSSARY

The language of environmental graphic design

The field of environmental graphic design has a lexicon all its own. While not an exhaustive or detailed list, these terms are often used during the planning, design, and implementation of signage programs and exhibits.

Acrylic
Generic term for certain workable plastics used in sign-making, i.e., Plexiglas R.

ADA
Americans with Disabilities Act, 1991 federal legislation requiring equal access to public facilities. Has specific requirements for signage and related design.

ADA signage
Certain signs and design standards that meet the intent and letter of the ADA, such as tactile letters, Braille, letter size, and contrast.

ADAAG
Americans with Disabilities Act Accessibility Guidelines. The specific design and implementation guidelines for accessible design as required by the ADA.

Ambient light
Existing or surrounding light in an area or space.

Animation
Moving images, real or electronic, on a sign or display.

Architectural scale
One of twelve drawing proportions used to draw objects larger than the page, i.e., 1/4" = 1'.

Area development
Exterior public circulation spaces and landscaped areas.

Art glass
Decorative graphic techniques, such as chipped glass.

Back of house
Nonpublic areas of a facility.

Backing
Internal structure added to a wall or ceiling to support the weight of a sign.

Bid
Price or firm estimate of price.

Bond
Guarantee by a third party (bonding company) that a contractor can and will complete a project.

Braille
Alphabet of raised, tactile dots for use by the visually impaired.

Breakaway
Structural component of a sign designed to fail in the event of impact or excessive wind, i.e., wood post on a roadside sign.

CAD
Computer-aided design or drafting.

Change order
Directive to change a scope of work, design in process, or ongoing construction.

Charrette
Intense work session usually conducted just before a deadline. Based on the French word for "cart," on which architecture students were said to roll their final projects into class while making last-minute changes.

Conceptual design
The initial or idea phase of the design process.

Construction documents
The combined package of construction drawings, specifications and bid instructions. Also: bid documents, contract documents, or bid package.

Construction drawings
Set of detailed instructional drawings that show how something is to be built. Also: working drawings.

Cost-plus contract
Contract type in which the designer or contractor charges for all costs incurred plus a percentage markup for profit.

Design-build
Construction business structure in which a single company is responsible for design and construction.

Design development
Phase of the design process in which the design is finalized and methods and materials are selected.

Design intent drawings
Drawings that show the visual intent of the designer but without substantial detail.

Design review
Review of the aesthetics of certain projects before construction, usually by a board or commission appointed by a local jurisdiction.

Digital media
Print or other graphics output composed of digital or pixilated images.

Division 10
Chapter in the Construction Specifications Institute–16 Division Format dealing with specialties such as signage.

DOT
Department of Transportation—local, state, or federal.

DOT symbols
Travel-related pictographs issued by the U.S. Department of Transportation, now standard in most U.S. airports.

Dynamic sign
Sign with changeable display capability, such as an electronic message unit or reader board.

Elevation
Drawing of front or side view of a building or structure; direct perpendicular view of a surface.

Façade
Front exposed surface of building or store.

Facilities impact
Refers to the impact the addition of signage elements has on a structure, usually weight and electrical load.

F. F. & E.
Furniture, fixtures, and equipment.

Fiber optics
Illumination technology based on transmitting light through plastic fibers.

FIDs
Flight information displays.

Field set
Set of construction drawings used at the job site, usually annotated with field notes and observations.

Finial
Decorative ornament attached to the end of a pole.

Finger sign
Directional sign made of individual pointed slats, each mounted to point directly in the direction of a destination. Also: pointer sign.

First surface
Front or exposed side of a sheet material.

Flag-mounted sign
Sign mounted perpendicular to a wall. Also: blade sign or outrigger sign.

Flips
Small hinged panels that, when lifted by guests, reveal captions or other information.

Flexible media
Nonrigid sign-making material, i.e., fabric banners or vinyl wrapping.

Footing
The hidden or underground structure that supports a sign or other freestanding object.

Freestanding
Ground mounted; without attachment to walls or ceiling.

GIS
Geographic information system. Refers to the integrated, multilayer computer mapping of a building, place, or city.

Hard costs
Costs associated with construction, fabrication, or purchase of physical facilities or components.

Hardscape
Paving, curbs, railings, and other "hard" outdoor surfaces or objects.

High-pressure laminate
Durable, decorative plasticlike material used for countertops and other high-use surfaces, i.e., Formica.

Icon
Symbolic graphic representation, simplified picture, or image. Also: a large distinctive object in an environment or space.

Interactives
Objects, controls, computers, and video that guests can move, activate, or affect in some way.

Interpretive design
Design discipline focusing on explaining or interpreting information, as in exhibit or museum design.

ISA
International symbol of accessibility. Used to indicate accessible routes, facilities, parking, etc.

Kerning
The spaces between letters in a word. Also: letter spacing.

Kiosk
Freestanding information structure such as a map directory, touch-screen display, or message-posting device.

Knockdown
A fabricated exhibit or object that is designed to be taken apart and rebuilt at another location. Also: KD or demountable.

LCD
Liquid crystal display. Electronic display screen capable of presenting complex, pictorial images and information.

LED
Light-emitting diode. Technology based on tiny light sources organized into a grid for the display of changeable messages.

Load
Amount of electricity needed to power something, usually expressed in amps. Can also refer to weight or accumulated weight in structural engineering.

Marquee
Identification sign.

Message schedule
A list of signs, by category, presenting the wording of each sign and often indicating additional information such as mounting type, references to other documents, etc. Also: message matrix.

Millwork
Cabinetry, counters, and other built-in woodwork.

Monument sign
Formal ground-mounted identification sign.

MUTCD
Manual of Uniform Traffic Control Devices. Federal or state guidelines for highway signage.

Not-to-exceed contract
Contract based on hourly billing, but with a limit that cannot be exceeded. Also: NTE.

Notice to proceed
Official written notice to start work previously approved by a contract. Also: NTP.

Patina
Effect of wear or aging on a surface. Usually refers to the warm and interesting appearance of aging seen in exotic metals such as bronze or copper.

Pattern
Full-size paper layout of the letters and messages of a sign for approval prior to fabrication.

Peer review
Review of designs or drawings by an independent professional peer; only seen in certain government projects.

Phenolic resin signage
Digital graphics embedded in high-pressure laminate material.

Photopolymer
Plastic that can be photoetched to leave tactile "high spots" for Braille and tactile letters.

Plan view
Drawing of a building or object viewed from the top or above. Also: top view.

Porte cochere
Roofed overhang at a vehicle entrance or drop-off. Also, carport.

POV
Point of view. Usually refers to the angle of view in an architectural rendering or photograph.

Professional liability insurance
Insurance that protects against errors and omissions by design professionals.

Programming
The process of organizing the signage needs of a project into types, locations, and messages.

Proposal
Written offer of services, costs, and schedule for a project or assignment.

Punch list
List of items for correction or completion, usually prepared at the end of a project.

Pushthrough (letters)
Refers to acrylic letters that have been "pushed through" matching letter shapes cut out of sheet material.

Pylon sign
Tall vertical sign or overhead sign on a pole.

Record drawings
A set of the construction drawings revised after construction is completed to reflect field changes made during construction. Also: as-built drawings.

Reflected ceiling plan
A drawing of a ceiling as if it were viewed reflecting off the floor or transparently through the roof.

Retro-reflective
The ability of a material to reflect light back toward its source, instead of away at an equal angle. Developed for night viewing of highway signs.

RFI
Request for information. Formal requests from contractors to designers or architects during construction.

RFP
Request for proposal.

RFQ
Request for qualifications.

ROI
Return on investment.

Scale
Relative size of one thing to another. See: Architectural scale.

Schematic design
Design phase that results in scaled drawings showing the basic appearance of a building or object. Includes visual details, but little information about structure or materials.

Screen-printing
Printing of images through a stenciled screen. Also: silk-screening.

Second surface
Back side of a transparent material.

Shell building
Structured walls, roof, and mechanical core of a building.

Shop drawing
Detailed fabrication drawing by vendor (not designer).

Short list
List of finalist candidates for a project or contract.

Sign code
Official limitations to signage on private property, usually as part of a municipal code. Typically includes limitations on sign size, quantity, location, and lighting.

Sign engineering
Structural or electrical engineering for sign structures, foundations, or electrical power.

Site plan
Drawing showing the configuration of a piece of property, including placement and shapes of buildings, streets, walkways, and landscape elements.

Soft costs
Costs associated with planning, designing, and managing a project.

Soft opening
Prepublic opening for training and shakedown of systems and equipment.

SOQ
Statement of qualifications.

Stick set (drawings)
Final, definitive set of construction drawings, including annotations, kept in the design office for reference. Refers to the wooden "sticks" that held large drawings in precomputer days.

Specifications
Written technical descriptions of the materials, fabrication techniques, vendor, and product performance requirements prepared as part of a set of bid or construction documents.

Square-foot sales
Method of measuring retail sales by dividing total sales by the square footage of the store, usually stated annually.

Stanchion
Leglike base for a freestanding sign.

Streakers, strollers, and studiers
Exhibit design shorthand for the three types of exhibit visitors.

Submittal
Official document provided as part of the design or approval process, i.e., a shop drawing or color sample.

Subsurface
Graphics printed on the back side of a transparent surface but read through the front surface. See: Second surface.

Tactile sign
Sign with information read by tracing one's finger along raised letters and/or Braille.

TCO
Temporary certificate of occupancy.

TDD
Telecommunications device for the deaf; allows telephonic messages to be displayed.

TI
Tenant improvements. Changes or "build out" that a tenant brings to a shell building, usually from a separate budget.

Touch screen
Electronic display technology activated by touch, as in an information kiosk.

Urban design
Design discipline that creates streetscapes, building façade improvements, and street furniture.

Value engineering
Process of simplifying a design to reduce cost while preserving design intent.

Vinyl letters
Letters cut from adhesive-backed vinyl. Also: die-cut letters or VDC.

Water feature
Fountain or other water-based design.

Wayfinding
Signs and other graphics for visitor circulation.

Wind load
Pressure applied to a surface by wind. Usually expressed in pounds per square foot.

Working drawings
See: Construction drawings.

ACKNOWLEDGMENT
Thank you to all who helped make this book possible, especially:

Karen Aseltine
Jack Biesek
Jennifer Bressler
Christina Chang
Rick Chavez
Jeff Corbin
Ann Dudrow
Virginia Gehshan
Todd Hays
In Sung Kim
Dinnis Lee
Jan Lorenc
Suzette Mason
Jerry McConnell
Michele Perez
Debbie Peters
Sherri Schottlaender
Perry Shimoji
John Temple
Carla Walecka
Heather Watson
Tzumin Wen